The Legislative Labyrinth

A Map for Not-for-Profits

Walter P. Pidgeon, Jr. Editor

JOHN WILEY & SONS, INC.

NEW YORK / CHICHESTER / WEINHEIM / BRISBANE / SINGAPORE / TORONTO

Copyright© 2001 by John Wiley and Sons, Inc. All rights reserved.

Published simultaneously in Canada.

This publication is designed to provide accurate and authoritative information in regard to the subject matter covered. It is sold with the understanding that the publisher is not engaged in rendering legal, accounting, or other professional services. If legal advice or other expert assistance is required, the services of a competent professional person should be sought.

Library of Congress Cataloging-in-Publication Data:

The legislative labyrinth : a map for not-for-profits / Walter Pidgeon, editor.
      p. cm. — (The NSFRE/Wiley fund development series)
   Includes bibliographical references and index.
   ISBN 0-471-40069-6 (cloth/CD-ROM : alk. paper)
      1. Lobbying—United States. 2. Nonprofit organizations—United States—Political activity. I. Pidgeon, Walter, 1897- II. Title. III. Series.

JK1118 .L44 2001
328.73'078—dc21

                                                                         00-064912

This book is dedicated to not-for-profit professionals who devote their careers to increasing the quality of life of the constituents they serve.

In particular, I dedicate this book to the professionals who are involved in the government affairs arena, for it is they who keep the democratic process alive and well.

About the Editor

Walter (Bud) Pidgeon, Jr. is a recognized authority on how not-for-profit organizations function. He conducts research on the subject and is credited with the first empirical research published on the benefits that volunteering provides the volunteer. He is a published author and consultant in the areas of government affairs, volunteering, fund-raising, strategic planning, and membership enhancement. His previous book, *The Universal Benefits of Volunteering: A Practical Workbook for Nonprofit Organizations, Volunteers, and Corporations,* was published by John Wiley & Sons, Inc., in 1998.

Dr. Pidgeon has had a distinguished career as a not-for-profit leader. He has held positions that required expertise in government affairs, finance, membership development, program enhancement, fund-raising, meeting planning, education, and administration. He served as the chief executive officer of five not-for-profit organizations. Dr. Pidgeon is currently president and chief executive officer of the Wildlife Legislative Fund of America (WLFA) and the Wildlife Conservation Fund of America (WCFA). WLFA, a 501(c)4, and WCFA, a 501(c)3, are national organizations that represent 1.5 million outdoor sports enthusiasts and wildlife management officials at both the federal and state levels. WLFA and WCFA's national office's are located in Columbus, Ohio, and their national and international affairs office are located in Washington, DC.

Dr. Pidgeon earned his bachelor's degree in human relations and nonprofit administration at Salem International University in Salem, West Virginia. His major was an American Humanics, Inc.–sponsored program. Dr. Pidgeon earned his doctorate in philanthropy, leadership, and voluntary studies at the Union Institute in Cincinnati, Ohio.

Dr. Pidgeon is currently certified by the American Society of Association Executives as a Certified Association Executive (CAE). He is also currently certified by the National Society of Fund Raising Executives as a Certified Fund Raising Executive (CFRE).

Dr. Pidgeon is an active civic leader and a volunteer in a number of professional, business, and social service organizations.

About the Co-Authors

John Chwat, a native Washingtonian, is a well-respected professional lobbyist who began his distinguished career on Capitol Hill in 1971. He has extensive experience at the federal and state level representing a multi-client base of corporations, trade and professional associations, industry coalitions, and foreign clients. As President of the government relations firm of Chwat & Company, he has maintained a strong Washington presence for the firm's clients, representing their interests at all levels of government.

Mr. Chwat has a unique background specializing on how the Congress works, having served both Democrats and Republicans as a "Hill Professional" in the capacity of Chief of Staff to former Congressmen, Rep. John Breckinridge (D-KY), Chairman of the House Antitrust, Small Business Committee and Rep. Bill Boner (D-TN), a member of the House Appropriations Committee. Mr. Chwat served as a legislative Aid to the late Rep. Seymour Halpern (R-NY), a member of the House Foreign Affairs and Banking Committees and staff member to the Senate Labor Committee under the late Sen. Jacob Javits (R-NY). He also served as a national defense and foreign policy analyst for the *Congressional Research Service (CRS) of the Library of Congress*. In this capacity, he authored congressional documents and researched projects for the US Congress with the *Central Intelligence Agency, Defense Intelligence Agency, Department of Defense, Joint Chiefs of Staff* and the *Department of State*. He was a senior specialist in congressional relations for the *Communications Satellite Corporation (COMSAT)* and also served in the Congressional Relations Office of the *United States Department of Agriculture*.

A graduate of *Georgetown University* with a Master's Degree in American Government, Mr. Chwat holds a Juris Doctor from *American University's Washington College of Law* and a Bachelor of Art degree in Political Science from *Long Island University*. He has taught courses on lobbying, the legislative process and American government at *George Mason University, Trinity College, Northern Virginia Community College and the Washington Center*.

John Chwat teaches lobbying techniques at industry and trade association conventions. He also speaks on government relations strategies before state and national groups, conventions, and board of directors' meetings. He serves on the *Government Relations Council of the American Society of Association Executives (ASAE)* and is Chairman of *ASAE's "Government Relations School."* He serves on the faculty of the *U.S. Chamber of Commerce's Institute for Organization Management*, providing seminars on government relations for Chamber members and associations. He is a past president of the *House Administrative Assistants Alumni Association* (representing former Chiefs of Staff to Members of Congress). He is also a member of the *American League of Lobbyists, the Capitol Hill Club*, the *United States Capitol Historical Society, the International Shakespeare Association*, and serves as president of *The American Friends of the Shakespeare Birthplace Trust, Inc.*

Robert K. Goodwin has served as President and CEO of the Points of Light Foundation since July 1, 1995. He joined the Foundation in March, 1992 as Executive Vice President and Chief Operating Officer. In that position, he managed every aspect of the Foundation's mission and operations.

Mr. Goodwin was instrumental in the development of the 1997 Presidents' Summit for America's Future, which celebrated a commitment to improve the quality of life for this nation's youth. He also created Connect America which has grown continuously and now involves more than 70 organizations.

He was twice selected as one of the 50 most influential people in the nonprofit sector by the *NonProfit Times*, and recently received honorary doctorates from the University of Notre Dame (2000) and Ripon College (1999).

Currently, Goodwin serves on the following voluntary boards of directors: Generations United, National and Community Service Coalition, National Assembly, National Urban Fellows, Inc., Parents and Friends of Lesbians and Gays, The Salvation Army, American Society of Association Executives, and the Interdenominational Theological Center.

Past positions include: executive director of the U.S. Department of Education's White House Initiative on Historically Black Colleges and Universities (HBCU's), assistant deputy chancellor for external affairs for Texas A&M University, director of public information and then as associate vice president for university relations at Prairie View A&M University.

Earlier in his career, Goodwin was publisher of his family-owned weekly newspaper, the OKLAHOMA EAGLE in Tulsa. While a student, he served as an associate pastor of several churches in Oklahoma and California.

Goodwin received his BA degree from Oral Roberts University in 1970, MA in Social Psychology at the University of Tulsa, and MA in Philosophy (Christian Ethics) from the San Francisco Theological Seminary and did further graduate study at Texas A&M University. He is the recipient of honorary doctorates from the University of Maryland-Eastern Shore and LeMoyne Owen College.

Bruce R. Hopkins, JD, LLM, is a lawyer with Polsinelli, Shalton & White in Kansas City, MO, where he specializes in the representation of not-for-profit organizations. He served as the chair of the Committee on Exempt Organizations, American Bar Association; chair of the Section of Taxation, National Association of College and University Attorneys; and president of the Planned Giving Study Group of Greater Washington, DC.

William P. Horn is a partner at Birch, Horton, Bittner and Cherot, in the Washington, D.C. office of an Alaska-based law firm. He also serves as Director of National and International Affairs and Washington Counsel for the Wildlife Legislative Fund of America. He previously spent 16 years in federal service working on Capitol Hill and the U.S. Department of the Interior. During his service on Capitol Hill he worked in the U.S. Congress most notably on the staff of the Interior Committee (now Resources Committee) in the U.S. House of Representatives. He served as Assistant Secretary for Fish, Wildlife and Parks at the U.S. Department of the Interior where he was responsible for the U.S. Fish and Wildlife Service and the National Park Service and as the Deputy Undersecretary of the Interior where he was responsible for the Department's programs in Alaska. He is a recipient of numerous awards, including the Outstanding Service Award of the Department of the Interior and the International Academy of Trial Lawyers Advocacy Award.

Jack Kalavritinos is the Director of Government Affairs for the American Consulting Engineers Council (ACEC), a national trade association representing 7,000 engineering firms employing over 200,000 people. Mr. Kalavritinos has authored articles and is quoted frequently in the trade press on behalf of ACEC. Kalavritinos received his Juris Doctorate degree from Catholic University in Washington, DC, and received his Bachelor of Arts degree in Political Science from Wake Forest University in Winston-Salem, North Carolina. He is the 2000-2001 Vice Chair of the American Society of Association Executives Government Affairs Section Council.

David L. Kushner is a certified association executive and certified meeting professional serving as President and CEO of the American Osteopathic Healthcare Association (AOHA) since 1990.

Through a subsidiary organization, the Osteopathic Services Corporation, he oversees the delivery of multiple association management services to the Association of Osteopathic Directors and Medical Educators, the American College of Osteopathic Pediatricians, the American Osteopathic Academy of Addiction Medicine, and the Foundation for Osteopathic Health Services.

Prior to joining AOHA, Mr. Kushner established and led The Kushner Group, a successful consulting practice with a specialization in leadership, organizational development, and human resources management. Past positions he has held include serving as National Director for Membership and Education with the American Federation of Government Employees and Regional Member Services Representative for New York State United Teachers.

Mr. Kushner is a member of the American Association of Medical Society Executives; the American Society of Association Executives; the Greater Washington Society of Association Executives; the Association Council of Montgomery County, Maryland; the National Speakers Association; and the Health Associations Lobbyists Organization.

Mr. Kushner holds a Masters degree from The George Washington University in Washington, DC and a Bachelors degree from Binghamton University, Binghamton, NY.

Rick Story has practiced the art of public relations for over 25 years on behalf of corporate concerns and non-profit associations. He holds a degree in public relations and journalism from The Ohio State University. Throughout his career, he has represented clients on numerous controversial issues. As vice president and board secretary of The Wildlife Legislative Fund of America and The Wildlife Conservation Fund of America, he has been an important player in the national struggle to defend wildlife management in the face of modern threats.

Acknowledgments

Government affairs is a vital part of the way in which individual and collective thought can be heard and acted on at the highest levels of government. It is the "art" of democracy, and it is the key to the continued protection of our fundamental rights. This publication would not have been possible if it were not for a number of individuals who helped to make it a reality.

First of all, let me express my thanks to the contributing authors. Each of them brought a different perspective and expertise on how to develop a successful government affairs program: David Kushner, CAE, president and chief executive officer of the American Osteopathic Healthcare Association, Chevy Chase, Maryland; William P. Horn, JD, managing partner, Birch, Horton, Bittner & Cherot, Washington, DC; Jack Kalavritinos, JD, director, Government Affairs, General Counsel, American Consulting Engineers Council, Washington, DC; Richard Story, vice president, Wildlife Legislative Fund of America, Columbus, Ohio; Robert Goodwin, president and chief executive officer, The Points of Light Foundation, Washington, DC; John Chwat, president, Chwat & Company, Inc., Alexandria, Virginia; and Bruce Hopkins, JD, Polsinelli, White, Vardeman & Shalton, Kansas City, Missouri.

A special thanks must go to the National Society of Fund Raising Executives' volunteer leadership for helping to publish this work.

Thanks to all of the sources that gave us permission to use their materials. The book would not have been the same without your contribution.

Thanks to the Wiley team, who smoothly assisted in the production of the book, to Martha Cooley our acquisition editor and to Scott Kramer, Adminstration Assistant. Also thanks to Lea Baranowski at Carlisle Publishers Services for her exceptional editing work.

A special thank you has to go to my family. To Susan Wallace Pidgeon, my wife of 32 years, who has provided advice and support on the project. To my son Walter (BJ) Pidgeon III, JD, for legal and editing support and to my son Spencer W. Pidgeon for providing various administrative duties on the project.

The publication was a team effort.

Contents

PART
II
▼ SUCCESSFUL METHODS USED BY NOT-FOR-PROFITS   53
WALTER P. PIDGEON, JR.

PART IV

▼ DEVELOPING A STRATEGIC PLAN FOR A NOT-FOR-PROFIT   175

WALTER P. PIDGEON, JR.

8 A Strategic Plan for Success / 178   WALTER P. PIDGEON, JR.

CONTENTS

Preface

Throughout history, humankind has been subjected to many forms of government. These governments were formed for both noble and not so noble reasons. Over time, tribal leaders gave way to monarchies and dictatorships.

As the new world began to take shape, a small revolution took place. What was different about this revolution was that its victors did not choose to dictate. Instead, they chose to form a new kind of government. They called this new form of government a democracy, and they called their territory the United States of America. The new form of government was designed to give a major part of its power to its citizens, to have limited federal power, and to ensure that each member state had rights within its territories. It was a noble idea—a government "by the people and for the people."

It is sometimes hard to believe today that our founding fathers envisioned a government, both in size and in process, that would not overpower its citizens, one that would help its citizens to live the lives that they choose. While life is much more complicated today, it is still a good idea.

The process of government relations continues to receive bad press. This is rather funny since "freedom of the press" happened through the government affairs process. Words such as *lobbying, special interest groups, right wing, and left wing* are used in a negative context to fuel the idea that groups working on behalf of their constituents to pass or defeat legislation are doing bad things. In reality, it is this very thing that keeps our democracy alive.

The founding fathers of our great nation created a form of government that has checks and balances and, above all, representation for the individual citizen. Alexis de Tocqueville's now classic book, written in the nineteenth century, titled *Democracy in America*, is believed to be the most penetrating and astute picture of American life at the time. De Tocqueville praised America for developing a form of government in which "the people reign over the American political world as God rules over the universe." He further noted, " If there is one country in the world where one can hope to appreciate the true value of the dogma of the sovereignty of the people, study its application to the business of society, and judge both its dangers and its advantages, that country is America." De Tocqueville saw something special in the role that America's form of government provides its citizens, a form of government designed to serve rather than dictate to its people.

The role of government affairs is as noble as the government that it works within. If it were not for government affairs, we would not have created the nation that is the envy of the world. The government affairs process is vital to our democracy. It should involve everyone.

The Government Affairs Process

For the purpose of this book, we will define the government affairs process as any act that is conducted to influence one or more parts of a government entity or function. The process is the method by which government affairs is performed.

When the government affairs process is considered by the general public, government affairs often brings up visions of large, powerful lobbies that have unlimited funds to influence legislators. This may be a trade association or business lobby who wishes to protect their area of interest.

While this type of government affairs is done every day in Washington, DC, and in every state capital in our nation, this will not be the focus of this book. While it is not the primary focus, it is important to note that this kind of lobbying is also a significant part of the democratic process. This book will focus, instead, on how not-for-profit organizations can become players in the government affairs process.

The Goal of the Book

The Legislative Labyrinth: A Map for Not-for-Profits is designed to provide a guide for not-for-profit leaders on launching or refining a government affairs program. While the material presented in each chapter encourages all not-for-profits to engage in the highest-level government affairs program allowed by the Internal Revenue Service (IRS), a special focus will be made on 501(c)3 organizations. These organizations tend to shy away from government affairs work. Many focus on programmatic roles or feel that such activity would jeopardize their IRS status. In the meantime, 501(c)3 organizations that are not taking advantage of the government affairs process could be harming their constituents.

Under law, 501(c)3 organizations have the ability to conduct a number of government affairs functions. The percentage of exempt purpose expenditures that an 501(c)3 can spend on lobbying varies, based on the following scale:

Exempt Purpose Expenditures	Nontaxable Amount
Not over $500,000	20 percent of the exempt purpose
Over $500,000 but not over $1,000,000	$100,000 plus 15 percent of the excess of the exempt purpose expenditures over $500,000
Over $1,000,000 but not over $1,500,000	$175,000 plus 10 percent of the exempt purpose expenditures over $1,000,000

In no event, however, can total direct lobbying expenditures exceed $1,000,000. Other provisions need to be examined to determine the extent to which 501(c)3 organizations can perform a government affairs function, however. The important thing is that these organizations can and should be involved.

This book is organized in four parts:

- Part 1: The Legislative/Government Affairs Process and the Not-for-Profit. This part introduces the government affairs process. It covers how the process can play a significant role in fulfilling a mission of an organization, the historical role of legislation, the roles that need to be played, the capabilities that are needed, volunteer involvement, and the state versus the federal level.
- Part 2: Successful Methods Used by Not-for-Profits. This part looks at the use of political action committees and grassroots lobbying, the use of communications and the media to win, and the development of partnerships for greater success.
- Part 3: The Legal Aspects of Government Affairs and Lobbying. This part provides information needed to design a program to meet Internal Revenue Service (IRS) scrutiny.
- Part 4: A Strategic Plan for Success. This part provides a guide to help develop or refine a government affairs program. Included are planning documents and fill-in forms that can be easily adapted to fit individual needs.

The CD-ROM Adds Additional Value

One of the features of the book is the CD-ROM, which can be found on the back cover of the book. The CD contains many of the exhibits in the book, including the strategic planning materials. It also contains other support materials, including successful campaign materials used by not-for-profits to win issues for their constituents. Feel free to use them. I ask only that you provide credit to the source when you do use them.

This has been an exciting experience for me to play both the editor's and author's roles. I know that all of the co-authors join me in encouraging you to take full advantage of the government affairs process. We hope that this book will help and encourage you to do so.

Walter P. Pidgeon, Jr., Ph.D., CAE, CFRE

▼ Foreword

Whether a trade association, professional society, or philanthropic organization, America's not-for-profit community is confronting public policy challenges at every level. From the court house to the White House and from the *Daily Advance* to the *New York Times*, policymakers and opinion shapers are questioning the operations, functions and performances of associations at every opportunity. And it is incumbent upon these membership associations and societies to deal effectively and professionally with the issues and concerns as they arise.

Non-profit organizations have always had the basic staffing structure to provide administrative oversight, meeting management, communications and volunteer relations. But treading into the arena of public policy has been one of the last organization structure changes for these groups. Today, more than any time in our 250-year history of volunteer organizations in America, we are needing guidance, expertise and definition to the process of influencing public opinion, promoting appropriate legislation, fighting inappropriate regulations and preserving the organizational integrity of the association. Walter (Bud) Pidgeon's *The Legislative Labyrinth: A Map for Not-for-Profits* is just what the doctor ordered.

Bud has assembled the collective wisdom of some of the most experienced executives in the profession of association management in presenting a range of issues from fundamentals of structure and course in the legislative arenas to effective creation of a public policy advocacy program for associations. We are given examples of specific programs that have been effective in preserving an organization or advancing a cause, and how to accomplish these objectives without bankrupting the organization's treasury or integrity.

The association community, thanks to Bud Pidgeon's efforts, will benefit and grow in its understanding of the vital role public policy management, strategy and initiatives now play in this environment. This collection is a must-read for the professional association or professional society executive as well as those whose interests in the field include understanding the impact of legislative and regulatory actions on our country's voluntary organizations.

Michael S. Olson, CAE

President and CEO

American Society of Association Executive

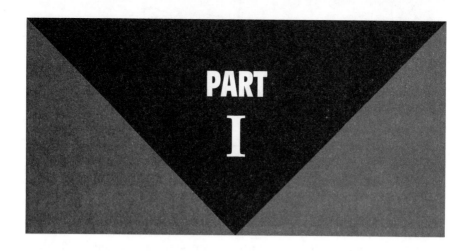

THE LEGISLATIVE/GOVERNMENT AFFAIRS AND THE NOT-FOR-PROFIT

WALTER P. PIDGEON, JR.

The human race has been in conflict since the beginning of time. Early humans found it best to group together in tribes to protect themselves from predators and the elements. Humans found conflict, however, particularly concerning who would rule and who would follow. In the beginning, humans who had the most strength tended to be the leaders. Nature and animals still use this criterion today.

The selection of the leader, based only on strength, gave way to other attributes. The human brain enlarged and became the predominate factor in who would rule. Larger groups of humans began to intermingle. Larger conflict often arose due to differing customs and beliefs.

Somewhere in the midst of the taming of humankind came the rule of law. In many cases, early law did not favor individual rights; it was more of a power struggle to maintain control over the group.

While early forms of government gave some rights to the individual, usually a few individuals were singled out to enjoy more freedom. It was not until the United States was formed that citizens were given greater individuals rights through a representative form of government.

Right from the beginning of our nation, it was determined that individuals who banned together to form alliances could strengthen their position. While the original organizations were mostly trade associations, they demonstrated the power of one voice for the common good.

While it seems that most not-for-profits engage in some level of government affairs, thousands do not. The greater numbers of those that do not engage in government affairs fall into the 501(c)3 IRS status. These groups often believe that government affairs has little value for their mission, or they are leery of losing their not-for-profit status by engaging in government affairs.

Not-for-profits that do not engage in some kind of government affairs role miss out on a great opportunity to represent their constituents. Most not-for-profit organizations have the ability to have a government affairs activity, including not-for-profit groups that are classified by the Internal Revenue Service as a 501(c)3 organization.

Chapter 1 begins the journey through the legislative process. The author, David Kushner, is president and chief executive officer of the American Osteopathic Healthcare Association, a national health-related association. He has extensive experience in the use of government affairs as a tool to represent his organization's constituents.

Think back to your early school days and the civic classes that you sat through. Remember the basic principles that were drilled into your head about the power of citizenship and the importance of voting. You were told that this simple act is one of the most powerful ways a citizen has to voice opinions on issues and to elect fellow citizens to represent him or her at the local, state, and federal levels.

During those early classroom discussions, at least in my experience, I don't recall a lot being said about the use of groups to represent us through that process, groups that could lobby for issues on our behalf, yet our system of government is designed to do just that. In order for a not-for-profit to take full advantage of this process, its leaders need to know the rules.

While Chapter 1 will provide an introduction to the rules, make sure that you review Chapter 7, dealing with the legal aspects of government affairs. In addition, consult with your legal and accounting services to make sure that you understand the rules as they pertain to your not-for-profit.

Make sure you also have a historical perspective on the role that not-for-profits have played in the government affairs arena. There are a number of books on the subject. This will help you to avoid making similiar mistakes and to build on the work that other not-for-profits have done.

A lot of discussion will take place on the capacity of a not-for-profit to perform a government affairs function. Don't be intimidated by the discussion. Not-for-profits vary in the size and dimension of their government affairs programs. Chapter 8 will assist you in making a decision based on the resources you have and the need to represent your constituents.

Chapter 2 details the legislative process at the state and federal levels. William Horn is the author. Bill is a partner at Birch, Horton, Bittner & Cherot and one of the leading lobbyists groups in Washington, DC. He begins his chapter by reviewing the steps of introducing a bill in Congress.

Not-for-profits can play a significant role in this process. On either side, the bill may be supported by one or more not-for-profits. The discussion and lobbying that take place help to pass, refine, or kill a bill. While rules may differ when you compare the federal process with the state process and states themselves may vary on how the process works, the overall rule is that a representative government cannot function without knowing what its citizens need and desire.

Not-for-profits can provide a valuable service to both their constituents and the general public through a quality government affairs program. Trade associations and other, 501(c)6 and 501(c)4, associations successfully represent their constituents on matters that affect all citizens' lives, from product safety to tax issues. While a number of 501(c)3 organizations have done the same, thousands have not.

Not-for-profit leaders need to consider seriously what role government affairs can play in their organizations. While it will vary, depending on a number of factors, a government affairs function should be part of almost all not-for-profits.

The Significant Role That the Legislative Process Can Play in Fulfilling the Mission of a Not-for-Profit

DAVID KUSHNER

Introduction

Ask yourself why you belong to a particular not-for-profit group, and I am certain there will be a variety of answers and valid reasons. One area—the legislative process—often dominates the list of motivating factors for joining and remaining in an organization. This chapter is intended to provide you with an overview of the components of a sound legislative agenda for an organization and the reasons that this arena is so important to both current and prospective members.

My experience with the legislative process and the not-for-profit world spans activities ranging from local community area school board politics, to state legislative matters, to federal-level regulatory and congressional activities. Throughout my 30-year career in nonprofits, the most easily identifiable theme has been the need for an effective legislative agenda coupled with member communication and education programs.

The legislative process fulfills a wide range of organizational goals. Not-for-profit groups serve as forums for highly specified professionals who conduct research, provide continuing education for licensure or certification along the lines of medical societies, and serve as a catalyst for action among employees through unions. Not-for-profits serve as communicators, educators, advisors, proposers, and mobilizers, depending on the goals of each group.

A significant goal that can be achieved through the legislative process is that of member involvement. Later in this chapter, there will be a more in-depth discussion of various ways to involve members in the activities of the not-for-profit using the legislative process. Members find this to be an opportunity to influence future legislative action, to gain prominence for themselves and the organization, and to advance or oppose specific agendas.

This chapter will cover the following areas:

- Historical roles that not-for-profits have played in the legislative process

- Multiple roles for not-for-profits at state and federal levels
- Essential capabilities not-for-profits need in order to develop a legislative agenda
- Volunteer opportunities resulting from legislative activities
- Attractions of prospective donors to legislatively active groups
- Examples of not-for-profits with successful legislative operations

In the complex and global society in which we live, an effective legislative capability is the norm in not-for-profits. Technological advances may improve the ability to individualize communications, yet separate us as citizens, and weaken the democratic processes that rely on consensus building. Through not-for-profit organizations, we are able to share information, debate issues, educate one another, and present a common message to various governing bodies. Regardless of successes or failures, a positive legislative program demonstrates an organizational mission in a concise and easily identifiable manner to members and the public.

Historical Role Not-for-Profits Have Played in the Legislative Process

Not-for-profit roles in the legislative process are not reserved solely to today's sophisticated lobbying programs with the accompanying high-tech member communications. Considering that associations are formed by people who share common concerns and needs, it is logical that associations have been active legislative participants for many years. Their successes today are the result of a record of years of building accomplishments.

Whenever a void exists in an industry or a profession, one of two routes can be followed to resolve the matter. The government can assume the role of rule maker, standard setter, or accrediting body, or a not-for-profit group can establish various industrywide or professionwide standards and secure government approval or acceptance. Recognizing that it is far easier to modify rules or standards that are voluntarily set and adhered to, as opposed to changing legislation through a cumbersome and time-consuming process, it is easy to see why not-for-profits have assumed active legislative and sometimes quasi-governmental status. The following sections describe some sample historical roles filled by not-for-profits.

Professional Standards: National Education Association (NEA)

Before the advent of modern teacher unions, there were associations of educators, which acted to advance the educators' professional lives. Teacher associations built a historical record of political activism first at the local school district level, gradually expanding to state-level associations and finally to national groups, such as the National Education Association. The successes of these groups included establishing teacher retirement plans and setting standards for entry into the profession.

Education and Lobbying: National Rifle Association (NRA)

The National Rifle Association has built a long record of legislative successes at all levels of government. Whether one looks at gun safety standards, education for new hunters and gun owners, or state and federal laws regarding gun ownership, the National Rifle Association has built a very strong grassroots organization, which is able to reach legislators at all levels of government to enact favorable measures or to defeat efforts to restrain gun ownership. As this chapter progresses, you will find other examples of the effectiveness of groups such as the National Rifle Association in areas such as communications, member involvement, and the development of targeted messages.

Industry Standards: National Spa and Pool Institute (NSPI)

The area of industrial standards development is exemplified by the National Spa and Pool Institute. Through the NSPI, companies have banded together through a not-for-profit association to set industrywide standards for continued safety and reliability. Consumers and the government rely on the National Spa and Pool Institute to enforce these standards to ensure public safety. Additionally, many smaller governmental jurisdictions have adopted the National Spa and Pool Institute standards as regulations. The standard-setting role of this association forms the basis for an effective legislative program.

Accreditation—Assuming a Quasi-governmental Role: American College of Surgeons (ACS)

Medical societies structured as 501(c)(6) associations conduct lobbying; however, those established as 501(c)(3) education or research organizations also have active roles in the legislative process, which extend back for many years. An excellent example of this is the American College of Surgeons. Early in the twentieth century, its efforts were focused on ensuring hygienic conditions in the hospitals in which surgeons practiced. Its leadership resulted in the formation, by a group of other related not-for-profits, of the Joint Commission for the Accreditation of Healthcare Organizations. Today, this organization, known as the JCAHO, is the standard setter for healthcare institutional accreditation assessment and regulation.

Multiple Roles

At both state and federal levels of government, not-for-profit groups fulfill a number of important roles. The complexities surrounding most of the issues that are before legislators have shifted the governing process from individual citizen commentary and involvement to a more focused and often highly specialized approach. Media identification of *special interest groups*—a term often used by candidates in a pejorative manner—frankly refers to the not-for-profit groups that have the technical knowledge or specialized research that is essential to understanding legislative matters at all levels of governance.

The roles that will be covered in this section include

- Serving as advocates for members and the public
- Conducting independent research
- Seeking public opinion
- Providing information to legislators
- Modifying proposed legislation
- Mobilizing grassroots constituencies
- Serving as information disseminators and educators

Serving as Advocates for Members and the Public

One of the most easily identifiable roles for not-for-profits is that of member advocate. Individual citizens find themselves removed from the governing process today. Whether the reasons are lack of time or interest, an inability to grasp the complexity of a particular issue, frustration with the pace of legislative activity, or unfamiliarity with the issues under consideration, we as members of society are less and less personally active in state and federal affairs.

Through participation in a membership group, however, the process of advocacy on issues is enhanced. Rather than each individual's taking action, the collective expertise of paid staff and dedicated volunteers can be brought to bear on elected leaders. Beyond advocacy for members, often the public as a whole benefits from the legislative work of not-for-profits because of the broad implications of many government actions.

Conducting Independent Research

Once an issue has been identified as potentially affecting members of a not-for-profit, it may be necessary to conduct independent research. This may include basic scientific research, review of available literature, contacts and/or discussions with experts or spokespeople on the matters under consideration, or studies comparing the proposed actions with other options that should be considered.

Consider that a new regulatory rule for a particular industry is under deliberation by either a state or a federal body. To assess the impact of the proposed regulation, a coalition of companies or membership groups representing those with vested interests may form a not-for-profit group. Specialized research is then conducted to support the position and is then publicized through the vehicle of the coalition in an effort to sway public opinion or legislative deliberations.

Another example is research on the effects on children of riding bicycles without protective headgear. Once the data on injuries and deaths are collected, verified, and publicized, groups such as the American Academy of Pediatrics then seek legislation that mandates helmet use, or they oppose legislation that does not require protective headgear.

Seeking Public Opinion

Another area of research is the assessment of public opinion through surveys. Not-for-profits conduct extensive membership research through mail and telephone surveys, focus group sessions, Internet responses, and anecdotal comments from meetings or correspondence. The term *public* here is more discreetly defined than general public opinion surveying because of the individual's predisposition to join with like-minded people through a not-for-profit. Nonetheless, from the perspective of an association, the resulting information that is collected is valuable to those who are considering legislative or regulatory matters.

Providing Information to Legislators

The previous two roles for not-for-profits, conducting research and seeking public opinion, naturally lead to the provision of pertinent information to legislators. Once the data or opinions have been collected, assessed, and formulated, the information needs to be synthesized and summarized into easily understood and useful formats. Legislative bodies are inundated with information and have scant time to pore over detailed, lengthy reports. One of the most important roles for the not-for-profit is to serve as the source of pertinent information that is reliable and easily digestible. Legislators depend on not-for-profits for extensive background pieces on a variety of topics. This activity may, in fact, be a very effective legislative program on its own.

Modifying Proposed Legislation

Another role that logically flows from the previous examples is that of modifying language and proposals that are before a government body. Once the not-for-profit has completed its research and public opinion gathering, quite often it is clear that alternatives should be brought forward for consideration. Experienced staff can draft new language or work with appropriate legislative staff to modify existing material to reflect the need of the members of the not-for-profit.

Effective advocacy requires that the organization's leadership know when it is most appropriate or effective to provide alternative language. This process may include "floating trial balloons" among groups of legislators to determine which approach or terminology will be most effective for members and acceptable to the deliberators. One could argue that this role of modifier/proposer must include serving in an advisory capacity to elected leaders. A seasoned legislative affairs staff member knows whether the best opportunity is to offer alternative language or to advise a key drafter of the original language on how best to modify the legislation in a manner that will protect members.

Mobilizing Grassroots Constituencies

Another role is that of mobilizing grassroots constituencies to either promote or oppose specific issues under consideration. Once the research process is completed and delivered to the appropriate parties, it is essential that association members be asked to support the association's positions. Contacting the local offices of elected officials at the state and federal levels is best accomplished by those who are actually eligible to cast ballots in future elections.

The mobilization process is usually the not-for-profit's most complex role. A specific plan of action, time line of activities, and process for publicizing the positions to be taken are required before embarking on this task. With today's instantaneous and low-cost communications capabilities, the mobilizing of opinion can be conducted rapidly. This role has sprouted a variety of highly technical and specialized vendors, who are available to advise not-for-profits or to act on their behalf throughout the grassroots efforts. (See Exhibits 1.1 through 1.4.)

Serving as Information Disseminators and Educators

Not-for-profits serve an essential educational role for members through the dissemination of both proposed and enacted rules, regulations, and laws at both state and federal levels. This vein of member communications expands the distribution channels for important pieces of legislation beyond those normally used by government. In addition to direct member communication, the "readership multiplier effect," of more than the intended audience having access to any printed materials, helps to spread the message.

In the association I work for, we hold "Hot Topics Seminars" to highlight issues that are in the spotlight. Two recent examples include a seminar of the effects of rulings that allow medical residents to unionize rather than be considered students in an education program. Although there was

EXHIBIT 1.1   Mobilization: Call to Action

ACTION ALERT

A SPECIAL ALERT FOR MEMBERS OF THE GRASSROOTS OSTEOPATHIC ADVOCACY LINK.

CRITICAL CALL TO ACTION!

WITHOUT YOUR HELP TODAY, PATIENTS' RIGHTS WILL DIMINISH!

If a congressional committee does not reach an agreement between the House and Senate Patients' Bill of Rights before Memorial Day recess May 26th, the chances of a Patients' Bill of Rights being approved will be greatly diminished.

For months, the osteopathic medical community has tirelessly worked to convince Members of Congress the importance of meaningful patients' rights legislation. But we MUST continue to work for patients' rights. We are at the moment that counts. Whether you have acted in the past or not, your policymakers NEED to hear from you! Your action will decide if patients will have the protections for which they have long fought. Whether you act *or not* speaks volumes to our Nation's leaders.

This call to action is so critical that the AOA is challenging EVERY member of the osteopathic medical community to participate in the action items listed below. Help us convince Members of Congress to accelerate their negotiations and support the House Norwood-Dingell provisions! The osteopathic medical community must communicate to all policymakers, not just conferees, that patients deserve a meaningful Patients' Bill of Rights NOW, not next year!

If you have any questions about this call to action, please call Heidi Ecker, AOA's Director of Grassroots and Washington Communications at 800/962-9008 ext 225.

TAKE ACTION! FOLLOW THESE STEPS!

1. Identify your Members of Congress by visiting the AOA's Patients' Rights Action Center at www.aoa-net.org or calling the Washington Office at 800/962-9008. Don't forget, you can also lookup the policymaker that represents your place of employment.

2. Contact the Washington Office at 800/962-9008 or visit the above mentioned Patients' Rights Action Center to identify whether your policymakers are lead negotiators in the debate, how your policymakers voted on the House and Senate Patients' Rights bills, and other important patients' rights information.

3. Decide on your method of communication: There's more impact with a phone call, but letters also make a difference! Please see the attached talking points and sample letter to take action!

4. Regardless of how you communicate there are two very important things to remember: a) always include your name and mailing address on your correspondence; and b) share your communication and any responses with the Washington Office of AOA.

DEPARTMENT OF GOVERNMENT RELATIONS, AOA, 1090 VERMONT AVE., NW, SUITE 510, WASHINGTON, DC 20002, PHONE: 800/962-9008, FAX: 202/544-3525

EXHIBIT 1.2   Mobilization: Example Talking Points for Telephone Calls

ACTION ALERT
A SPECIAL ALERT FOR MEMBERS OF THE GRASSROOTS OSTEOPATHIC ADVOCACY LINK.

TALKING POINTS FOR TELEPHONE CALLS

If you'd like to talk to your Members of Congress about patients' rights, call 202/224-3121 and tell the Capitol Hill Switchboard your zip code or the name of your policymakers. Once you are connected to the appropriate office, ask the receptionist to speak with the health LA (legislative assistant).

For House Norwood-Dingell supporters, tell the staffer:

1. "As a voting constituent and an osteopathic physician I applaud your efforts to approve managed care reform. **I am very pleased my Member of Congress voted to pass Norwood-Dingell.**"

2. "As you know, Norwood-Dingell provisions will make a tremendous difference in quality patient care. Please convince your colleagues to support Norwood-Dingell in the compromise."

3. "I expect my policymakers to hold Sen. Nickles' feet to the fire with regard to his promise of a patients' bill of rights compromise by the already-passed Easter recess. This slow-moving conference MUST accelerate. **We need patients' rights now, not next year.**"

For those in the House that did not vote for Norwood-Dingell, tell the staffer:

1. "As a voting constituent and an osteopathic physician I am disappointed that you did not support the Norwood-Dingell Patients' Bill of Rights."

2. "The Norwood-Dingell patient bill of rights is meaningful legislation that allows physicians to determine medical necessity, holds health plans accountable for their actions, provides a fair and independent appeals process to patients, and ensures these basic protections apply to all Americans."

3. "I expect my policymakers to hold Sen. Nickles' feet to the fire with regard to his promise of a Patients' Bill of Rights compromise by the already-passed Easter recess. This slow-moving conference MUST accelerate. **We need patients' rights now, not next year.**"

For Senators, tell the staffer:

1. "As a voting constituent and an osteopathic physician I commend the Senate for taking a step forward towards patient protections. However, the Senate bill does not provide the greatly needed patient protections outlined in the Norwood-Dingell legislation."

2. "The Norwood-Dingell Patients' Bill of Rights is meaningful legislation that allows physicians to determine medical necessity, holds health plans accountable for their actions, provides a fair and independent appeals process to patients, and ensures these basic protections apply to all Americans."

3. "I expect my policymakers to hold Sen. Nickles' feet to the fire with regard to his promise of a Patients' Bill of Rights compromise by the already-passed Easter recess. This slow-moving conference MUST accelerate. **We need patients' rights now, not next year.**"

DEPARTMENT OF GOVERNMENT RELATIONS, AOA, 1090 VERMONT AVE., NW, SUITE 510, WASHINGTON, DC 20002, PHONE: 800/962-9008, FAX: 202/544-3525

EXHIBIT 1.3   Mobilization: Sample Letter

ACTION ALERT

A SPECIAL ALERT FOR MEMBERS OF THE GRASSROOTS OSTEOPATHIC ADVOCACY LINK.

SAMPLE LETTER

[Date]

[Insert Member of Congress' name]
United States [House of Representatives/Senate]
[Insert address]

Dear [Insert Representative's or Senator's name]:

As an osteopathic physician in your state, I write in support of the provisions of the "Bipartisan Consensus Managed Care Improvement Act of 1999" (H.R. 2723) included in the "Quality Care for the Uninsured Act of 1999" (H.R. 2990). As the conference committee continues considering the Senate's "Patients' Bill of Rights Plus Act" (S. 1344) and H.R. 2990, please hold firm for the H.R. 2723 protections in the final compromise. Patients need and deserve this meaningful and comprehensive legislation.

As a voting constituent, I expect my policymakers to hold Sen. Nickles' feet to the fire with regard to his promise of a Patients' Bill of Rights compromise by the already-passed Easter recess. This slow-moving conference must accelerate! Patients deserve meaningful protections now, not next year!

I also expect my policymakers to support the following points, as they are essential to securing meaningful patient protections:

- Reviews of claim and treatment denials should be independent, fair, binding and timely;

- Medical necessity should be determined using a prudent layperson standard in accordance with generally accepted standards of medical practice;

- Health plan accountability should remedy the inequity that results from the ability of plans to make medical decisions while remaining unaccountable for injuries they cause;

- Enrollees in managed care plans should be offered a point-of-service option enabling them to obtain care from physicians outside the health plan's network of participating physicians; and

- All Americans should be covered by any patient protection legislation passed by Congress, not just those enrolled in ERISA or "self-funded" ERISA plans.

In closing, I would like to express our appreciation for your efforts to promote fairness in managed care. I am hopeful a bipartisan bill that advances the rights of patients comes forward. All patients must be guaranteed the protection of the law. The osteopathic medical community is committed to working with you on this critical issue.

Sincerely,

[insert your name]
[insert your mailing address]

CC: Heidi Ann Ecker, AOA, Director of Grassroots and Washington Communications

DEPARTMENT OF GOVERNMENT RELATIONS, AOA, 1090 VERMONT AVE., NW, SUITE 510, WASHINGTON, DC 20002, PHONE: 800/962-9008, FAX: 202/544-3525

EXHIBIT 1.4   Mobilization: Example Issue Background

ACTION ALERT

A SPECIAL ALERT FOR MEMBERS OF THE GRASSROOTS OSTEOPATHIC ADVOCACY LINK.

ISSUE BACKGROUNDER

Now that the U.S. House of Representatives and the U.S. Senate have each approved a version of patients' rights legislation, the two are negotiating a compromise. According to the AOA, a meaningful Patients' Bill of Rights allows physicians to determine medical necessity, holds health plans accountable for their actions, provides a fair and independent appeals process to patients, and ensures these basic protections apply to all Americans. A House-Senate Conference Committee is responsible for reconciling differences between the House (HR 2990) and Senate (S 1344) bills. Members of this special panel, also known as conferees, are selected to serve by House and Senate Leadership.

The House Plan

After a drawn-out House debate and rejection of three alternate measures, the House adopted "The Bipartisan Managed Care Improvement Act," as its solution for patient protections. Sponsored by Representatives Charles Norwood (R-GA) and John Dingell (D-MI), the AOA-backed legislation promises Americans broad safeguards when dealing with their managed care plans. The Norwood-Dingell legislation applies to all Americans with private health insurance, allows physicians the ability to determine medical necessity, provides independent external review by doctors of the same license, and holds health plans accountable for decisions that harm or hurt patients. The House-approved Norwood-Dingell measure was attached to another House-approved health tax-and-access package sponsored by Rep. James Talent (R-MO) (HR 2990). "The Quality Care for the Uninsured Act of 1999" expands tax breaks for health insurance expenses and provides self-employed individuals and small businesses with lower health insurance rates when health coverage is purchased with others. H.R. 2990 is the vehicle for compromise between the House and Senate versions of patients' rights.

The Senate Plan

In July, the U.S. Senate rejected Minority Leader Tom Daschle's (D-SD) version of the House-approved patients' rights bill (S. 1344). The "Patient's Bill of Rights Act of 1999," sponsored by Majority Leader Trent Lott (R-MS), provides only basic protections, fails to make health plans liable for their actions, and does not apply to all Americans for health insurance. While the AOA commends the Senate for taking a step forward toward establishing patient protections, the Senate bill does not provide the greatly needed patient protections outlined in the Norwood-Dingell legislation.

Work Lies Ahead for Conferees

Patients' rights conferees have agreed on legislative concepts of access to emergency room services and pediatricians, prohibition of discrimination against providers and external review. They have not reached an agreement on whether protections should apply to all Americans with health insurance or on health plan liability. AOA firmly believes meaningful patients' rights legislation must provide patient protections to all Americans and hold all health plans accountable for medical decisions that harm or injure a patient.

In March, patients' rights conferees agreed on four main principles: 1) parents can select a pediatrician; 2) the prudent layperson definition stands for emergency room services; 3) if a hospital isn't part of a plan, the hospital must call the plan within one hour of stabilization and three hours after that time frame to determine services; and 4) a plan can not ban certain licensed health professionals from being in a network (that's GREAT news for D.O.s!). In April, conferees agreed on four concepts of external review: 1) medical decisions should be made by doctors; 2) the sanctity of the contract is maintained; 3) the external review is medical in nature; and 4) the standard of review is based on science and evidence. *It is important to understand that the conferees agreed in principle, but these are solely summaries of agreements and not actual legislative language.*

Timing is of the essence! Contact your policymakers TODAY and tell them patients deserve a meaningful Patients' Bill of Rights NOW, not next year!

DEPARTMENT OF GOVERNMENT RELATIONS, AOA, 1090 VERMONT AVE., NW, SUITE 510, WASHINGTON, DC 20002, PHONE: 800/962-9008, FAX: 202/544-3525

widespread press coverage of the ruling, members wanted more in-depth information and the opportunity to share concerns with colleagues. The result of this one seminar was a sharing of the information throughout the facilities the attendees came from. The second example deals with proposed legislative actions based on a report released by the government regarding the frequency of medical errors. The furor over the study could easily have resulted in stringent new rules placed on an already heavily regulated environment. The original information was widely disseminated based on the study, but the Hot Topic Seminar allowed thoughtful discussion, analysis, and development of counterarguments to new rules. (See Exhibit 1.5.)

Essential Capabilities Not-for-Profits Need to Develop a Legislative Agenda

There are basic capabilities of an organization that are prerequisites to the development of a legislative program. The board of trustees or other governing body must carefully assess these components before embarking on a legislative journey. There are factors associated with a nonprofit establishing an outreach program that must be considered, such as costs for program development and maintenance, public and membership perceptions of the effort, and potential negative reactions that may result from unexpected sources.

A good legislative program requires a complex, matrix management approach to the allocation of resources and other elements. Seven components will be discussed to give you a perspective on the scope of issues that must be reviewed prior to implementing the effort.

Interested Membership

The most fundamental aspect of a not-for-profit legislative effort is the assessment of member interests and expectations. It is critical to the success of lobbying activities that senior management and volunteer leaders have a firm grasp on the priority of the issues members face. This can be accomplished via telephone or mail survey, group discussion at meetings or conferences, or focus groups. The information that is gleaned should be reviewed, summarized, and prioritized by category, using the services of an experienced survey firm. This may help the organization avoid a common pitfall—having in-house staff, with vested interests, attempting to impartially present survey data. The results of this initial stage of investigation should be further reviewed with members and leaders to permit an educational assessment about potential organizational positions. In my experience with this, in one case, a group of elected leaders promoted an agenda they felt was appropriate, only to find themselves surprised by the lack of member support. An even cursory survey would have revealed a large conservative group within the association, which

EXHIBIT 1.5   Hot Topic Seminar Announcement

Take advantage of small-group interaction on topics in the forefront of healthcare today at the

American Osteopathic Healthcare Association's Hot Topics Seminars

Thursday, January 27, 2000
The Hyatt Regency, Columbus, Ohio

SCHEDULE:

8:00 A.M.–8:30 A.M. Morning Registration

8:30 A.M.–12:00 P.M.
Seminar #1:
Reducing Medical Errors and Improving Patient Safety
In light of the recently released IOM report on medical errors calling for Congress to create a Center for Patient Safety to set national goals for patient safety, attendees will be provided with clinical performance data to assist them in identifying emerging risks and developing strategies for reducing patient injuries and improving outcomes.

12:00 P.M.–1:00 P.M. Lunch on Your Own

1:00 P.M.–1:30 P.M. Afternoon Registration

1:30 P.M.–5:00 P.M.
Seminar #2:
New Challenges in Healthcare Labor Relations
On November 29, the NLRB determined that interns and residents at Boston Medical Center are entitled to collective bargaining rights under the National Labor Relations Act. Subsequently, BMC's house staff voted 177–1 in support of unionization. This is a session that healthcare administrators and medical educators can't afford to miss.

Register today to guarantee seating for either session or both—a reduced fee is available if you choose to stay for both important seminars.

had not been previously identified because of a propensity toward passive membership. The outside image of this organization's legislative program was one of disarray based on a leadership team that espoused liberal program support but which could not muster member participation or financial contributions. The long-term negative image that resulted was quite costly to correct and had an impact on membership recruitment and financial support for other activities.

Experienced, Educated Staff

Building a core legislative staff would seem to be an implicit assumption for success. Although that may be true in some cases, it is not in all. Not-for-profits across the country often depend on volunteers who demonstrate an interest and a willingness to engage in lobbying and other government relations tasks.

At the core of a program must be experienced and educated staff who will be responsible for the design and implementation of government relations activities. Whether the activities are at the local, state, or federal level of government, engage staff with experience that is as directly related as possible and ensure that their experience is augmented by appropriate continuing education offered by groups such as the American Society of Association Executives or state or local groups of association government relations personnel.

Members who do not have the requisite experience to serve as full-time representatives play important roles in the outreach efforts of the not-for-profit, and this will be covered in more depth in a later section of this chapter. Problems sometimes result from volunteers' assuming status that exceeds their experience. Volunteer spokespeople may overstate positions, misinterpret legislative language or intent, or not be current on the deliberations or passage of related legislation. Although the volunteer's intent is good, it is very difficult to challenge the statements of a fellow member, even when staff are fully aware of erroneous statements. Each not-for-profit should take care to provide oversight to members who speak on behalf of the organization and to offer support to those with experience.

A successful not-for-profit government relations program requires that staff be assessed on a set of specific goals that has been cooperatively developed with the volunteer body that oversees the government relations activities. While it might be perceived as power sharing for volunteers to involve the staff, my experience has been that only jointly planned programs result in success. This allows volunteers to set the goals for the programs while considering the opportunities, resource requirements, and potential opposition or constraints that are assessed by staff leaders. Too often, programs run independently by either group fail because volunteers' expectations are unrealistic or because staff are not held accountable for the results.

Board Support and Strategic Oversight

The main role of a board of trustees or directors is to set the policies for the organization. In the not-for-profit world, the need for ongoing board education in the area of legislative action is critical. While staff may be aware of the nuances of a particular issue, volunteer leaders must have a thorough grasp of the overall matter in order to provide valid oversight. Regular staff briefings of the board or direct oversight group are an excellent means for accomplishing this. With today's instantaneous communications technologies, boards and volunteers can be advised more frequently about the status of issues. In addition, adequate time at board and committee meetings should be set aside to allow thorough discussions about the pros and cons of all legislative matters. The days of a twice-yearly written report to a board or committee are over because the pace of all levels of government action are rapid and intricate, thus calling for more continuity and frequency of communications.

A Clear Message Tied to the Mission or Vision

Tied closely with proper board education is the need for a clear, concise message that is to be delivered via the not-for-profit's legislative activities. As the policymaking body for the group, the leaders are responsible for connecting the legislative program and messages to the organization's mission, vision, and strategic direction. Recalling the earlier segment on the assessment of member interests and support leads us to the capability to align overall legislative goals with organizational policy statements. Associations that fail to connect mission to message, especially in legislative matters, find themselves with confused members, frustrated staff, and an outside audience that views the program with little credibility.

Sources of Funding

It is essential that adequate resources be provided to support a legislative program. Costs for staff, travel, printing, membership in various political groups, research, meetings, and publications, to name a few areas, should be included in a prospective budget. Since these are not one-time or start-up costs (which must be considered as well), ongoing sources of income need to be identified and allocated to government relations activities.

Board and committee members should delineate the sources of potential income and then verify availability before implementing legislative projects. There is a wide range of income sources to be considered, including the following:

- Allocations of a percentage of membership dues revenue or other nondues revenue sources

- Solicitation of funds through the establishment of a regulated political action committee (PAC). (See Chapter 7 for a more detailed discussion of the legal requirements for establishing and operating a PAC.)
- Development of a non-PAC, government affairs–type fund, which is able to accept corporate contributions but can be used only to offset the administrative costs for operating the official PAC itself
- Encouragement and/or coordination of individual member contributions to targeted elected officials' campaign funds while including a message that indicates membership in and support of the not-for-profit's goals or positions on issues

Since the fund-raising arena is carefully regulated at both state and federal levels, you are encouraged to read Chapter 7 very carefully and consult with legal counsel before collecting or allocating any funds. This entire activity—funding for a legislative program—needs to be a key component of board-level consideration and deliberations.

Communications Vehicles

All not-for-profits have established methods for communicating with members. With the explosion of new options that are tied to the Internet, this is a capability area that may not pose a problem for groups but is still a part of the initial assessment phase. Although traditional newsletters, web sites, broadcast fax, and regular mail are all viable means of reaching members, it is important to determine the legislative agenda and messages that are best for reaching members.

In my organization, we have produced a concise, one-page information sheet that is broadcast faxed to all members bi-weekly. Exhibit 1.6 is a copy of the Washington Update, as it is named. From our member surveys, we have learned that it is the most widely read publication we produce. Additionally, it has achieved an even broader audience through pass-along distribution channels. Other options include publishing a regular report for financial supporters of the legislative activities or some type of insider's report, which goes beyond normal publications to offer in-depth analysis of issues.

In the event your association blends its government relations messages into already existing publications, one good approach is to set up this information in an easily identifiable format that is also in the same location in a publication for each edition.

Earlier I suggested that a sound government relations program requires the involvement of both volunteer leaders to set policy and experienced legislative staff for practical guidance, as well as finance and publications staffs to insure continuity throughout the headquarter's operations.

EXHIBIT 1.6   AOHA Washington Update

AOHA WASHINGTON UPDATE
July 14, 2000—A biweekly member service of
The American Osteopathic Healthcare Association

AOHA and AODME represent the interests of osteopathic healthcare facilities and medical educators on Capitol Hill.

- Fueled by reports of a federal budget surplus of $211 billion, the Administration has called on Congress to provide $21 billion in Balanced Budget Act (BBA) relief to health care providers over the next 5 years ($40 billion over 10 years). The proposal also includes a comprehensive Medicare prescription drug benefit and a "lockbox" to preserve the Medicare surplus for the program's exclusive use. Of the $21 billion, $9 billion would be earmarked for hospitals and other specified health care institutions, with the additional $12 billion subject to negotiation with Congress. For FY 2001, the President's plan would:
    - increase hospital inpatient payment rates to the full market basket rate;
    - eliminate the reduction in the indirect medical education (IME) adjustment;
    - freeze Medicaid disproportionate share hospital (DSH) allotments at the FY 2000 level; and
    - eliminate reductions in Medicare DSH payment rates.
  $1 billion would be reserved over 10 years for policies supporting rural health care providers. Home health agencies (HHAs) also would benefit, with a FY 2001 payment rate increase to full market basket and a one-year delay in the scheduled 15 percent reduction in payments. Skilled nursing facilities would see a full market basket increase and an additional one-year delay in implementation of caps on therapy services.

- June Gibbs Brown, Inspector General (IG) of the Department of Health and Human Services (HHS) has stated that the Office of Inspector General (OIG) will not take legal action against providers for "innocent errors, mistakes, or even negligence" leading to billing errors under the new outpatient prospective payment system (OPPS). In a June 23 letter, Brown assured hospitals that neither the False Claims Act nor the Civil Monetary Claims Law imposes sanctions unless offenses are committed "with *actual knowledge* of the falsity of the claim, *reckless disregard* of the truth or falsity of the claim, or *deliberate ignorance* of the truth or falsity of the claim." According to Brown, the OIG is "very mindful of the difference between innocent errors and negligence (erroneous claims)" on the one hand, and "reckless or intentional conduct (fraudulent claims)" on the other. Where erroneous claims occur, the hospital will be asked to return the money; however, no civil or criminal penalty action will be initiated. The new payment system is scheduled to go into effect August 1.

- Final regulations implementing a home health care prospective payment system (PPS) were published in the Federal Register July 3. The new system will replace a BBA-mandated interim payment system in effect since October 1997. Under the final regulations, HHAs will be paid for each covered 60-day episode of care a beneficiary receives. As long as beneficiaries remain Medicare eligible, they may receive an unlimited number of medically necessary episodes of care. Payment for each 60-day episode will be based on national payment rates, ranging from about $1,100 to $5,900 depending on intensity of care, with adjustments for area wage differences, Outlier payments will be made when the costs of care are significantly higher than the specified rate. Medicare will begin paying HHAs under the PPS on October 1, 2000.

- Two articles in the July 5 *Journal of the American Medical Association* present very different pictures of the accuracy of last fall's Institute of Medicine (IOM) report on medical errors. According to the report, 44,000 to 98,000 Americans die in hospitals each year from adverse events, many of them preventable. While researchers from the Indiana University School of Medicine were critical of the report, calling underlying data greatly exaggerated and recommendations premature, one of the report's authors stood by its findings, stressing the need to avoid blame and address systemic flaws that cause errors. Though a number of medical error bills have been introduced in Congress, thus far, legislators have failed to agree on how best to deal with the issue.

> With summer here and the end of the Congressional session fast approaching, unless there's stop-the-presses news, *Washington Update* will be moving to an every-three-weeks schedule. Look for the next issue in early August.

Prepared by Margaret J. Hardy, JD, Director of Government Relations
5550 Friendship Boulevard, Suite 300, Chevy Chase, MD 20815-7201
Phone: (301) 968-2642 Fax: (301) 968-4195

Specific Goals and Milestones

This discussion has focused on careful planning, implementation, and communications related to a not-for-profit's legislative program. Groups at all levels have faithfully followed this logical approach and yet failed to achieve membership recognition or valuation of their efforts. Most frequently, this is because of a lack of measurable goals and milestones, which are necessary to conduct an assessment of progress.

It is incumbent on the leadership—that is, volunteers—to insist that, once policy goals are set, milestones be established to allow the regular tracking of activity. Staff involvement is required to ensure that all factors are considered in setting timetables and task assignments. However, once this is done for a particular legislative cycle, the assessment process needs to be overseen by both the chief executive officer and volunteer committees. If the situation, issues, or other pertinent factors change, the organization needs a mechanism to allow for reconsideration. Remember, all government relations programs are fluid and require constant monitoring and adjustment.

Volunteer Opportunities

The range of opportunities for volunteer participation in a not-for-profit is greatly expanded through a comprehensive legislative program. An aura of excitement surrounds political events, regardless of party affiliations, positions on issues, and conservative or liberal leanings. The energy that can be generated through volunteer participation also creates vitality for the association.

Speaking to Legislators at Local, State, and National Levels

A well-rounded legislative effort often involves arranging visits with legislators for volunteers. Although the organization may have professional government relations staff, the most effective outreach is accomplished through a member who is a voting constituent in the legislator's home district. Whether the visit is held at a legislator's local, state, or national office, face-to-face interaction is essential and appreciated by those who have the opportunity to participate. Members who deliver the organization's positions on issues become more committed to the overall program and give the organization credit for a successful endeavor—even if the original goals are not achieved.

A significant amount of planning must be done by staff to ensure that the visits are productive. A checklist of previsit activities is included as Exhibit 1.7. Detailed planning and follow-up are necessary because schedules for legislators are fluid and often change at the last minute. This calls for an educational effort by staff to prepare volunteers for a variety of possible scenarios, including cancellation with no or short notice. Provide concise presentations to participants to help ease their concerns and to deliver a specific message, and always prepare a postmeeting summary for each legislative visit. See Exhibit 1.8

EXHIBIT 1.7   Prelegislative Visit Checklist

Legislator to be contacted/visited:

_____

Office location:
Address: _____

_____

Phone: _____ E-mail: _____

Date/time of visit: _____ Time: _____

Name of member who will attend: _____

Address: _____

_____

Phone: _____ Fax: _____

E-mail: _____

Staff assigned to visit: _____

Phone: _____

Issues to be covered:

1. _____

2. _____

3. _____

Advanced information sent to member: Yes _____   Date: _____

No _____

Travel/lodging reservations:
Hotel: _____

Airline: _____

Arrival: _____ Departure: _____
         Date/time   Date/time

Pre-meeting briefing to be held:
When: _____ Where: _____

EXHIBIT 1.8   Postlegislative Visit Checklist

Member's name: _____

Address: _____

_____

Phone: _____ Fax: _____

E-mail: _____

Date of visit/contact: _____ In person: _____ Phone: _____

Location: _____

Individual visited: Legislator: _____ Staff: _____

Party Affiliation: _____

Local _____ State _____ National _____ level office

Name of not-for-profit staff member in attendance: _____

Issues presented:

1. _____

2. _____

3. _____

Areas of interest expressed by legislator/staff:

1. _____

2. _____

3. _____

Follow-up actions: _____

_____

_____

Thank-you letter sent to legislator: Yes _____ Date: _____

for a sample meeting report form. Completing a summary sheet provides a historical record for the association and facilitates proper follow-up.

Participating in the Election Process—Voting

Although it may appear not to be necessary, it is critical to encourage members to vote. Statistics demonstrate that voter turnout at all levels has declined and, thus, fewer people than ever make the actual decisions about issues and candidates. There is value in the organization's communicating to its members positions on campaign issues. Throughout the campaign period, reminders about these issues help to build a momentum for voting.

The association's policymaking body must establish positions on issues and authorize communications to members. Because of the inherent sensitivity of some issues, staff should not be given sole responsibility for positions; their role is to research, draft, help with communications, and track and coordinate activities.

There is a heightened level of member sensitivity about being "told how to vote" by a membership organization. Care needs to be taken to avoid this perception by focusing on the connection between specific positions on matters before the legislative body or electorate and the organization itself.

Communicate the facts on issues, provide supportive information, and let members vote as they wish. If you have presented the matter in a balanced yet clear manner, the membership will act accordingly. One post-election option is to conduct an anonymous member survey to determine how people voted on targeted issues. This activity provides valuable data for the staff to assess efforts and to plan for future actions. And be sure to report the results, whether positive or negative, to members, giving enough detail to explain the results.

Fund-Raising

Depending on the legal status of the not-for-profit, members can become effective fund-raisers for political action. You must be aware of the legal constraints and appropriate methods to be used for fund-raising. You will also find that some members have an aversion to asking for money. Those people should be assigned other tasks, and a separate cadre of interested fund-raisers should be used to solicit contributions.

Fund-raising can be done for a registered political action committee established under Federal Election Commission rules. This type of undertaking is more complex than other kinds of solicitation and requires extensive member education beforehand and monitoring throughout the process to avoid legal problems. Since there will be more technical advice provided in this book in other chapters, this section will not provide detailed discussion of political action committee rules.

If an association operates a political action committee (PAC), it is permissible to establish a separate fund to provide assistance with the costs for administering the PAC itself and for other administrative costs, such as memberships for staff and leaders in party organizations. This type of government affairs fund cannot be used for contributions to candidates but can be quite useful for the not-for-profit political activities.

Fund-raising can be done by telephone or mail solicitation; through person-to-person efforts at member locations or meetings held by the association; through raffles, drawings, or other fun activities; or as part of annual dues solicitations as long as the contributions are separated from normal dues. Members should be provided with detailed background information about why the fund-raising is necessary and what the money will be used for. This certainly helps solicitors answer questions from potential donors and eases the potentially difficult process for many volunteers.

My experience has been that not-for-profits have the greatest success in fund-raising when contributors see the activities as supportive of critical positions, backed by supporting documentation, and fun to participate in. It is best to remember that you have to make it easy to contribute and to have fund-raising be seen as a respectable and realistic undertaking for the group.

Delivering Political Contributions to Elected Officials

A natural follow-up to successful fund-raising for the organization is the process for delivering contributions. A few years ago, a long-time Democratic member of my organization was asked by staff to arrange to deliver personally a PAC check to an incumbent candidate running for re-election, who was also a Democrat. After several attempts were made to arrange the appointment, as it was also our intent to use this meeting to explain a position, the member became frustrated. He called the association headquarters, commenting that the lack of timely response by the candidate was troubling. At his suggestion, and with the approval of the appropriate leadership, the contribution was changed to offer it to the challenger. The challenger not only was willing to arrange the appointment but actually went to the member's office—a very smart political move. The member was very pleased with this turn of events, and a long-term relationship was started that proved beneficial to all parties—except the incumbent, who lost in a narrow election.

I relate this story to illustrate that there is tremendous benefit to the organization if members are asked to personally help with the distribution process. They enjoy the exposure, see the actual results of fund-raising efforts, and serve as spokespeople. Whenever possible, involve your members in the process of presenting campaign contributions. This will strengthen the members' connection to the candidates and to the association. And it gives the elected individual a "face" to attach to positions taken by the not-for-profit.

Serving as Public Spokespeople

An excellent array of volunteer opportunities to participate in the legislative process is opened through serving as spokespeople for the not-for-profit. Members are often willing to serve in the role of representing the association before the public. This allows members to speak before groups, to endorse the organization's positions on issues, and to achieve personal recognition. Each of those is interconnected and mutually beneficial to the not-for-profit and the individual. Examples of presentation opportunities include the following:

- Speaking before local membership groups, such as the Kiwanis or Rotary Clubs, church organizations, and other not-for-profit groups
- Participating in radio or television news or interview opportunities, such as radio call-in programs and local cable TV programming
- Acting as expert witnesses before selected panels or at legislative hearings on issues
- Serving as presenters or moderators at association-sponsored meetings or conferences where the audience is composed of other members

Although these suggestions appear to be quite easy to accomplish, there are many potential pitfalls that staff must avoid. First, not all members are capable of serving as spokespeople, and this reality can cause problems if, for example, volunteers who are not selected become angry. Second, even good speakers need extensive preparation to effectively deliver the association's messages. Staff should take care to brief volunteers fully on all aspects of the issues to avoid embarrassing moments during questioning periods following a presentation. The best messenger is someone who supports the association's positions, who is a good speaker, and who has been properly briefed and supported by knowledgeable staff.

Participating in Survey/Focus Group Research

Political campaigns, news organizations, polling firms, and not-for-profit groups all use client, customer, or member research information. There are a number of ways to collect the data needed to prepare accurate reports; however, one approach—focus group research—is often engaging for members.

Focus group interviewers gather a number of individuals for a session of questioning about particular issues and seek comments or observations, which are audio- or videotaped. Providing members with the opportunity to participate serves multiple purposes:

- The research results are valuable to the organization's policymakers.

- Members view this is as an engaging and fun way to assist the organization.
- It is a tangible example of the organization's use of sophisticated research techniques.
- It brings together members from different political perspectives to accomplish a goal of the association.

The intent of this section is not to disregard other forms of research, especially since, in most cases, the data from those alternative approaches are more valid and reliable. Focus group research techniques are more subjective, but they do provide members with personal involvement.

Engaging in Election Activities

As a final segment in this section on volunteer opportunities, let's review the actual election process. Members can be actively involved at this juncture in a variety of ways that serve both personal and organizational goals. Members enjoy

- Helping in "get out the vote" projects
- Serving as polling place watchers
- Working in election or campaign offices
- Serving as event planners or helpers (especially when these are sponsored by the association)
- Working as volunteer callers on telephone banks
- Assisting with production and distribution of large mailings

Before embarking on any of these activities, it is helpful to assess the likelihood of actual member participation. The old adage of throwing a party and having no guests show up is poignant for an association undertaking such activities. Factors such as geographical dispersion of members, their level in the organizations they work for, whether membership is individual or institutional, and the organization's previous political activities should be considered. This type of organizational profiling serves as a basis for developing a range of appropriate legislative opportunities. Keep in mind, as well, that offering a choice of activities may be a good way to encourage members at all levels to become active.

Whatever legislative approach you ultimately decide to use, always think of how to offer members the opportunities to participate that are easy for them to complete and that support the organization's strategic initiatives.

The Attraction of Prospective Donors to Legislatively Active Groups

Attracting donors, whether individual or institutional, to a not-for-profit is a highly competitive business. Groups must seek every available advantage to distinguish themselves from others who also seek the largesse of prospective donors. This section will outline several advantages that may result from the operation of a successful legislative program.

Strength/Purpose of the Organization

Although donors may not be personally aware of it, they are more willing to support an organization that is perceived as having a strong sense of purpose, as well as effective operational management. Assessments of annual reports, financial statements, research studies, and the overall image presented by the organization's publications may convert prospective donors into actual donors. An active legislative program provides many opportunities for the not-for-profit to demonstrate its ability to leverage its messages and membership toward specific goals.

A previous section covered opportunities for volunteer involvement in legislative efforts. Each member activity also serves as an opening for future donations to the organization. The absence of a legislative program may significantly curtail potential interactions with members.

Message Clarification

One of the most critical elements in building a donor base is developing a concise organizational message. If prospects are confused about the group's vision or goals, they will be hesitant to contribute. Preparing the association's policy statements, which serve as the basis of lobbying activities, requires a thorough analysis of the messages that are to be delivered to elected officials. The resulting focus on a specific legislative goal or agenda facilitates drafting the distinct messages that will be used for donor prospecting.

Measurable Achievements or Progress

Another advantage that results from a legislative program is the ease of keeping score about organizational achievements. At the start of each legislative session, a series of goals can be identified for members, tracked throughout the process of deliberations, and then assessed at the conclusion. Measuring the legislative work of the not-for-profit may create concerns for staff but is essential for members' understanding of the value of lobbying and the difficulties of achieving political goals. Since the legislative process is often deliberative and may include reverses, small advances must be acknowledged and celebrated to encourage continued support. If you wait to recognize only a final or significant achievement, the legislative program will lose support.

Political or Social Movements

Prospective donors find that being part of a political or social movement is exciting and encourages greater involvement. The activities resulting from a not-for-profit's legislative program provide options for a wide array of member interactions, which are essential to building an expanded donor base. Contributors must be convinced that the organization has value, is energized, and is one they can be proud to be a part of. The perspective of fulfilling a social movement is usually reserved for individual membership groups, such as unions, and other issue advocacy venues, such as support of children or people with disabilities.

Public Recognition

Coupled with member satisfaction that results from legislative efforts is the establishment of public recognition. Not-for-profits are usually formed around the needs of particular groups or specialized business issues. The result is that public recognition is initially limited to those distinct in-house audiences. The arena of legislative activity, however, expands the potential for achieving public awareness of the not-for-profit's issues. Because of public disclosure laws, the media are more able to learn of specific proposals for legislation and, if the disclosure is properly planned, can become sources of enhanced public recognition.

When one considers the extensive coverage that negative stories receive, such as the leadership problems faced by the United Way some years ago, the need to proactively build a positive public image is clear. Boards of trustees will want to design a legislative agenda based on the association's overall strategic direction, as outlined in an earlier section. The rationale for doing so should now be clearer, as one envisions greater public awareness of the activities of the organization.

A Particular Point of View

Expressing a particular point of view on issues is a privilege that most not-for-profits enjoy because of the nature of their development and organizational structure. Through careful planning and ongoing assessment, leaders are able to track the results of actions on behalf of, or in opposition to, specific pieces of legislation.

Taking what might be perceived as partisan positions, however, should be done with caution. An organization's position on an issue is generally expected by members, yet there may be divisions that exist over the same matters. A program of extensive internal communications on the positions taken is therefore essential for legislative success. Additionally, it is important to reassess member opinions consistently. The use of a number of survey techniques highlights shifts in member perceptions about targeted legislative issues long before these are obvious to the leaders. One further benefit of this use of member surveys is the fact that members themselves recognize that the organization's agenda is based on their input and opinions.

Examples of Not-for-Profits with Successful Legislative Operations

Not-for-profit organizations with records of successful legislative operations can be found across all aspects of individual or organizational membership or cause-based groups. Though it would appear to the inexperienced eye that measuring successes would be the easiest method to determine such a list, the truth of the matter is that many successful legislative operations are built on overcoming setbacks, such as legislative or regulatory losses. A number of factors affect an organization's ability to reach a level of success that is recognized by both members and outside audiences. In this section, I will provide examples of several legislative operations to give you a broader perspective on the issue of measuring success.

American Hospital Association (AHA)

The American Hospital Association has one of the most successful legislative divisions in the country. Representing more than 5,000 healthcare institutions, the AHA has the necessary financial and human resources to achieve its goals, but its success has been built on membership involvement and commitment to common goals, despite the wide range of hospital and health system sizes that are present in the AHA. Over the years, the AHA has increasingly focused its communications, meetings, educational seminars, and public positions on the political arena.

The AHA's experiences in relation to 1997 congressional actions are good examples of our topic. The Balanced Budget Act of 1997 drastically reduced Medicare funding for hospital services and reimbursement for medical education costs. Although the overall goal of Congress to reduce the federal deficit was ultimately successful, the impact on hospitals was negative. The AHA developed a comprehensive plan of action to recover from this devastating legislation, involving members from across the country to do so. (See Exhibits 1.9–1.11.)

One of the most effective tools the AHA used was spotlighting the financial impact at the local hospital level. This attracted the attention of local leaders, the communities served by the hospitals, and the elected officials

EXHIBIT 1.9A   Issue Background

Moving Beyond the Down Payment: BBA Relief 2000

AHA

Advancing Health in America

Small or Rural Hospitals

Issue

Small or rural hospitals are often the hub of the local health care delivery system and major employers in their communities. Because they are small, these hospitals have difficulty absorbing the impact of changes in payment and coverage policies, managed care, or government regulations. They are more severely affected by shifts in local demographics, health status, practice patterns and the loss of health professionals. And because there often are few or no reasonable alternatives to care, small or rural hospitals are the source of essential health care services and lifelines for community wellness.

The Balanced Budget Act of 1997 (BBA) posed additional challenges for the rural health care delivery system. Deep Medicare payment reductions and mounting regulatory requirements have hurt the fragile rural health care delivery system, particularly access to inpatient and outpatient services and post-acute care. While the Medicare, Medicaid and SCHIP Balanced Budget Refinement Act of 1999 (BBRA) provided some much-needed relief for small or rural hospitals, it did not remedy all their ills.

AHA View

For 2000, the AHA has identified the following issues as priorities for small or rural hospitals.

Updating and improving Medicare payment policies – Many of the current rural hospital classifications are based on antiquated criteria, and Congress is interested in updating current classification requirements. The enhanced Medicare reimbursements provided to special designations (e.g., Sole Community Hospitals, Medicare Dependent Hospitals, Rural Referral Centers and Critical Access Hospitals) are vital to maintaining the integrated network of services essential for rural communities. The AHA will work to ensure continued access to these programs, maintenance of Medicare payments, and elimination of arbitrary barriers that prevent other isolated hospitals from receiving assistance under these programs.

Post-acute care – Rural communities depend on several types of providers, such as hospitals, nursing facilities and home health agencies. Unlike metropolitan areas, only a handful of such rural providers exist, and in many cases, the local hospital sponsors all post-acute services. One of the most troublesome aspects of the BBA is its collective impact on the rural health care delivery system and its contribution to a patient's inability to access a network of coordinated services after discharge.

(Over)

A New Century of Caring for People

KEEPING OUR COMMITMENT ★ FACING NEW CHALLENGES

EXHIBIT 1.9B   Issue Background (continued)

AHA View
con't

The BBRA increased payments to hospital-based skilled nursing facilities (SNF) for medically complex patients, and delayed the BBA-mandated 15 percent reduction to home health agencies. The AHA has identified additional Medicare administrative and payment changes that should be made in 2000. These priorities include:

- reducing certain data collection requirements for small rural hospitals
- allowing the option to exempt swing bed services from the SNF prospective payment system
- providing enhanced payments for critical access hospital-based home health agencies
- expanding coverage for telehealth services where applicable

Ambulance Services – The BBA requires ambulance costs to be paid under a fee schedule beginning in 2001, which is a year later than originally mandated. Many hospital-based ambulance providers do not charge Medicare beneficiaries the full costs of ambulance services because Medicare reimburses the providers on a reasonable cost basis, and therefore the providers are able to recoup most of their expenses. However, the fee schedule will not allow for this recoupment, and rural hospitals, in particular, will be unable to make up these losses due to their low volume of services. Because rural hospital-based ambulance providers are often the only ambulance providers in the community, it is essential that beneficiaries have access to this vital service. Through our participation in the Health Care Financing Administration's negotiated rulemaking committee for ambulance fee schedule, the AHA is pushing for an adjustment for low-volume rural providers that recognizes the readiness, or standby, expense of ambulance services.

Critical Access Hospitals (CAH) – The Medicare Rural Hospital Flexibility Program, established by the BBA, allows rural hospitals to be reclassified as limited-service ("critical access") hospitals and still provide important inpatient care. Last year's BBRA included several changes that improved program flexibility, such as a 96-hour *average* length-of-stay limitation, and permitting hospitals that recently closed or downsized to a clinic to convert to a CAH. The AHA will advocate for additional technical refinements, such as:

- restoration of Medicare bad debt payments for CAHs
- special treatment of swing bed costs
- adjustments for an increase in admissions due to seasonal effects
- paying ambulance services on a cost basis, as opposed to a fee schedule
- revising the all-inclusive rate billing option for outpatient services

EXHIBIT 1.10   Responding to Legislation: Example

AMERICAN HOSPITAL ASSOCIATION

2000 ANNUAL MEETING ★ ADVOCACY MESSAGES

BBA RELIEF 2000: THE BBA <u>STILL</u> HURTS!

✈ **KEY MESSAGES**

- ► **Thank** lawmakers who were helpful last year in our efforts to secure relief.

- ► **Explain** to them why we are back looking for more... the BBA continues to threaten hospitals and patient care. In many communities, hospitals are in crisis.

- ► **Educate** them on what's necessary to keep pace in providing care for our communities.

- ► **Outline** the two key policy recommendations we believe need to be enacted this year to respond to our concerns.

✈ **WHAT WE NEED**

A COST OF CARING ADJUSTMENT, an adequate update factor, achieved by increasing the Medicare payment updates slated for this year and next. Current updates and adjustments do not allow hospitals and other providers to keep pace with rapidly growing costs of caring for patients.

FREEZE THE CUTS in the Medicaid disproportionate share hospital (DSH) program for two years. Medicaid DSH payments help reimburse hospitals' costs of treating Medicaid and low-income patients, particularly those with complex medical needs, and make it possible for communities to care for their uninsured.

A New Century of Caring for People

KEEPING OUR COMMITMENT
FACING NEW CHALLENGES

EXHIBIT 1.11   Responding to Legislation: Example

America's Hospitals and Health Systems

AMERICAN HOSPITAL ASSOCIATION

2000 ANNUAL MEETING ★ ADVOCACY MESSAGES

EXPANDING ACCESS AND COVERAGE

Tackling the problem of the uninsured must go hand-in-hand with addressing the current underfunding of health care services. With greater resources, we can continue to improve access to services through investment in our facilities, technology, and our health professionals...who are the unsung heroes on the front lines, providing health care to patients seven days a week, 365 days a year.

✱ **MESSAGES**

► By 1998, the number of Americans without health coverage had grown to 44 million, of which 11 million were children.

► Eighty-three percent of the uninsured live in families that are headed by workers.

► The uninsured are concentrated disproportionately in low-income families – more than 40 percent earn less than $20,000.

► Statistics suggest that the U.S. can extend health care coverage by making insurance more affordable for employers and employees, and by bolstering efforts to enroll adults and children in public programs like Medicaid and the Children's Health Insurance Program (CHIP).

A New Century of Caring for People

KEEPING OUR COMMITMENT
FACING NEW CHALLENGES

✱ **WHAT WE NEED**

For Children...

► Expand CHIP coverage for legal immigrant low-income children.

► Mandate the current option to allow children 12 months of continuous enrollment in Medicaid, regardless of their family's changes in income, and extend the mandate to CHIP.

► Strengthen outreach efforts to enhance CHIP enrollment.

For Working Families and Individuals...

► Develop a refundable tax credit that makes insurance more affordable for low-income individuals and their families.

► Offer tax credits for small employers that purchase group coverage premiums.

► Accelerate the deductibility of health payments for the self-employed.

► Require employers to allow part-time employees to buy in to employer-sponsored health plans.

► Create purchasing cooperatives that can give small firms and individuals more leverage in negotiating health care insurance contracts.

► Offer federal grants for state high-risk pools.

► Provide incentives and flexibility to states to extend Medicaid coverage for individuals and families moving from welfare-to-work.

► Expand CHIP coverage for low-income pregnant women and legal immigrant low-income pregnant women.

For Early Retirees...

► Create a refundable tax credit for the purchase of health care insurance through the Federal Employees Health Benefit Program.

► Extend COBRA coverage to early retirees.

from those areas. Through a series of town hall–type meetings, a national print advertising campaign, regular Washington gatherings of targeted leaders, and a constant flow of factual information to Capitol Hill, the message began to be heard. In 1999, Congress passed the Balanced Budget Relief Act, restoring some of the original cuts and delaying the implementation of planned future additional reductions.

As you can see from the dates of the two actions, the AHA invested two years of intensive, grassroots membership work to achieve a partial restoration of funds.

This example provides several essential components of successful legislative actions:

- The need to have a carefully crafted plan with specific, measurable goals
- A commitment of resources, both financial and human, to the effort
- Membership communications and education about the organization's plan
- A series of activities that focuses on delivering the key messages in legislators' home areas
- Preparation of factual materials for legislators
- The need for a continued commitment of resources to pursue further governmental action that will benefit members

Smaller Organizations:
Families USA and the Children's Defense Fund

Two smaller not-for-profits with successful legislative records—Families USA and the Children's Defense Fund—are more cause-related than the AHA. As their names indicate, they are not-for-profit groups dedicated to advancing the needs of families and children on a variety of issues. Both organizations have individual members and donors, who provide support for the operations and legislative agendas of each group.

Using these organizations as examples of legislative programs is an opportunity to illustrate the need for policy-level guidance, which should be targeted by the not-for-profit. One can well imagine that either group could find itself deluged by the myriad challenges that face families and children. [Lacking the resources to engage all the issues, each organization is required to conduct a careful assessment of the options and to select only those that will benefit the largest number of constituents or which has the greatest expectation for success.]

Families USA provides a good example of the value of working with a perceived antagonist organization to advance the not-for-profit's legislative agenda. In a coalition with a separate association that represents the insurance industry, Families USA sponsored a national meeting on the issues related to the number of individuals and families without insurance coverage. Because of the high media and legislative interest in this area, coupled with sponsorship of the meeting by two groups traditionally not seen as bedfellows, the meeting drew a large audience and broader coverage than would have been expected. This clearly advanced the legislative agenda of this cause-based group by positioning it as a national player on the issue of the uninsured.

The Children's Defense Fund has built a national board consisting of high-profile political advocates and is led by an individual who is well known as a child advocate. The organization exemplifies another effective political approach through the use of widely known volunteer leaders, who bring their own resources and audiences to the benefit of the organization. By having thought leaders or issue makers on the board, the organization increases both its appeal to potential donors and its opportunities to receive publicity.

National Rifle Association (NRA)

An example of an individual membership organization that has an exceptionally powerful and successful legislative operation is the National Rifle Association. Despite its sometimes controversial media reputation, the NRA continues as one of the nation's most effective staff and grassroots lobbying operations. This group uses a variety of political action techniques, including the following:

- Mobilizing a national grassroots membership base to repeatedly contact government leaders on specific issues
- Using a nationally recognized spokesperson to speak to members, the media, and government on association issues
- Focusing activities on a very distinct and limited range of issues
- Demonstrating a willingness by policymakers in the association to confront controversial issues and organized challenges
- Employing highly skilled staff experts to advise the organization.

Regardless of how you feel about the issues of the NRA, from the focus of assessing legislative operations, this organization has built a reputation as a powerful political force.

Conclusion

This chapter provided an introduction to the significant roles that the legislative process can play for not-for-profit organizations. Average citizens view the processes of governing and government as plodding, confusing, frustrating, and far too sophisticated for their everyday involvement.

Through the work of organized not-for-profits, the legislative process can be made more personal and understandable. In addition, the groups' missions are advanced through the cooperative efforts of staff and members.

We began with a review of the historical role that not-for-profits have played in the legislative process, such as conducting research, serving as accrediting bodies in a quasi-governmental capacity, and providing continuing education to meet license requirements.

The next section outlined a variety of roles that are filled by not-for-profits at both state and federal levels. Whether serving as seekers of public opinion, advocates for varying publics, or mobilizers of grassroots efforts, not-for-profits are essential components of a democratic governing process. For those who are involved in these organizations, it is important to understand the optional roles that are available.

Once you have an understanding of both the historical basis for association legislative action and the roles that can be fulfilled, a thorough review of the essential capabilities that an organization must have before acting is helpful. Unless the group's policymaking body makes a commitment to employ experienced staff, allocate necessary resources, provide communications to members, and prepare plans and set goals, a legislative program will not be successful.

The chapter then analyzed a number of volunteer opportunities that result from legislative activities. Not-for-profits broadly expand membership involvement by venturing into the political milieu. Individuals enjoy speaking to their legislators on issues they feel are important to them, and both members and legislators appreciate the information and education the association provides. For certain members, the challenge of raising money is exciting and rewarding, especially when it is done to support a favorite group or issue. Direct election campaigns and voting actions are also good openings for engaging members in short-term and specific legislative projects.

Beyond recruiting members and retaining their involvement through government relations, not-for-profits become more visible and attractive to donors through high-profile events. Political action offers a wide variety of this type of event. The chapter dealt with the need to clarify organizational messages, establish measurable goals, and create public recognition.

Finally, the chapter provided examples of successful legislative operations to show how all the components come together. From large institutional members represented by the American Hospital Association to the issues of children and families, the examples should help stimulate creative ideas.

▼ 2 Introduction to the Legislative Process

WILLIAM P. HORN

Introduction

It is reputed that either Mark Twain or Otto Von Bismarck remarked that there are two things one should never watch being made—sausage and the law. Given the German propensity for wursts, it was probably Otto. And, yes, the process is messy, but the absence of efficiency is deliberate. It assures all interested parties an opportunity to participate and seek to have their viewpoints incorporated into pending legislation before it becomes codified in statute. At the federal level, the founding fathers created the bicameral legislature (i.e., two separate houses), gave each body different authorities, and required presidential approval of passed bills. The often protracted process guards against precipitous action and assures that all points of view get at least some level of consideration. When many cooks are seeking to prepare the same soup, and often using competing recipes, the kitchen will often look like a disaster area and the quality of the final product hard to predict. So it is with the legislative process.

This chapter is designed to provide insight into this unique process at both the federal and state levels. You will be introduced to basic terminology and the steps common to enacting a bill into law in most legislatures. Like many things, the enterprise is fundamentally simple but is often encrusted with arcane features and complications that obscure the simplicity. The objective is to render the process transparent and enable you to become a penetrating observer, able to understand and use the process to your benefit.

U.S. Congressional Process

Basic Legislating

Virtually every civics textbook outlines the 11-step sequence associated with the enactment of a bill into law:

1. *Bill introduction*—An idea or a concept is rendered into appropriate legal language and introduced as a bill. In the House of Representatives, all bills are referred to as "H.R. _____," meaning House of Representatives bill number x. Bills introduced in the Senate are referred to as "S. _____ ." Only Representatives can introduce a bill in the House, and only Senators can drop in a bill in the Senate.

2. *Referred to a committee*—The House and Senate each has a number of standing committees with jurisdiction over particular matters. (See Exhibit 2.1). Tax measures, for example, are within the purview of the House Ways and Means Committee and the Senate Committee on Finance; National Park issues are assigned to the House Resources Committee and the Senate Energy and Natural Resources Committee: Each newly introduced bill is reviewed for its subject and sent, or referred, to the committee with the appropriate jurisdiction. A bill that touches on multiple topics, and jurisdictions, can be referred to more than committee.

3. *Committee hearings*—Consideration of an introduced bill traditionally begins with a legislative hearing. A committee (or one of its subcommittees) invites witnesses to appear before it and provide testimony about a particular bill. Testimony usually involves a statement of support or opposition, as well as descriptions of particular benefits or problems with the bill. Many witnesses offer suggestions about changes or amendments to improve the pending legislation. The number of witnesses appearing in person before committees is limited, but virtually anyone can submit a written statement for the record about a bill. The witnesses' statements—oral and written—as well as the transcript of the hearings, including questions from the members and answers by witnesses, are recorded and become the hearing record.

4. *Committee markup*—On completion of the hearings, a committee or subcommittee meets to "mark up" the bill. This is literally going through a bill line-by-line, section-by-section and marking it up (i.e., amending it via additions, deletions, and language changes). A common practice is to have the committee chairperson (and staff) significantly rewrite a bill based on what was learned during the hearings and to begin the markup with a chairperson's amendment—a complete substitute bill. The bill number often stays the same, even though the text might have been changed substantially.

5. *Committee report*—At the conclusion of markup, the committee acts on the amended bill. If the committee supports the measure, it reports the bill "favorably," meaning that the committee recommends that the bill be passed. Once the committee votes to report it, a committee report is prepared describing the bill, explaining what happened during the hearings and markup, explaining how the bill changes existing law, and outlining what the provisions of the bill mean ("congressional intent"). The committee report is a very important document and is usually the main source of legislative history about a bill. In most cases, bills must be reported favorably from a committee in order to be moved to the floor. There are highly specific rules and

EXHIBIT 2.1   **Congressional Committees**

House Committees

Committee on Agriculture
Committee on Appropriations
Committee on Armed Services
Committee on Banking and Financial Services
Committee on the Budget
Committee on Commerce
Committee on Education and the Workforce
Committee on Government Reform
Committee on House Administration
Committee on International Relations
Committee on the Judiciary
Committee on Resources
Committee on Rules
Committee on Science
Committee on Small Business
Committee on Standards of Official Conduct
Committee on Transportation and Infrastructure
Committee on Veterans' Affairs
Committee on Ways and Means

Senate Committees

Agriculture, Nutrition, and Forestry Committee
Appropriations Committee
Armed Services Committee
Banking, Housing, and Urban Affairs Committee
Budget Committee
Commerce, Science, and Transportation Committee
Energy and Natural Resources Committee
Environment and Public Works Committee
Finance Committee
Foreign Relations Committee
Governmental Affairs Committee
Judiciary Committee
Health, Education, Labor, and Pensions Committee
Rules and Administration Committee
Small Business Committee
Veterans' Affairs Committee
Indian Affairs Committee

Special, Select, and Joint Committees

Joint Economic Committee
Joint Committee on Printing
Joint Committee on Taxation
Joint Committee on the Library
Senate Select Committee on Intelligence
Senate Select Committee on Ethics
Senate Special Committee on Aging
Special Committee on the Year 2000 Technology Problem

procedures for discharging a bill from committee and taking it straight to the floor. Successful use of the discharge mechanism is extremely rare.

6. *Floor consideration*—The next stop for a reported bill is the floor of the respective house (i.e., House of Representatives or Senate). A bill is brought to the floor, debated, made subject to amendment, and voted on. However, there are very specific rules regarding the floor consideration process, which can be quite complex. All of the rules, though, have a common feature—a bill that gets sufficient votes (a simple majority, in most cases) is considered passed.

7. *Conference committee*—In a bicameral legislature, the House and Senate can pass differing bills. These differences have to be resolved before a single bill can be passed by both and sent to the president for signature and enactment. A House-Senate conference committee is the standard vehicle for resolving any differences, and a panel of members from each house is appointed by the respective leadership to serve on the conference committee. It meets and negotiates the differences, ultimately producing a single, mutually agreed-to measure. This agreement is written up in a conference report, which outlines the text of the unified bill, as well as explanatory text about how and why differences were resolved.

8. *Passage of conference report*—Each house then takes up the conference report, debates it, and may amend it before voting. A simple majority is usually sufficient for passage. However, if the bill has been amended, it may be necessary to reassemble the conference committee to resolve any new differences that may have been created.

9. *Enrollment*—Following passage of a bill by the House and Senate, the measure is "enrolled" and presented to the president for consideration and signature. Commonly, this occurs within a week or so of passage. However, some bills (e.g., emergency funding bills to keep the government running) get enrolled and presented within hours. Others may not be enrolled for weeks to achieve political objectives.

10. *Presidential signature*—The enrolled bill is presented to the president for consideration. The president may sign the bill, at which point it is considered enacted into law and assigned a Public Law number. The president may also choose to disapprove or veto the bill. If Congress is in session and the president takes no action, the bill becomes law.

11. *Veto override*—A vetoed bill is returned to the Congress. The legislature then has three options: (a) try to override the veto, which is accomplished by having a two-thirds majority vote in each house to enact the bill over the president's disapproval; (b) amend or change the bill to accommodate the president's wishes and pass, enroll, and present a modified measure; or (c) accept the veto.

EXHIBIT 2.2   Congressional Legislative Process

1. Bill is introduced.
2. Bill is referred to a committee.
3. Committee holds hearings on bill.
4. Committee holds markup on bill.
5. Committee votes on and reports bill.
6. Bill is considered, debated, passed.
7. Conference committee is convened to work out differences in House/Senate versions of bill.
8. House/Senate considers and passes conference report.
9. Bill is enrolled and presented to the president.
10. President signs or vetoes the bill.
11. House/Senate may consider veto override.

See Exhibit 2.2 for a complete list of the steps in the congressional legislative process.

Forms of Bills

The basic process is used to enact the four standard forms of bills: authorizing, appropriations, tax, and joint resolutions. (see Exhibit 2.3). Each of these forms of legislation has a specific purpose and comes with specific rules regarding the enactment process.

An authorizing bill is the basic garden variety measure. Authorizing bills set new penalties for selling drugs, create new healthcare programs, establish national parks, deregulate the airline industry, and set the rules for the Internet. They are referred to as authorizing bills because they invariably

EXHIBIT 2.3   Types of Legislation

Public bill—used for new law/statute
- Authorization bill
- Appropriations bill
- Tax bill

Private bill—Used for new law/statute

Joint resolution—Used for a constitutional amendment

Concurrent resolution—Used for regulation of Congress as a whole

Simple resolution—Used for regulation of the chamber of origin contain a provision authorizing a government agency to spend money to implement the program or plan spelled out in the bill.

An appropriations bill is a money bill. It actually appropriates money from the U.S. Treasury to each agency or program. In many cases, a law authorizes the expenditure of funds, but, unless the funds are actually appropriated by Congress, no funds may be spent. This power of the purse is conferred on Congress by the Constitution and is the primary source of institutional authority for the House and Senate. The House traditionally acts first on these bills, and the Senate responds to the House initiative. In reality, both houses work on parallel tracks, but these bills are always passed with H.R. numbers.

Each year, Congress must enact 13 appropriations bills to fund the many divisions of the federal government for the coming fiscal year. One bill provides funds for the Defense Department (the Defense Appropriations bill); another funds National Parks, National Forests, and related natural resources programs (Interior and Related Agencies Appropriations bill); and so on. Since the federal fiscal year begins on October 1, these bills must be enacted (passed and signed into law) before that date, or the government cannot operate. These measures are a frequent source of conflict between Congress and the president and give rise to much political brinksmanship each September. If a final appropriations bill for a division of the government cannot be enacted in a timely manner because of disagreements, a temporary spending bill, called a continuing resolution (CR), is frequently passed to fund government operations for a week or two. In Washington parlance, a CR creates an interim period, during which Congress and the president try to resolve their disagreements and enact a full fiscal year appropriations measure.

Tax bills also have their own set of rules. The Constitution requires that tax measures must arise in the House. In practical terms, it makes the House Ways and Means Committee especially powerful, as it is the starting point for amendments to the U.S. tax code, which now raises nearly $2 trillion annually in federal revenue.

The last primary form of bill is a joint resolution. This expresses the U.S. position on a given issue (e.g., condemning terrorism) and requires passage by both houses and signature by the president.

Interest groups do not generally seek the passage of an entire bill. Most lobbying is focused on the passage or defeat of specific sections or amendments to a bill. For example, each year there are attempts to add amendments—referred to as "riders"—to the appropriations bills. In recent years, these have included anti-abortion provisions, gun control items, and animal rights matters. Since most interest groups have fairly narrow objectives, a specific amendment or rider will achieve these goals without having an impact on the broader bill.

The process of seeking such amendments begins at the earliest stages of the legislative process. When someone learns that a Senator is working on a bill regarding a new national park, affected interests will try to influence the text of the bill regarding the boundaries, special rules for land acquisition, protection of property rights of inholders, continuation of fishing and hunting, and so on. If unsuccessful at the introduction stage, the same groups will try to influence committee markup to get their changes incorporated into the bill at that stage. This can continue all the way through conference committee and is why perseverance is a critical element of all successful legislative lobbying.

Amendments to bills or bill language is an attempt to have specific words actually enacted into law. Many times, however, an interest group can achieve its goal by including in a committee report specific language expressing a point of view or directing or suggesting to the administrative agencies that certain actions be taken or stopped. And no issue is too arcane to be addressed. One disagreement broke out between the U.S. Fish and Wildlife Service and bird dog fanciers over dog competitions on certain public lands. The federal agency had decided that these dog trials are an inappropriate use of the lands. Bird dog and hunters organizations were outraged; in a recent House of Representatives bill affecting administration of the Service, there appeared Committee report language telling the agency that bird dog field trials are an appropriate and traditional use of the public lands in question. Report language is especially important in the appropriations context, where it is common for Congress to appropriate millions of dollars to a general program in the bill or statutory language and then suggest to the agency how to allocate those funds in report language. Because of the power of the purse, federal agencies are very sensitive to suggestions from the committees that provide annual funding.

Legislative History

As noted previously, committee reports (and conference reports) are the primary sources of legislative history about a bill. This history is often used by administrative agencies and federal courts to determine congressional intent regarding the interpretation of a bill's terms and provisions. Another source of legislative history, and another window of opportunity for lobbyists, is statements on the House or Senate floor during consideration of a bill. The primary sponsors of a bill frequently describe the purposes and intent of their legislation during the floor debate. These contemporaneous expressions of congressional intent can be very important. In contrast, explanations offered months after passage are generally accorded no weight by agencies and federal courts.

One highly structured form of a floor statement is a colloquy between two Representatives or Senators during debate. It consists of a series of inquiries and responses, usually from the committee chairperson with jurisdiction over the subject bill, about particular features or sections of the bill. The members are usually reading from painstakingly prepared scripts; as such, these interchanges are looked at carefully by agencies and courts.

House Features

Taking a bill to the floor in the House of Representatives is a rigidly controlled process. There are multiple forms of consideration, and the traffic cop is the Rules Committee. This highly specialized committee has no basic legislative jurisdiction but sets the rules on how each bill will be handled when it reaches the floor. For example, it prescribes how much debate will be allowed (e.g., four hours) and whether any amendments to the bill will be allowed (or "in order"). When no amendments are in order, the bill is considered under a "closed rule," meaning that the bill is closed to any further amendments. The parliamentary rules of the House are referred to as Jefferson's Manual because the first set was written by Thomas Jefferson, and these rules set forth a daunting list of procedural do's and don'ts. If a provision in a bill violates one of these rules, it may be subject to a "point of order" on the floor and stricken from the bill. However, the Rules Committee can waive such points of order and allow an otherwise offending provision to remain in a bill. By long bipartisan tradition, the majority party and the Speaker of House dominate the Rules Committee, allowing them to exert strong control over legislative procedures.

For general purposes, there are four forms of floor action in the House. First is the standard form of consideration, which prescribes some hours for debate divided between proponents and opponents and allows amendments relevant, or germane, to the bill (e.g., it's against the rules to appropriate or spend money on an authorizing bill); a simple majority is necessary for passage.

Second, bills that are largely noncontroversial are placed on the Suspension Calendar. They are considered without a specific rule from the Rules Committee (hence, under suspended rules), they cannot be amended on the floor, debate can last no longer than one hour, and passage requires a two-thirds vote. When the House takes up the Suspension Calendar, it often passes a dozen or more bills in an afternoon.

Third, certain bills, primarily Conference Reports, are privileged and can be brought up quickly, even if it means pushing other measures aside.

Fourth, and last, is the concept of Unanimous Consent, or UC (i.e., where there is complete agreement or unanimous consent by all members). An enormous amount of procedural business gets done (and a few bills are passed) by Unanimous Consent. All kinds of rules, restrictions, and time limits can be dispensed with if there is UC. Without it, business in the House can grind very slowly, and traditionally the minority party uses UC as leverage to ensure that its rights and interests are respected. But *unanimous* means just that, and a single member of Congress among the 435 can object.

Senate Features

The U.S. Senate operates dramatically differently than the U.S. House. It styles itself as the world's greatest deliberative body, and its critics agree that it certainly knows how to be deliberate. Whereas House bills are governed by rules limiting debate, all Senate bills go to the floor for unlimited debate. Theoretically, Senators may talk forever and postpone a vote on a bill. Accordingly, the key items in Senate operations are time agreements, cloture votes, (i.e., a vote to cut off or close debate) and UC.

Since unlimited debate is the norm, agreements must be reached among Senators to limit debate to a certain amount of time. These time agreements are usually negotiated among the leadership (majority and minority leaders) and the senior committee members. Once negotiated, the agreements are adopted by unanimous consent. Obviously, the interests of all 100 Senators must be accommodated to achieve UC.

In a limited number of cases, a time agreement cannot be achieved, but a majority of Senators want to vote on a bill. Unlimited debate (referred to in these circumstances as a filibuster) can be cut off by a vote on a cloture petition. Senators desiring to cut off debate and vote file a cloture petition. That petition is then voted on, and 60 votes are required to pass it. If the requisite 60 votes are not obtained, debate (filibuster) continues.

Another Senatorial device for slowing down bills is the "hold." Over time, a tradition has developed that Senators may place a hold on a bill or a nomination pending confirmation. When a hold is in place, the affected bill will not be scheduled for floor action until the hold is released. As you may imagine, this provides each Senator with an enormous amount of power. Holds may be placed secretly (only the leadership knows who has put a hold in place), and usually the interests or concerns of the Senator placing the hold must be dealt with before it is lifted. On major bills, holds are generally insufficient to hold up action, and a determined Senator must be prepared to engage in a filibuster in order to prevent a vote on a bill.

Presidential Action

When a bill has passed Congress and has been presented to the president, most of the work is over. On receiving a measure from the legislative branch, the president has four options: (1) sign the bill into law; (2) let it pass into law without signing it; (3) veto it; or (4) in special circumstances, pocket veto it. A pocket veto can occur only at the end of a congressional session, if the president takes no action to sign a bill when Congress has adjourned the bill does not become law and the inaction becomes the equivalent of a veto.

These rules, or options, all originate in Article I, Section 7, Clause 2 of the Constitution. If a bill is presented to the president and the president approves of it, he signs it. This occurs literally with an engrossed copy of a bill printed on heavy stock, red-lined paper put before the president, who physically signs the bill, making it into law. Signing ceremonies in the White House Oval Office or the Rose Garden are just ceremonies, but affixing of the signature is a constitutional requirement.

If Congress is in session, the president has a 10-day period to approve and sign or disapprove and veto the bill. Should the president take neither action in this period, the bill becomes law without presidential approval or signature.

A presidential disapproval is referred to as a veto, although in the Constitution the word *objections* is used. The president returns the bill to Congress, with a message explaining his objections. Congress then has the option of trying to override the veto by a two-thirds vote in each House to overcome the president's objections.

A pocket veto can occur only at the end of a congressional session. If a bill is presented to the president and Congress has adjourned, the president may "put the bill in his pocket" and not sign it; at the end of 10 days, it is considered vetoed. Congress has to start from scratch in its next session if it wants to overcome a pocket veto.

Influence on the Federal Process

Contrary to popular myth, shoveling wheelbarrows full of dollars into campaigns is not the only way to influence the legislative process. Its probably not the most effective means and is not an option for most nonprofit entities. Strange as it may seem, sound ideas, attention to details, substantive knowledge, and energized constituents have always been extremely effective in advancing a legislative initiative or agenda on Capitol Hill.

A lesson we all learned early in school is the cornerstone of effective lobbying: do your homework. A thorough understanding of issues and the demonstration of substantive expertise are the critical elements of successful lobbying by not-for-profits. You generally cannot raise boatloads of campaign money, and most not-for-profits are small enough that you also are not going to inundate Congress with thousands of postcards or letters on your issue. What you can sell is a sound idea and a clear articulation of why your legislative initiative ought to be enacted or why a particular bill or amendment is simply bad.

Members and staff of Congress greatly appreciate solid substantive homework. They are often overworked and asked to consider dozens of issues every day. These pressures make it difficult for them to focus on one matter, consider it thoroughly, and do the necessary supportive paperwork. For example, the introduction of a bill requires that someone draft it as well as an introduction statement. At the same time, a press release on the measure and other explanatory materials are needed to present to congressional offices, the press, and other interested parties. None of these documents and materials prepare themselves, and staff often has insufficient time to get it done on your timetable.

After introduction of a bill, there will be a need for testimony at committee hearings; statements during floor debate; responses to criticisms of your bill or amendment; letters to editors; subsequent rewrites on your bill or amendments to address certain issues, political or substantive; and so on. A lot of work is entailed in pushing a bill through the arduous legislative process. One of the answers is for you to prepare these materials—ghostwrite them—and present them to the member or staff of Congress with whom you are working. Your drafts will undoubtedly be altered, but you will have pointed the effort in the right direction.

Two warnings are necessary. First, no successful lobbyist or interest group ever tells the public that he or she drafted a bill or wrote any statements and press releases. Everyone knows that this is what happens every day, but it is extremely poor form, and politically damaging, to acknowledge it. Think of the famous scene in the movie *Casablanca* in which Claude Rains is "shocked" to discover that gambling is going on in Rick's Café. Second, make absolutely sure that your work products are accurate, factual, and truthful. If you put a member of Congress, the Senate, or their staff out on a limb and it gets sawed off, no one is going to rely on you or your work products again. For a big city, Washington, DC, is a pretty small town, and a reputation for inaccurate or shoddy work spreads very fast.

The House and Senate consist of 435 and 100 members, respectively, as well as thousands of staffers. Very few interests, and virtually no not-for-profits, have the resources to lobby this many people effectively. A second key to success is to focus your efforts, energy, and resources on key members—those who are interested in your issue, or can be made to be interested, and those who sit on the committees that have jurisdiction over your subject; then, the universe of members is much smaller and more manageable. If a funding or appropriations item is your issue, the respective House and Senate Appropriations Subcommittees will be your targets. In the House, there are typically 9 to 14 Representatives on these subcommittees and about 15 on their Senate counterparts. And, within these subcommittees, the critical members are usually the chairperson and the ranking minority member. Focusing your efforts on two to two dozen members is a manageable task.

The same pattern holds true for the authorizing committees. A limited number of members are the recognized experts or leaders on certain issues. Similarly, a limited number of members are likely to have constituents affected by your proposed action. You will need to find the right focus for your effort.

Within this limited group, you also need to identify and recruit your leader or leaders. Every successful legislative effort has a "horse," a "spear carrier": one or more members, and key staff, who become committed to pushing through your (now their) bill or amendment. Without a legislative champion, failure is inevitable. Finding your leader early in the process is the one indispensable step to success.

At this point in the process, you have done your homework, identified the key members and committees, and recruited your leader. Its time to examine your expectations and commitment. Expectations must be reasonable and consistent with the reality of the legislative process. Very little happens fast and, for significant stand-alone bills, years are often required from conception of the idea to signature into law by the president. What you may think of as a relatively small single provision or amendment may take two or three years to enact. You must be realistic in your assessments of success and needed time. The primary requirements for successful participation in the legislative process are perseverance and patience. It's a slow, arduous process that takes time and commitment, and failure to understand these facts will lead to nothing but frustration.

Since this is ultimately a political process, you will also need to demonstrate a level of support among the body politic. Elected representatives want to know that, among those pulling the voting levers, there is support for your bill, provision, or amendment. Two ways to achieve this are old-fashioned grassroots politics and coalition building or, in modern parlance, networking. The process of energizing the citizenry to show its support for your effort is considered to be developing and demonstrating grassroots support. Computer technology has greatly facilitated this task with e-mail and Internet communication. Getting your message to the public, which in turn delivers the message to elected representatives, is much easier today than just a few years ago. However, Capitol Hill remains a traditional place, and there is no substitute for a personally composed letter from a constituent to a Representative or Senator. Be aware that congressional members have their own expectations about what constitutes a groundswell or public concern. On big national issues backed by well-funded interests, congressional offices expect to be inundated with form letters or postcards. On your kinds of specific issues, though, a dozen personally composed letters to an individual office will carry substantial weight. Do not discount your efforts at grassroots mobilization because you cannot generate hundreds or thousands of pieces of mail to each targeted office. Even in a big state, a Senator will take note if he or she receives a couple of dozen non-form letters on a particular bill or amendment.

In addition to firing up your grassroots support, it is useful to reach out to other like-minded interest groups and organizations seeking support for your initiative. James Madison's Federalist Paper No. 10 accurately predicted that American politics would be dominated by ever shifting coalitions of interests pursuing their objectives with the national government. Lining up other interests to support your effort demonstrates broader support and provides assurance to Congress that your bill or provision is mainstream. It allows you to establish and broaden connections with elected congressional members via your coalition partners. A good coalition not only helps to expand support but it also creates a better intelligence network, so you learn sooner of problems with your bill or emerging opposition. A network of eyes and ears is a big help in a difficult legislative battle.

Nothing about the congressional process is rocket science. It is really a series of commonsense rules and principles that simply need to be comprehended before you start. There are, however, two last features of working "The Hill" that should be noted. First, congressional staff, especially in

---

EXHIBIT 2.4   Typical Congressional Office Staff Positions

Administrative assistant/chief of staff	Legislative correspondent
Legislative director	Caseworker
Legislative assistant	Staff assistant

the House, are relatively young. Many chiefs of staff, or administrative assistants (AAs), are in their late twenties or early thirties. Legislative assistants (LAs) are usually younger, and many are very recent college graduates. Senate staff tend to be a little more senior, but not much. The worker bees of Capitol Hill are a young bunch. Know that going in and you will not be surprised. More than one gray-haired CEO has gone to DC and been dismayed to be making a pitch to a 25-year-old LA. And do not alienate the staff. They are the gatekeepers and avenue to the elected bosses.

Second, interchange with staff is the norm because congressional members are extremely busy and often unavailable. Do not expect to have the majority of your Hill meetings with Representatives or Senators. Be prepared to meet with staff, especially those listed in Exhibit 2.4. Eventually, especially with the leaders of your effort, you will spend more time with the elected principal. Access to elected members is often easier at home in their districts or states than it is in DC. Keep that in mind when planning appointments.

State Process

State Legislatures

The process for enacting bills into law at the state level is comparable to the congressional process. The sequence of introduction, committee action, floor vote, reconciliation between the houses, and presentation to the governor (instead of the president) is essentially identical. All states except Nebraska have bicameral (i.e., two-house) legislatures; Nebraska operates the nation's only unicameral legislature.

Committee authority is one area of substantial difference between the federal Congress and the states. Within the states, there are two basis committee models: (1) the committee "stranglehold" model and (2) the "advisory" model. The stranglehold model confers enormous power on the committees; in these states, a successful lobbying program must work effectively with the appropriate committee and its leadership. The advisory model features weaker committees, with the real authority retained by the leadership for the whole legislature.

Under the stranglehold model, no bill may be brought up on the floor unless it is reported favorably by the committee of jurisdiction. Committees become graveyards for most measures, and only those supported by the committee chairperson or the leadership stand much chance of passage. In these situations, the committee leadership and its members are necessarily the first targets of attention if your plan is to either move a bill or kill it. Attention must be paid to the entire membership in order to assure a majority vote on the floor; however, in this game of first-round elimination, having a majority of votes ready on the floor means little if the measure gets bottled up in committee.

In the advisory model, committee action is not dispositive. Obviously, favorable action can help in securing votes for ultimate floor passage, but the real test is on the floor among all the members. The committee will consider the bill, report on it, and move it to the floor with a recommendation that it be passed or defeated. Legislatures organized in this fashion typically have more powerful leadership (e.g., speakers, majority leaders) and less formidable committee chairpersons.

Influence on the State Process

The principles outlined for influencing the federal/congressional process hold true for the states. These, too, are political institutions and respond in essentially the same manner to substance, leadership from key members, energized constituents, and well-organized coalitions. If there is one crucial difference, though, it is that the states operate under highly compressed time schedules. The average state legislature meets once a year and may be in session only 4 to 6 months. Some meet only every other year. In contrast, the U.S. Congress is usually in session for 10 to 11 months in nonelection years and 9 months in election years. It is imperative that a state legislative effort factors in the limited time available for action.

This compressed time frame ensures that a state effort is generally short and intense. What might take months at the federal level often occurs in weeks in a state capital. By necessity, successful action in state legislatures requires substantial advance preparation. A lot of advance contact and communication with legislators and staff is needed to set the stage for action during the short session. To move quickly, your key congressional members should be identified and on board when the legislature convenes. Substantive materials should also be ready, as well as your energized grassroots and coalition partners. At the state level, one who hesitates is lost and will wait months, if not a year and a half, before being able to try again.

Management of Lobbying

A successful venture into the legislative arena is not for amateurs. It requires a mix of procedural and substantive knowledge, honed political skills, and the ability to manage an enterprise that may involve a multiplicity of individuals and organizations. Entities that dabble in the process do not get results or are just monitoring or watching developments without attempting to exert substantive influence.

For the small to modestly sized nonprofit organization, there are three basic approaches to securing the skills of effective lobbyists. The first is to hire one or more staff members and task them with the job of running the group's legislative or political operation. Such a one- or two-person staff is generally sufficient to monitor activities and periodically "show the flag" (e.g., testify at a hearing, submit comments on a bill, communicate periodically with key elected representatives) on behalf of the group. Over time, a small professional political staff can develop a network among key legislators as well as a solid substantive reputation and be able to get things done on a modest scale.

Many not-for-profits (and profit-making entities) are unwilling to dedicate the resources to full-time personnel for this purpose and will employ a second approach. When the need for legislative action arises, an alternative is to simply retain a lobbyist. This is a way to secure instant expertise, a political network, and a representative with a good reputation if the right person is selected. Much like attorneys (and many attorneys are lobbyists), legislative services can be secured on an hourly basis, a single flat project fee, or a monthly retainer. Each has its benefits and costs for the client.

The third approach is to join a larger coalition of similarly situated or interested entities and have the group secure professional services by hiring full-time staff or retaining lobbying professionals. Washington, DC, is full of national trade associations organized for this purpose.

Be aware of the need to comply with lobbying registration requirements, regardless of the approach used. Anyone hired to influence legislation within Congress is required to register with the Clerks of the House and the Senate as lobbyists. Registration requires the disclosure of the client, of the issues being worked on, and of a generalized range of expenditures on the effort. Many states have similar requirements, and the trend at both the national and state levels is for greater disclosure and tighter oversight of lobbying activities. (See Exhibit 2.5.)

In the same vein, learn the gift rules that govern each legislative body. Most have restrictions on the number and value of gifts, including meals, that legislators may accept from lobbying interests. It is political disaster for a not-for-profit to venture into the legislative arena and run afoul of lobbying and gift rules. Such transgressions generate news headlines, which can take a long time to erase.

Conclusion

A basic understanding of the institutions, procedures, and people make the legislative process transparent and comprehensible. The objective is most often to achieve a tangible end product in the form of an amendment,

EXHIBIT 2.5   Compliance with Lobbying Disclosure Act of 1995

The Lobbying Disclosure Act of 1995 (LDA—Public Law 104-65) was signed into law on December 19, 1995, and took effect January 1, 1996. The Lobbying Disclosure Technical Amendments Act of 1998 (Public Law 105-166) was enacted on April 6, 1998.

General Information on Compliance with the Lobbying Disclosure Act

- Lobbying reports must be filed every six months.
- If you have as few as two contacts on behalf of your organization within a six-month period with members of Congress, congressional staff, or high-level administration personnel, you may have to register.
- Depending on how much time you spend lobbying or how much your organization spends on lobbying or is paid for lobbying, you may have to register.
- The fine for failure to comply with the LDA can be as much as $50,000.
- More in-depth information on compliance with the LDA can be obtained through the Secretary of the Senate and/or the House Legislative Resource Center.

a provision, or a bill—or to stop any of these items. Critically, participants must remember that the legislative process operates by its own rules and pace. Adapt to those rules and the time constraints and the end product can be realized. Exclusive focus on the end product, in contrast, is a recipe for frustration. Bring the knowledge learned here to bear, add healthy doses of perseverance and patience, and the legislative process can be used to serve your interests.

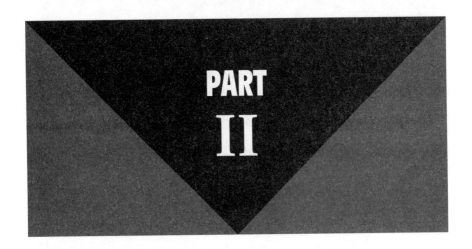

PART
II

SUCCESSFUL METHODS
USED BY NOT-FOR-PROFITS

WALTER P. PIDGEON, JR.

Part 1 was designed to provide a starting point in the development of a government affairs program, including a historical background of the process, the rules of the road, the capabilities that are needed, volunteer opportunities, fund-raising, and the way the process works at both the state and federal levels.

Part 2 introduces the leading methods that can be used in the government affairs process. These include the use of a grassroots network, the role that political action committees (PACs) play, the use of communications in government affairs activities, partnerships with other organizations and the use of outside consultants to achieve your goals.

Part 2 also highlights some of the methods that can be used to make your government affairs program come alive. The authors have taken the time to illustrate by examples the ways that their information can be used. Several examples cite 501(c)4 or 501(c)6 organizations. Does this mean that a 501(c)3 organization cannot perform these functions? Not necessarily, but it is important to discover the parameters that your organization has to obey within the IRS code.

Consult with your legal and accounting services to determine your opportunities. Several 501(c)3 organizations are performing successful government affairs programs well within the IRS ruling. Other 501(c)3 organizations have found themselves reaching the limit on the IRS ruling and have opted to transfer their government affairs operations to other organizations. Some have even developed new organizations, which have other IRS classifications. The bottom line is that, if a need exists to provide a government affairs function, it can be done well within the IRS rulings.

Pay careful attention to Chapter 3, which discusses grassroots lobbying and the use of political action committees (PACs). The author, Jack Kalavitinos, general counsel and director, government affairs, American Consulting Engineers Council, is an expert on PACs and the grassroots function. While the use of political action committees is a grand idea, not all not-for-profits can or should use them. If your not-for-profit falls into this category, think about how you can increase your grassroots network. In many cases, a well-developed grassroots network can be as effective as a PAC if you provide the support that is needed. In my association, we do not have a PAC, but we do have an extensive grassroots program, which promotes our issues.

Chapter 4 is a must. Government affairs campaigns are not conducted in a vacuum, you must gain the attention of your target groups. Its author, Rick Story, vice president of the Wildlife Legislative Fund of America (WLFA), notes that, if you wish to start or refine a government affairs program, communications are a key factor in its success. In addition, you will want to use the government affairs function to promote other areas of your operation. WLFA exploits the communications factor to the highest possible level. Most of the issues campaigns that it conducts have a major communications component, from grassroots postcard mailers to television spots. It is a very effective way to bring your story to your target audience.

Chapter 5 will provide you with the information that you will need to form partnerships with other organizations. The author of this chapter, Robert Goodwin, is president and CEO of Points of Light Foundation, a national organization that promotes volunteering and business involvement in community activities. Bob understands that, in the government affairs arena, working with other groups is the name of the game. Most not-for-profits cannot do it alone; they simply do not have the power. Grouping your resources with others' provides added power and visibility. Partnering is a vital part of the government affairs program.

Chapter 6 provides another option that not-for-profits can use to cover part or all of the government affairs function. Its author, John Chwat, president of Chwat & Company, demonstrates through experience and expertise the significant role that consultants can play, particularly at the state level. I have found in my association that consultants can significantly increase reach and effectiveness. The process of selecting and evaluating consultants needs to be clearly defined. Consultants can be a major asset in a government affairs function.

Achieving Impact through Political Involvement

JACK KALAVITINOS

Introduction

Americans enjoy a system of self-government unique in the world. Ours is the most successful democracy in history. For the past 225 years, Americans have used everything from letters, megaphones, e-mail, and handwritten flyers to exercise their rights as free citizens in a democratic republic. Using the power of the Internet, Americans continue to express their opinions to an even broader audience in record time.

This freedom of speech is the foundation of our system of government. Through this right and freedom of assembly, we are able to elect our own representatives. These members of Congress or the state legislatures debate, hold hearings, and vote on legislation. In turn, Americans, individually and collectively, seek to influence that legislation. Regular elections can serve as a public referendum on performance, through which the people decide whether to re-elect or replace their legislators.

This ability of groups of individuals within a democracy to exert their will on the legislative process has raised fears in the hearts of many since the beginning. In 1787, James Madison wrote at length about the tyranny of "the faction."[1] He warned that factions, or today's special interests, create "instability, injustice and confusion . . . the mortal diseases under which popular governments everywhere perished."[2]

Madison did not, however, mean to suggest the elimination of these "factions"; he recognized that their origins are "sown in the nature of man."[3] Thus, how can a free country temper the influence of a cauldron of special interests? By creating a democratic republic with a representative form of government. In Federalist Paper No. 6, Alexander Hamilton takes this concept one step further and describes how a "commercial republic"[4] actually provides stability through competing commercial interests.[5]

Almost 50 years later, Alexis de Tocqueville, renowned French observer of the American people and culture, noted the American penchant to join organizations—whether civic, political, charitable, religious, or recreational. While this tendency to coalesce obviously continues today, Americans also cherish individualism. This seeming contradiction yields a healthy conflict among forces that is visible today in the world of associations. An effective not-for-profit builds on both the belief in voluntary association and the efficacy of the individual.

The right of consulting engineers, doctors, wholesalers-distributors, dry cleaners, and every other imaginable trade or professional group to exercise their First Amendment freedoms to organize into groups to achieve representation for their issues is exactly what the founders predicted and wanted. Some groups, such as labor unions, have mastered the art of galvanizing their membership and effectively harness their numbers to make a difference in the political process. Trade and professional groups should take note of organized labor's success in this area.

In the American system of government, we may have an impact on legislation through effective communication with and education of elected officials. For association leaders, both volunteer and executive staff, there is no more significant exercise than advocating their issues before state and national policymakers. An association can serve its members well by creating a strong political program.

An important component of such a program is achieved by giving directly to candidates and the national parties. Through a political action committee, or PAC, associations can reinforce their message and highlight the importance of particular issues by supporting legislators who share their priorities. PACs provide opportunities for associations to participate in, and to influence, the political process.

Of course, 501 (c)(3) organizations are not able to form PACs. The IRS code allows certain 501 (c)(3) organizations to lobby government officials, as long as it is not a "substantial part of the activities" of the group.[6] The 501 (c)(3) must "not participate in, or intervene in . . . any political campaigns on behalf of any candidate for public office."[7]

However, options exist for such groups to make a difference in the legislative arena. One opportunity is through issue advocacy. Highlighting a certain issue at a particular time can help educate the public in advance of state and national elections. It is best to seek counsel from an attorney who specializes in association law to determine the ways that an industry or professional group can have an impact on the political system.

Impact Through Supporting Candidates and the Parties

Not-for-profits that seek to get involved in the political process or to increase their current involvement recognize that they must participate if they wish to be heard. As veteran Washington lobbyist Wayne Valis explains, industries and professions "need a broad-based presence. When a company lobbies individually, the company does not have the influence nor the standing." He continues by noting that an industry PAC adds legitimacy to that industry and helps to avoid what may otherwise be seen as a "one-company piece of legislation." He adds that PACS can ease the appearance of special interest lobbying when it's a broadbased group. Lobbyist Marlene Colucci, with the firm of Akin Gump Strauss Hauer & Feld, echoes his sentiments: "There is strength in numbers. Giving money through the PAC enables the association to speak with one unified voice. That voice is much louder if it comes from a PAC versus an individual donor."

According to Jan Baran, general counsel of the Business-Industry Political Action Committee (BIPAC), "Politics is the lifeblood of a democratic society. One sign of a vital society is the widespread involvement of citizens in political affairs."[8]

There is no single path to greater impact. Different groups offer political candidates different assets. According to Dirk Van Dongen, president of the National Association of Wholesaler-Distributors, and a prominent member of the association community in Washington, an association should "inventory and then develop a plan where you leverage your resources so you become part of the life support system of the candidate. It could mean being a trusted advisor. Or serving as an effective fundraiser. It could mean connecting the candidate with constituents at home. If the circumstances are conducive, then starting a PAC is key."

Political Action Committees

History of PACs

This section will explain the basics of forming a PAC and highlight some of the Federal Election Commission (FEC) rules regarding party giving and other political activities by not-for-profits. We will then look at using the resources effectively and strategically. One of the most effective ways that an association can participate in the American political system is to form an association PAC in order to pool the resources of its members and to contribute to congressional candidates.

Political action committees entered the scene in 1971 as a form of campaign finance reform. Congress passed a series of election laws, the cornerstone of which was to regulate the dollar amount of giving and to provide donor disclosure. The resulting system set strict limits and required that candidates and PACs file reports to the FEC disclosing pertinent information. Today, a PAC may give no more than $5,000 per election. For example, at the maximum giving level, Congressman Jones may receive $5,000 from XYZ PAC for the primary election and $5,000 again for the general election. Of note, these limits were set 26 years ago and have not been adjusted for inflation; some in Congress and political observers have advocated raising the contribution limits.[9]

Ways of Organizing a PAC

The best way to ensure that a PAC is properly run is to create by-laws. While not legally necessary, by-laws help to detail everything from the structure and operation of the PAC to the criteria for giving. In particular, by-laws should include the name of the PAC and the affiliated association; the structure; the general purposes; a stipulation that procedures are in compliance with FEC rules; the composition of the governing board; the terms and duties of the trustees or officers; and provisions for amending the by-laws.[10] The bottom line is that the creation of by-laws add credibility within the association for the political program.

Ways of Complying with the Regulations When Fund-raising

Two of the most difficult challenges in raising money to bolster your association's political muscle are (1) achieving your members' buy-in for the goals and (2) complying with the complicated rules regulating a PAC's ability to raise money from its members. The FEC allows for the solicitation of noncorporate and partnership members at any time.[11] However, an association PAC must first ask its members for permission to solicit them for contributions. This requirement can burden an association when considering mail solicitation as well as face-to-face requests at association meetings. Jerry Jacobs, general counsel to the American Society of Association Executives, offers the following rules:

- A PAC can accept contributions only from individuals, not from corporations. The caveat is that a PAC may accept contributions from sole proprietorships and partnerships and their families without restriction.
- Prior approval to solicit for funds must be in writing, although the FEC is considering online approvals. Each member of the association may give approval for only one federal association–related PAC per year.
- When soliciting corporations, the PAC may solicit executive and administrative personnel or stockholders only after receiving prior approval from an executive in the corporation.
- An association PAC may solicit funds only from association members; review the FEC's strict definition of a member (a member firm is one that can vote for association officers).
- A federation of associations' PAC may solicit the restricted class of members of any state, local, or regional association in the federation.[12]

A myriad of other technical rules exist. Please consult with legal counsel and the FEC's materials not only when creating a PAC but also when deciding how to raise funds. The FEC provides advice over the phone and offers interested parties a full range of information through its website (www.FEC.gov).

Ways of Using Your PAC Strategically

There is certainly a correlation between a union's or trade association's PAC size and the perceived power that it exerts in Washington. However, after analyzing several PACs it is clear that, beyond the sheer size of the PAC, three basic elements are present in strategically effective PACs. Strong PACs (1) have a mission, (2) make a difference in key races for key candidates, and (3) build relationships with members of Congress.

Does Your PAC Have a Mission?

You need to give your PAC a sense of direction, a sense of purpose. The former chairman of American Motors, Gerald Meyers, once told the following story in a speech before the Society of American Business and Economic Writers:

> The story is about a knight who returned to the castle at twighlight in a state of total disarray. Dented armor, helmet falling off, face bloody, horse crippled, and the knight himself about to fall off the limping horse.
> "What hath befallen you, Sir Knight?" asked the lord of the castle.
> "Oh sire," answered the knight, "I have been laboring in your service, robbing and plundering and pillaging your enemies in the West."
> "You've what?" cried the lord. "I don't have any enemies in the West."
> "Oh," said the knight. "You do now!"[13]

As this anecdote suggests, a clear purpose is essential to using your resources effectively. According to lobbyist Wayne Valis, "The best PAC is guided by an idea or a philosophy. If you have an amorphous, shapeless giving program, your lobbying program will tend to follow."

Creating a PAC mission is the first step toward deciding which candidates you support. Having a strong PAC philosophy enables the association to better target its funds to the right candidates. This focus also "enables a PAC to say 'no' to requests that come from Members of Congress who are not supportive of the association's legislative agenda," notes Marlene Colucci.

Based on that mission, define a list of criteria for giving to candidates that meets your association's goals and objectives. As an example, the Business and Industry PAC of America (BIPAC) has developed such a set of criteria as part of Project 2000, a political operations steering committee composed of representatives from the nation's business community. See Exhibit 3.1.

Working with their lists of criteria, organizations then use a variety of ways, such as rating systems, to evaluate candidates and elected officials.

EXHIBIT 3.1   Bi-PAC PAC Criteria for Evaluating Candidates

- Voting records and position on issues
- Attitude regarding seniority
- Importance of committee assignments
- Relationships, access, friends of friends
- Unopposed, safe, somewhat competitive, vulnerable
- Well-funded, somewhat in need, very needy
- Interviews, word of mouth, PAC kits, other input
- Habits, legacies, entitlements

Source: *Excerpted from Project 2000, Direct Contribution Toolkit (2000).*

At my organization, the American Consulting Engineers Council (ACEC), we ask our nearly 50 PAC trustees to make recommendations from their own states of candidates whom they believe meet the criteria. Some organizations use key votes in order to rate members of Congress on their priority issues. As the director of government affairs for the Associated General Contractors (AGC), Jeff Shoaf explains: "Ratings are useful in helping politicians understand that we're keeping score, that we're watching. We're here to make sure that decisions in Washington are not being made in a vacuum. . . . Recommendations come in and despite poor ratings we sometimes contribute. Our members argue that the Members of Congress take their calls and so despite the low ratings they're not a lost cause." A list of giving criteria supported by an evaluation method provides a tool that enables critical thinking and greater consistency in making funding determinations.

Refer to BIPAC.org for an overview of BIPAC's sophisticated system of ranking all members of Congress.

Making a Difference: Be Essential to Candidates

"The way to become consequential to a candidate is to become part of his political life support system," Dirk van Dongen said recently. He added that the myriad of ways to become essential "pivot off of the individual association's circumstances." He suggests that industry and professional groups should carefully study the assets that their membership and executive staff bring to the table and determine, to the extent possible, how their group can be essential to political candidates.

Avoid diluting your impact by giving to too many candidates at very low amounts. If a member of Congress is particularly important, demonstrate your association's support. If the member is a chairperson of a key committee, a sponsor of important legislation, or a member of the House or

Senate leadership, your PAC may want to recognize that person and support him or her at a higher level. Additionally, consider looking at key challengers and candidates in open seat races. If a candidate meets your criteria, then contribute, and contribute early.

As a guide for timing your PAC's contribution, the following is a summary from BI-PAC of key moments in an election cycle to give and the advantages of each moment:

- After a candidate announces. This has a big impact on how viable a candidate appears to be to allies and adversaries.
- After candidate filing, so the individual is an official candidate. Many PACs get burned when a number of incumbents retire rather than run but wait until the last minute to announce their decisions.
- During a primary, if the district is not a two-party competitive seat in the general election. Choosing to support a candidate during the primary may be the only time to have an impact on the election. In many congressional districts, the primary is the real election.
- Right after a primary, especially if the primary strongly defined the candidates and the campaign for the general election. Primaries are useful for sorting out a candidate's stand on issues. Early money to a candidate after a primary can give him or her money to replenish depleted campaign war chests.
- About eight weeks out from the general election, if the candidate is still doing well in the polls and needs a final push for media or get-out-the-vote activities.
- Debt retirement, if the PAC missed giving to a candidate during the election year. While it is not the most courageous time to contribute to a candidate, the contribution will be appreciated by the campaign.[14]

On a related note, many associations have a policy that requires that PAC checks be delivered to elected officials in their home states rather than in Washington, DC. The reason is obvious: while there is a connection made in Washington, a local association member can either solidify an existing relationship or build a new one. It also has the benefit of showing that the national PAC has relevance for members at the local level, and that their hard-earned money is coming back to the state to support their favorite candidates.

Building Relationships with Members of Congress

It is not unusual for association lobbyists or their team to spend every Tuesday, Wednesday, and Thursday attending breakfasts, lunch meetings, and receptions or dinners for political candidates. While the large events, or cattle calls, have their place, seek opportunities to either host or co-host small events for candidates whom your PAC supports. At a minimum, focus your attendance on smaller events that more effectively maximize your group's PAC dollars. By increasing the time you can interact one-on-one with a member of Congress, you improve your ability to understand and be understood.

Consider working closely with the candidates' fund-raisers to help establish a relationship early that could be instrumental when you want to put together smaller, industry-specific breakfasts or dinners for a candidate. Association professionals who employ outside lobbyists should not lose sight of the ability to leverage their dollars by working with their outside counsel. Marlene Colucci adds: "Supporting a fundraising event hosted by the outside lobbyist gives the association the chance to get to know the elected official through their own consultant who often has a strong relationship."

Following the Winning Habits

Gary Andres, one of Washington's premiere lobbyists, lays out Seven Habits of Highly Effective PACs. His philosophy is echoed by political pros around town who distinguish themselves through smart giving. His Seven Habits provide a clear summary of how to add more strategic vision to your PAC:

- Habit One: Develop a contribution philosophy.
- Habit Two: Avoid the anonymous donor syndrome.
- Habit Three: Lead with Leadership PACs.
- Habit Four: Leave the herd behind.
- Habit Five: Get a little help from your friends.
- Habit Six: Spread yourself fat, spread yourself early.
- Habit Seven: Choose your friends wisely and stick to them.

Depending on the skills of your professional staff and your volunteer leadership, pick the right approach that allows you to be consequential to candidates. The bottom line is that too many associations spend all of their precious time raising the funds and give little thought as to how to spend it. Once your association decides its PAC recipients, you need to be sophisticated about how you contribute. By following suggestions—such as giving checks in the district, going to small industry events, sponsoring your own events, and helping challengers and incumbents in close races—you are truly maximizing your PAC dollars.

Fund-raising Methods

"I have a reputation for being straightlaced, but actually I come from a very tough state. In Utah—you think it's easy raising money from people who are all sober?" asked Senator Orin Hatch.[15] Members of not-for-profits often need strong motivation to counter their aversion to giving to politicians. Some members would rather give at the state level, and others do not like the idea of making political contributions. A strong, cohesive advocacy program that follows a well-defined mission developed with association leadership can help to build the support needed to reduce the reticence to give. The key is activating your association's members by having your PAC trustees and the elected volunteer leadership serve as ambassadors for the PAC. The association staff plays a key role in devising and implementing the strategy, but the volunteer members themselves are instrumental in persuading their colleagues to contribute. It's critical for association members to understand and see the beneficial impact of their PAC. When asked about the strongest appeal that is made to the general contractors, their chief lobbyist Jeff Shoaf answered that it's not about coming up with new appeals—they know why they need to give. "They see it as a duty. Our members used to wear GIPGOB (Get Into Politics Or Go Out Of Business) pins."

For many not-for-profits, fund-raising at annual meetings is vital to the entire endeavor. It allows for both the actual fund-raising and donor recognition. The positive energy that is created at conventions and the high concentrations of the association's most active members provide an environment conducive to building support. Typical fund-raising events at association meetings include live and silent auctions, golf tournaments, PAC booths, and receptions. The former vice president of government affairs at Associated Builders and Contractors provides a list of creative fundraisers in Exhibit 3.2.[16] However, your PAC-building strategies must also include other methods that reach out to members who never attend your annual convention.

Important guidelines that must be followed in order to raise money from members. Membership associations that are individual member–based can solicit all of their members without restriction. As noted earlier, trade associations with corporate members must have a representative from each corporation

---

EXHIBIT 3.2   Creative Ideas for PAC Fund-raising

- Skeet shoot
- PAC auction
- Boston tea party—an example of a Boston event that can be tailored to the historic attraction in your location
- Miniature golf tournament
- Blue marlin fishing trip
- Pig roast
- Golf getaway promotion
- Biking for dollars
- Sporting events
- Casino night, depending on state laws

Source: *Creating and Managing an Association Government Relations Program.*

give prior approval before any kind of solicitation for funds. This one rule has greatly limited the true fund-raising potential of many PACs. According to a recent survey, association PACs receive permission to solicit from only 50 percent of their members.[17] Before such an association can solicit its entire membership through a mass-mailing, for example, prior approval must be garnered from 95 percent of the members. With the widescale use of e-mail, the potential to streamline and facilitate the prior-approval process is a possibility.

Practical tips for running convention activities include the following:

- Always schedule to reduce conflicts.
- Ensure volunteer leadership is able to participate.
- Have a PAC booth set up for members to stop by during the event.
- Use a professional auctioneer unless one of your members has relevant experience.
- Have PAC meeting at the beginning of convention.
- Create a festive atmosphere.
- Consider selling raffle tickets before and during the convention to help generate excitement as well as reach those association members unable to attend.
- Add to PAC administrative account by allowing corporate sponsorships of events.

Again, you would be advised to consult with the FEC rules and rulings to ensure that you comply with the letter and spirit of the law. The FEC's *Campaign Guide for Corporations and Labor Organizations* as well as Jerry Jacobs' *Association Law Handbook* are excellent resources.

Donor Clubs

It is essential to acknowledge your members for giving to the PAC. Establish a system that both recognizes member support as well as differentiates among giving levels. Such a program can help reinforce the importance of the PAC to the overall association's advocacy approach and can promote greater participation and amount of giving. Associations can learn from university and party donor programs in order to reinforce the value of tiered-giving programs.

A donor club can be a particularly effective approach. For example, at AGC, their organization has had a PAC of over half a million dollars for approximately the past 10 election cycles. According to Jeff Shoaf, a whopping 85 percent of the AGC contributors donate $1,000 per year. These contributors are members of the "535 Club." They receive special access to a members-only hospitality suite at the association's annual convention, which includes breakfast, an open bar, a business center, and a club lapel pin. Recently, AGC has been making a concerted effort to increase its PAC size by cultivating lower dollar contributions: "At our last convention, our fund-raising goal was $175,000. We surpassed it on the second day of a four-day convention," says Shoaf. In addition, in order to encourage members to complete prior-approval forms for PAC solicitations, AGC's PAC gave away two Palm Pilots to randomly selected members.

At my organization, the American Consulting Engineers Council (ACEC), our $200,000 PAC grew steadily in the late 1990s. However, the entire PAC consisted of funds collected during the two conventions each year with a relatively small average contribution. We had a myriad of donor categories with little further distinction beyond giving pins to our members. While our members were appreciative, we were losing opportunities both to recognize more fully those donors who gave larger amounts and to build momentum. As a result, we started an elite group called the Millennium Club in November 1998.

At ACEC, for a $2,000 contribution over two years (1999–2000), members received a number of benefits: complimentary golf registration at the spring and fall conferences; a special PAC reception with a key member of Congress in conjunction with our ACEC spring legislative fly-in; a substantial gold name tag; plenty of recognition at meetings and in print; and free sweepstakes tickets twice a year. This program was advocated by our PAC trustees chairman, Art Brooks, an engineering firm owner from Arizona, and has led to the biggest fund-raising success in the history of our PAC.

PACs at State and National Levels

The consulting engineers council of Indiana executive director recently informed me that her organization had set up a state PAC. Initially, thoughts of competing for the same funds raced through my mind. However, I quickly realized that this is a mutually beneficial opportunity. First, it is good for the state organization. It allows for coordinated giving by the state industry group. It is also helpful for the national PAC because it *conditions* the state members to recognize the importance of giving to a PAC, as opposed to exclusively giving individual contributions to particular members of Congress. Jeff Shoaf, chief lobbyist for the Associated General Contractors (AGC), notes that the existence of state AGC PACs are not harmful because "we've been around longer" and that the state PACs do not support federal candidates.

Web-Based Fund-raising

"Quietly, but with accelerating speed, the Internet is changing the business of politics,"[18] proclaimed a recent front-page story in the *Washington Post.* Web-based fund-raising is the newest area of fund-raising. With the explosion of e-commerce, Internet political fund-raising has become increasingly successful, and associations are only now getting into the act. Even the associations that are selling products over their webpages remain reluctant about entering the PAC e-fund-raising business. One of the pioneers in this area is Trey Richardson, president of e-contributor.com.

Although making PAC donations over the Internet is still in its infancy, the growth potential is huge. According to Richardson, political candidates raised, at most, 2 percent over the Internet in 1998, compared with 20 percent in 2000.

ACEC is one of the first trade associations to set up a full-scale Internet fund-raising operation for its PAC. While still in the preliminary stages, we see this new tool as the number one method of reaching out to the thousands of members who pay their dues, read our publications, and even participate in our grassroots efforts but never make it to one of our two annual conventions. We envision this approach as the best way to reach out to all members with targeted messages based on their responses to instant polls available on the ACEC website.

The advantages of fund-raising over the Internet are remarkable. In essence, it's less expensive, faster, more effective, and targeted. In particular,

- *Cost.* It's much cheaper (currently, econtribute.com charges .08 of each dollar raised with no start up fees, versus .70 per dollar for telemarketing and .50 per dollar for direct mail).
- *Speed.* Whether your association member wants to contribute while on the webpage at work or at home, or if the association sends an e-mail solicitation or a grassroots alert that includes an appeal for funds, the speed and accessibility cannot be matched.
- *Data tracking.* One of the great missed opportunities for an association deluged with paper results from an inability to track who has given PAC funds and to use the information effectively. A well-designed, web-based fund-raising site can enable the association to maintain accurate records, follow up with previous donors with tailored messages, and reach out to new donors as never before.

Adding Internet fund-raising to your association's arsenal is worth considering. However, initially donations over the Internet represent only a small part of the overall total; over time, it should increase significantly. Take great care to design your PAC website to ensure that you meet all the relevant FEC rules, particularly the requirement that only prior-approved members are solicited. Additionally, existing tenets of fund-raising remain important; encouraging significant donations warrants a personal touch. As one fund-raiser recently said, candidates—or PACs, for our purposes—are always "looking for the magic bullet—right now it's Internet fundraising. I say, yes, we will have to have websites, but you still have to call people."[19]

Importance of Political Education Fund

Some associations decide to create a fund that may be used for issue advocacy or get-out-the-vote campaign efforts or that may be given to one or both political parties. Some associations establish separate accounts for these activities, and others place the funds under an assortment of names such as line items for "co-sponsorship" or general accounts for legislative affairs.

Every four years, the presidential elections return, and unique opportunities arise for associations. During the primaries, there are opportunities for your Iowa and New Hampshire associations to work with the major candidates and try to encourage them to support one or more of your key issues. You may also be able to secure one or more candidates at an industry event—such as a breakfast, lunch, or dinner function; a press conference; or an issue conference. Some groups, such as the U.S. Chamber of Commerce, are particularly effective in this area. Additionally, smaller groups in the key primary states are also successful in having an audience with the candidates because the groups make the effort to extend the invitation.

After the primaries end in the early spring, new opportunities exist to reach out to the two major candidates. Whether you help your members participate within the candidates' fund-raising apparatus or reach out to their issues departments, your organization can seek ways to find common ground with one or both candidates. By helping during the election process, you lay the groundwork for greater understanding of your issues when one of the candidates eventually wins the White House.

Your association might also want to send its top government affairs official and appropriate volunteer leader to the national conventions and help co-sponsor activities. Corporate America has been sponsoring events for years, and savvy associations not only attend but also help to support key congressional members' events or events sponsored by one of the campaign committees. The players are present, and, while not necessary to maximize your association's impact, your association should be there as well.

During the 2000 election season, we saw a very strong use of these funds for issue ads and get-out-the-vote drives. "Still smarting from the successful get-out-the-vote drive that unions used in 1998 to help narrow the Republican margin in the House, business groups are planning a grassroots drive coupled with issue advertising to offset the expected $30 million labor effort designed mainly to help Democrats," writes Peter H. Stone in the January 2000 issue of the *National Journal.* Stone adds, "Deep-pocketed business groups, such as the Business Roundtable, the National Association of Manufacturers, and the U.S. Chamber of Commerce, plan to boost spending to influence this year's elections. Besides their own drives, these groups and others are trying to better coordinate their political activities through the Business-Industry Political Action Committee, or BIPAC. Most business efforts are labeled bipartisan, but they are expected to overwhelmingly benefit GOP candidates."[20]

Grassroots Activism

Building a strong grassroots effort is a key complement to any government affairs program. An association needs to have the issue development, the political muscle, and the ability to mobilize the group's grassroots members to make up the well-worn phrase "three legs of the stool." However, for our purposes, we will focus not on grassroots advocacy to affect a single legislative issue but, rather, to affect elections.

Internet

The Internet is quickly changing the face of grassroots mobilization and the method of communicating with members of Congress. The professional and business communities can learn a great deal from the labor unions. In February 2000, the AFL-CIO made a major announcement regarding its new venture—workingfamilies.com. This operation includes as members 20 unions with a total enrollment of 9 million members. "Soon we'll be able to communicate instantaneously with our members with the click of a button, and we can also recruit volunteers, register voters, and raise money for our PACs," said AFL-CIO president John Sweeney. He added, "We have the ability to mobilize, educate, and organize our members electronically, and the implications for legislative and political action are enormous." In particular, the union controls the "start up screen"—the first image the union member sees—for members who take advantage of the inexpensive Internet access and computers. On the start up screen, union members see the daily "message."[21]

The trade association community is also recognizing the importance of this medium with its Project 2000, a high-tech grassroots program. Dirk Van Dongen noted that, in 25 years of participating in efforts to mobilize the business community, this is the best he has ever seen. Considering that more business executives and professionals are currently hooked into the Internet, "the business community actually has an advantage—a fleeting advantage," he concluded.

Grassroots Political Action

"It is very important that we hear from people, but it is very important that people try and really spell it out in as brief a way as possible. And I think that really is where these associations play such a significant role in terms of their ability to really impact legislation and . . . help us and assist us in our role in trying to make good laws," explains Rep. Ray LaHood (R-IL).[22] (See Exhibit 3.3.)

One of the leading grassroots experts in the country, Michael Dunn, has advised clients and others in developing effective grassroots programs. As he told the Public Affairs Council, although grassroots advocacy has evolved into a "key, strategic lobbying tool," for most associations, the central aspect of grassroots has not changed. According to Dunn, the three core principles are as follows:

- For many people, asking them to participate in politics is akin to "asking them to perform an unnatural act."

EXHIBIT 3.3   Political Influence Model

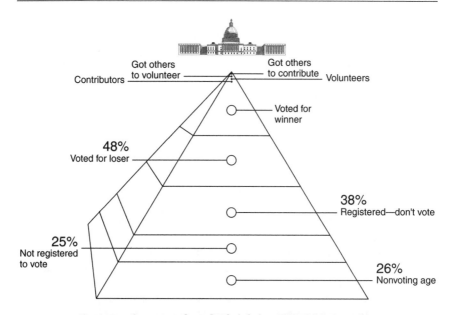

Contributors — Got others to volunteer — Got others to contribute — Volunteers

Voted for winner

48%
Voted for loser

38%
Registered—don't vote

25%
Not registered to vote

26%
Nonvoting age

Average Congressional District—565,000 People.

This model can apply to lawmakers at the federal, state, or local level.

Source: © *Michael E. Dunn & Associates, Inc.*

- The primary purpose of grassroots efforts is to have an impact on legislation.
- Grassroots advocacy includes many kinds of activities, with the most effective approach involving association members who are constituents with a real interest and often an economic stake in the issues and who will communicate them to their elected representatives.[23]

An essential part of being the political lifeline to a member of the legislature or a member of Congress is the power of your association's grassroots advocacy system. Can your group mobilize for or against a particular issue? Do you use the latest in technology in a way that fits with the culture of your member organization? Establishing a grassroots program and securing the willingness of your members to participate is not accomplished rapidly; however, once it is in place, even the smallest associations can make their voices heard. (See Exhibit 3.4 for more details).

EXHIBIT 3.4   **Advice on Grassroots Advocacy**

A successful grassroots program is not built overnight. With commitment and desire to succeed, your association will prevail.

Grassroots is about mobilizing constituents at the local level to contact their legislators in order to affect the outcome of a public policy debate. Grassroots organizing plays an increasingly important role in the legislative process. In today's legislative climate, a grassroots program is essential in transmitting your association views to your elected officials. Your grassroots program needs to be based on a continual educational process to ensure that members have a basic knowledge of the political process, so that, when they are called to action, they will know how to respond. The following factors are essential ingredients in a successful grassroots program:

- *Buy-in from the top.* Support is measured by what the chief executive officer is willing to do. Top management support means a renewed commitment to public affairs and government relations. This support from the top will speak volumes to your grassroots army.

- *Communication.* Don't expect people to stay involved in a grassroots program without being kept informed. A monthly newsletter or fact sheet is essential, complete with information about issues, the political process, and your association's position on the issues and the role your members can play. Many associations today use a broadcast fax system in communicating with their members. If you don't have a broadcast system set up, now might be the time to get one. In the legislative process, you don't always have the time to wait for the mail to be delivered. You might also use e-mail and the Internet to communicate with your members. More and more associations are going in this direction and are saving money in postage and long-distance fees.

- *Training.* It is important that your grassroots network understand its role in the legislative process. Your members need to feel comfortable writing or talking to legislators. Be specific, with some role-playing and "how-to" sessions when you meet with them. Your return on investment will be tremendous.

- *Materials.* As the grassroots manager, you are responsible for getting the current status of any issue to your grassroots network. These materials include position papers, fact sheets, and action alerts.

- *Recognition and feedback.* For a grassroots network to flourish, its members must be thanked. At the very least, send thank-you letters when your members take a grassroots action. Additional recognition (e.g., at your organization's annual meeting or legislative conference) is up to you. Feedback lets your grassroots members know why their communication is important. It also lets them know what has happened since their last action.

EXHIBIT 3.4   (Continued)

- *A database.* Use a database to keep track of your members, their elected officials, and any relationships that they may have with those officials.

There are many types of grassroots programs, with varying degrees of effectiveness. The two most commonly referred to are the key-contact program and the broad-based program. The key-contact program is based on personal relationships among your members and their elected officials. A key-contact person will meet at least the following criteria:

- Lives in the members' district
- Contributes financially to the elected official's re-election campaign or candidates' election campaign
- Is on the legislator's re-election campaign or the candidate's election campaign
- Has a personal relationship with the official (e.g., went to the same school, lives nearby, goes to the same church or synagogue, belongs to the same organization)

The key-contact members of your grassroots program will do the heavy lifting on your issue. They will meet face-to-face with legislators to ask for a commitment. They should also invite legislators to your organizational functions and events. Broad-based programs, on the other hand, focus on getting a majority of your members to understand and get involved in the political process. Once educated and called to action, your grassroots network will be inclined to write or call their legislators on a specific issue as needed.

Broad-based programs emphasize a quantitative approach. The main purpose of such a program is to activate your members, so that they will communicate with a legislator's office quickly. A broad-based program is ideal for doing group sign-on letters, phone-call campaigns, and letters-to-the-editor campaigns. A combination key-contact program and broad-based program can be most effective.

It is important for your association to decide what will work best for your members. The grass-roots program will succeed only if you can get your members to participate. Members will participate if they enjoy doing it. When they see grassroots success—especially in defense against a known threat—they will become part of the team and support your efforts.

The key to your grassroots program is your volunteer network—and the best way to reach your elected officials is through your volunteers. Legislators listen to their constituents—that's how the good ones get re-elected.

Source: *Raymond Towle, American Consulting Engineers Council*

Calls for Reform

While campaign finance reform has been a campaign issue for quite some time, it never achieved the prominence that it has received in recent years. Whether it was Ross Perot railing against lobbyists in Gucci loafers, the Clinton administration's 1996 campaign finance scandal, or Senator John McCain's (R-AZ) 2000 primary campaign, the issue of campaign finance has risen in the public consciousness. Network and cable news programs, as well as the written press,have dedicated significant time to the issue, and in certain demographic groups this area for reform has resonated.

This issue is affecting the ability of associations to mobilize their members as cynicism about the political process has grown. The debate rages regarding whether campaign finance reform will be achieved in the near future. Some believe it's right around the corner. Earlier in 2000, the *National Journal* addressed the issue: "This newfound salience for the once-yawn-inspiring issue has brought a sense of joyous expectation to the enthusiasts who are accustomed to being politely ignored. 'Regardless of who is elected,' exults Meredith McGehee, the legislative director of Common Cause, 'the possibilities next year are greater than they've been in ages that some kind of reforms will be enacted.' "[24] Her following comments underscore the extent to which some view this entire arena in a far different light than do most organized groups. She adds, "Imagine the nation's extortionate, subterfuge-filled, dishonesty-inducing system of financing campaigns at long last being revamped."[25]

The major proponents for reform are talking primarily about "soft money," or unlimited contributions to the political parties—not PAC contributions. When asked during the 2000 presidential campaign, Senator McCain scoffed at the notion that relatively small PAC contributions from any given source are the problem. For him and others, the problem is unregulated corporate contributions.

However, even proponents of the most dramatic reform do not think that banning soft money will make a dramatic difference. Ellen Miller, whose group, Public Campaign, advocates public financing of elections, concedes that life "wouldn't be much different." She adds that, even with the $100,000 donations, soft money was only 11 percent of the $2.4 billion raised in 1996.[26]

However, most association soft contributions are not of the magnitude referenced by the reformers. Bolstering an association's political power by contributing funds out of a political education fund as well as a political action committee can help to round out an association's effectiveness.

Conclusion

Participating in the political process—whether it's through PAC contributions or grassroots efforts—provides an opportunity for your association to communicate your priorities to public officials. If the notion of seeking to exert influence in the legislative process makes you uncomfortable, studies have shown that money does not change votes. Nor should it ever. Political money follows policy, not the reverse, says former Congressman Bill Frenzel (R-MN).[27] The point is that, by helping to elect and re-elect an industry or a "profession" friend on some or most issues, a group of like-minded taxpayers can exert the rights that our country's founders envisioned in the first place.

An association or a professional society with a critical stake in a public policy issue should have a presence in the political system, so that its voice can be heard in the debate that shapes the outcome. From the moment members of Congress go to Washington, getting re-elected is a top priority as they seek to fulfill their own legislative agendas. Whether it is through a PAC exclusively or in conjunction with a political education fund, it is your group's right to support members of Congress who support your priorities.

Due to the restrictions on the formation of PACs, consult an expert in creating one and ensure that your government affairs professional works with your members to devise a mission for the PAC and disburses the funds in an effective manner. New technology presents opportunities worth exploring to conduct these activities more efficiently. The key is to find the appropriate level of political participation for your organization that supports the strategic objectives of your membership.

Endnotes

[1] Alexander Hamilton, James Madison, and John Jay, *The Federalist Papers* (New York: The New American Library of World Literature, 1961), 77.

[2] Hamilton, Madison, and Jay, 77.

[3] Hamilton, Madison, and Jay, 79.

[4] Hamilton, Madison, and Jay, 56.

[5] Hamilton, Madison, and Jay, 56.

[6] Jerry Jacobs, *Association Law Handbook* (Washington, DC: American Society of Association Executives, 1996), 383.

[7] Jacobs, 383.

[8] Business-Industry Political Action Committee, Direct *Contribution Toolkit 1* (Washington, DC, 2000), V. Wayne Valis, interview with author, June 2000. Marlene Colucc; interview with author, June 2000. Dick Van Danger, interview with author, June 2000. Marlene Colucci, interview with author, June 2000. Jeff Shoaf, interview with author, June 2000.

[9] Eliza Newlin Carney, "Congress—the Outer Limits on Campaign Reform," *National Journal* (27 March 1999).

[10] Jacobs, 184–85.

[11] Sheryl A. Fowle (Information Division), *Campaign Guide for Corporations and Labor Organizations* (Washington, DC: Federal Election Commission, August 1997), 25.

[12] Jacobs, 190–96.

[13]Roger Ailes, *You Are the Message* (Homewood, IL: Dow Jones-Irwin, 1988), 40.

[14]Business-Industry Political Action Committee, *Direct Contribution Toolkit 1* (Washington, DC: 2000), 26–27.

[15]"Off the Record," *Campaign and Elections* (February 2000): 80.

[16]Charlotte Herbert, "Political Action Committees and Campaign Involvement," *Creating and Managing an Association Government Relations Program* (Washington, DC: American Society of Association Executives, 1998), 115–22.

[17]Business-Industry Political Action Committee, 12.

[18]Susan B. Glasser, "Consultants Pursue Promising Web of New Business," *Washington Post* 3 May 2000, A1.

[19]Glasser, A14.

[20]Peter H. Stone, "Lobbying: Business Confronts Labor's Clout," *National Journal* (8 January 2000): 104–105.

[21]Neil Munro, "The Electronic Lobbyist," *National Journal* (22 April 2000): 1264.

[22]American Society of Association Executives, Videotape, 1999.

[23]Michael Dunn, "Developing an Effective Grassroots Program: Templates for Success," The Public Affairs Council, October 1999.

[24]Burt Solomon, "Campaign Finance: Forever Unclean," *National Journal* (18 March 2000): 858.

[25]Solomon, 858.

[26]Solomon, 860.

[27]Solomon, 862.

Adding Light to the Heat: Using the Mass Media to Support Your Issues

RICK STORY

Introduction

Will Rogers said, "All I know is what I read in the papers." For Americans living in a media age, these words are more true today than when they were spoken during the 1920's.

Because of the ever increasing influence of the media on our culture over the past 50 years, one rule reigns supreme in affecting public sentiment: perception *is* truth. And the media *force* perceptions. As a campaigner venturing into a public policy labyrinth, you cannot assume that people will automatically see and understand the worth of your proposal or the evil of a proposal you combat but will take their opinion-forming cues from the news and entertainment media's reporting of your issue.

As a result, your mission as a campaigner is very clear when dealing with the media: your job is to be aggressive when trying to negate bad press and, wherever possible, generate positive press for your issues. There are several reasons:

1. Public policy debates do not exist in a vacuum. Legislators, administration officials, and others who hold in their hands the fate of your issues are deeply affected by what they see and hear on television and radio and in newspapers and magazines.

2. The public, which will ultimately decide an issue's passage or failure, is also affected by media coverage of the issues. Whether people will generate calls or letters to policymakers to oppose or support an issue is highly affected by what they see and hear in the mass media.

3. Your own association's members and constituents are vastly more apt to be responsive to your calls to arms if they understand the importance of the issue at hand. Media coverage proves to them that the important issue you have asked them to support with their calls and letters is, in fact, important. Coverage legitimizes your issue and tells them that it merits their concern and action.

However, keep one thing in mind when attempting to reach these audiences. After weeks or months of wrangling, the opponent becomes, literally, the enemy. Reporters, producers, and editors love to report on the fight and infighting inherent in a public policy campaign, and too many combatants give them plenty to report on. In the passion of battle, it is easy to forget that the campaign is being played out on a public stage on which what you say and how your campaign conducts itself will reflect well or poorly on your association and on your chances of winning.

Therefore, one of the key goals of the public relations element of your issue campaign is to frame your messages in reasonable terms and to make certain that you adhere to the high principles for which you and your measure stand. Your job, as a public relations-minded manager is to keep your campaign on the moral high road, outwardly and inwardly. If the media, the public, and public officials see your role as "adding light to the heat" of the battle, you are on the road to winning.

A Good Foundation: The Keys to Communication

Successful communication through the mass media has two components: *impact* and *frequency*.

Impact of Your Message

Impact means the strength of your message. No matter how complex the issue, your message should be boiled down into three to five key, easily understood points. These become your campaign's mantra; your spokespeople will become dreadfully tired of repeating them long before the public becomes fully aware of your message. The *power* with which these points are presented represents the impact of your message.

There are several rules for communicating powerfully and effectively:

- *Tell them "What's in it for You."* "Senate Bill 123 will save thousands of lives by giving doctors the resources necessary to treat heart disease" is more compelling than "Senate Bill 123 allocates $2.3 million a year to compensate physicians for services rendered to public health agencies' heart disease awareness programs."
- *Make your point immediately and clearly.* "House Bill 421 is bad for children because it robs education funds" gets people's attention faster than "A measure to reallocate $50 million in federal dollars intended to be used in programs to acquire textbooks by rural school districts will result in a loss of educational tools necessary for students in low-income areas of the state."
- *Use powerful words and phrasing.* "The scientific community agrees that Assembly Bill 456 *is the single most important* environmental

protection measure *of the century"* grabs attention more effectively than "Some ecologists believe that Assembly Bill 456 can be helpful toward protecting critical habitat for endangered species."

Back up your contention with details, but always lead in to your powerful, impact-filled message with strong, declarative statements.

Frequency of Your Message

The frequency with which your powerful message is delivered is even more important in making people believe what you say and in affecting their view of your position. Political strategists have learned that most people are not even aware of, let alone feel compelled to act on, most media-borne messages until they have heard and seen them at least four times. This is why marketers of products and services use saturation advertising to *drive* their messages into the public consciousness.

Advertising is terribly expensive, however. A single 30-second television spot in a major metropolitan area at prime time can cost upwards of $30,000. If you can afford advertising to support your legislative issue, use it. If not, redouble your efforts with local news media to package and repackage your news to get the most frequent coverage possible. Develop a strategy at the start of your campaign. How many different angles can the media cover relative to your issue? Create newsworthy events and release information at intervals to enable the media to offer the most comprehensive coverage possible.

Inside the Media

Working the media is a game; it is important to know the playing field.

The Media as Adversaries and Allies

A 1990 survey of American business leaders by the Roper organization, a major polling firm, revealed that over three-fourths of top corporate executives hated the news media. Survey results showed that the business leaders believed the media to be shallow and unfair. These results are troubling because such executives, by and large, are dependent on the mass communication to tell their story about their products and services.

However, down the corporate ladder a rung or two are personnel who do not see the media and media people in this light. Public relations people, marketing staff, and others have long learned that, despite the news media's problems, they still have strengths, and the company must learn to get along if the corporate story is going to be told.

Working the media is a game, and it is one media people know how to play. After all, it's their game, their field, and their rules. To play the game well, the issues management professional must learn how to play the game by the media's rules and learn to play it well enough to win.

Media people tend to have relatively few biases. That may sound strange to those who believe that reporters and editors enter every story with a pre-conceived notion of how it will be reported. The fact is, media people are not well enough informed on most issues to have hard and fast opinions about very many of them. Consider that, in one month, the typical reporter will cover police news, local education, transportation, environmental topics, and more. Mix in feature stories on topics ranging from personality profiles of interesting local characters to community events and you can see how difficult it is for a media person to be expert on any one topic—other than reporting the news.

However, media people are no different from other members of society. Many form snap judgments based on relatively little information, but like most Americans, their depth of conviction about any one issue tends to be shallow. When confronted with facts presented in a clear, logical way, they can easily see your point and can be swayed to report fairly and accurately.

The more compelling your case and the more clearly you present it, the better is your chance of fighting through any media bias. Don't be intimidated by the idea that you won't be able to get a fair shake by a reporter, an editor, or a producer. Tell your story as convincingly as you can and you will be delighted with the results.

What the Media Want from You

The job of newsmen and newswomen, particularly for those who are news managers, is very simple. Every day, their job is to fill the *news hole*, media jargon for the amount of time or space that is left over after the advertising has been sold.

It is true that the newspaper or news segments of the daily programming of a TV or radio station survive only if advertising is sold and the outlets make money. However, in the mindset of the news staff, that is someone else's problem. Reporters and news managers I have known see their jobs as much loftier than the money-oriented activities of the paper's or station's sales personnel. This is a key fact of life when dealing with news personnel; in many ways, it should guide how you approach and work with these people.

In the course of filling the news hole, editors, reporters, and producers are looking for trouble, or controversy. News people have learned that more people are interested in an airplane that crashes than an airplane that flies. However, audiences can be just as interested in an airplane that flies—if it is a brand new space shuttle rather than a production model Boeing 727. Packaging your news so that it is fresh and exciting is a big part of the media coordinator's job. You must be continually looking for ways to make your news as useful as possible to the news people with whom you will be working.

What Is News?

News is not complicated; it is *interesting information,* nothing more. If you expect news of your issue to be covered in print and on the air, you must always remember that your interesting information is in competition with every other scrap of information the news outlets receive each day. If your news is more interesting than that of someone else trying to get his or her story placed, your story will be told.

You have to *make* news, to create it. Do not merely respond to what your campaign's opponent is doing; make your opponent respond to what your campaign is doing. Experienced campaigners know that, if they get to the media first with an interesting story, they stand an excellent chance of not only being covered but also of receiving major treatment. If the other side gets there first, you will get 1 or 2 inches of a 10-inch newspaper story merely so that the reporter can give the story balance.

There are four kinds of news. Every newspaper, radio, and television news program identifies news in the same four ways:

- *Hard news: front page material, the meat of the newspaper or broadcast news report.* It is often something negative; something bad has happened. It is more difficult to control this kind of news; you have to *deal* with it.
- *Feature news: good news—entertainment, fashion, food, personality profiles, community events.* More editors and reporters are working in this area of the news than in any other.
- *Sports news: coverage of professional and amateur sports, including auto and horse racing, outdoor reports.*
- *Business news: news of companies and the financial world.* This includes banking and investment stories, personnel news, and the like.

Concentrate on placing your story via hard news formats. Even if your news has appeal to business, sports, or feature editors, you will reach more of the readers if your story appears in the hard news sections of the newspaper or broadcast report. Sports fans and business leaders pay attention to hard news, too. Also, policymakers and opinion leaders will assign your news additional weight if it appears in the forums in which they are accustomed to seeing important issues covered.

How the Media Work: Television

TV is the major source of news for over 50 percent of Americans. Many public relations professionals consider, however, that there are problems with television news. The typical network television news report is under four minutes long. In that four minutes, the viewer is supposed to know everything worth knowing about the latest turn in an event that has shaped the world. Perhaps the most frightening aspect of the fast-food information age in which we live is that most Americans believe they are well informed on the strength of watching these brief reports.

Television is much more interested in rhythm and flow than in information. This fact guides every aspect of TV news production. Television decision makers have learned that people are relaxed and receptive when watching TV, and they do not want to *work* at gleaning information. TV reports must be punchy and move quickly to keep viewers' attention. Two phenomena have accelerated this: the remote control and cable TV. The news is in competition with all that cable has to offer, and it is only a finger touch away—sports, music videos, and first-run movies.

If the news is not exciting, the ratings go down. When the ratings fall, the price of advertising plummets, as does the station's income. The net result is unemployment in the news operation. Thus, reporters, anchors, and producers have learned that, to keep their jobs, they are better off to be shallow, incomplete, and maybe inaccurate, as long as they are punchy and lively.

Who's Who in TV

Go inside any TV newsroom. The newsroom at KMOV in St. Louis is similar to any TV station in Indianapolis, Los Angeles, or Albuquerque. Some staffs may be more highly paid and slightly more numerous, but the jobs are the same and the way those jobs are done is virtually identical. The following are the major players at a network affiliate news operation:

- *General manager* (GM). He or she runs the show. Sometimes the GM is the owner or has past ownership of the channel. This is becoming more rare as chains gobble up television stations around the world. The GM is not involved in news gathering but has management jurisdiction over all operations—programming, sales, personnel, and the rest of the operation, in addition to news. A relationship with the owner or general manager of a television station can go a long way toward securing favorable or neutral coverage of your issue. Never be afraid to try this route if you can establish contact directly or through an intermediary.

- *News director.* The news director runs the newsroom and the entire news operation. In large markets, such as Dallas, San Francisco, or Detroit, he or she is an administrator, with hiring, firing, and bottom line responsibility. In smaller markets, such as Wheeling, San Antonio, or Buffalo, the news director may be deeply involved in the news-gathering and production processes and probably serves as executive producer of the news program. He or she takes an active hand in gate keeping, or the selection of news stories, and is involved in editing the various news spots for airing.

- *Assignment editor (AE).* The AE keeps the calendar and assigns the stories to the reporters for the day. He or she maintains a large calendar on a board in the newsroom called the Futures File. It has 31 slots—one for each day of the month. The slots contain notes on the news that is likely to happen each day. The AE knows about these events because people like you have provided prior notice. A lot of the news you will see on television this evening was alerted 10 or more days ago. The AE is a critical contact at television news operations. Get to know this person. He or she is one of the principal vehicles by which your story gets, or does not get, on the air. The better your working relationship with the AE, the better your chances of good treatment.

- *Producers.* These are the people who put the news show together. The reporter brings in the tape, and the producer and editing technician piece it together to make a cogent story. This work begins about two hours prior to airing. There is always a mad scramble each day to finalize the broadcast. Make it a point to avoid calling for any of the news staff within two hours of the noon, evening, or late news programs unless your story is nothing short of earth-shattering.

- *Anchors.* Anchors are the on-air personalities of the news program. People watch a specific news program because they like the anchor; the anchor's popularity is the most important factor in the ratings game. Know which news programs consistently grab the highest ratings in your campaign's area and direct your attention to these programs. Over the long term and well before you venture forth with a campaign, try to develop a relationship with the anchors. People trust and believe the news anchor of their favorite television stations and will look more kindly on your campaign if it has received passing or even tacit approval from this person.

- *Reporters and camera operators.* Reporters take direction from the news director, assignments editor, and executive producer. They bring in the tape to be transformed into a news report. The camera operator is every bit as important to you as the reporter. He or she can make you look either bad or good, and looking good on camera is often more important toward making the public respond positively to your message as anything you will say. Take a moment and speak with the camera operator. Offer a cup of coffee or a soft drink. Most people ignore the cameraperson, and he or she will appreciate your recognition of the importance of his or her work.

Television News Deadlines

Never call in a news story at deadline. Find out the deadlines for your local television stations and live by this rule. If you do call, chances are good that no one will speak with you. If someone does take your call and you do not have a story like "It's the End of the World and I Can Prove It," you can forget doing business with that station in the future. If you call with a mediocre story at deadline, you are guaranteed to receive little or no response.

To avoid conflicts with deadlines do not schedule a news conference or any campaign event within two hours of broadcast. The best times for events are 9:00 A.M. to 11:00 A.M. and 2:00 P.M. to 4:00 P.M. (EST).

Weeknights are prime news nights. The ratings are up, and the staffs are at full strength. Your chance of attracting coverage is best during the week. Weekend news shows have poor ratings, and the news operations are not staffed at full capacity then. For example, one network affiliate in Columbus, Ohio, reaches an average of 230,000 homes on its 6:00 P.M. Wednesday news show, but, on Saturday at 6:00 P.M., it reaches 75,000 homes.

How the Media Work: Radio

Two-thirds of Americans get their morning news from radio. Twice as many people listen to the radio between 7:30 A.M. and 9:00 A.M. as at any other time.

Radio has been changing over the past 30 years. Among the reasons for the change is the rise of FM and fragmentation. Fragmentation means that radio stations have targeted specific audiences. Today there are African American, Spanish, religious, all sports, all talk, and many other types of stations. Each is designed to reach a distinct segment of the public.

In the average city, one or two radio stations are serious about covering the news. Most are AM stations. Radio stations on the AM dial concentrate on information—news and talk formats. Stations on the FM dial focus mainly on music. The AM stations that feature locally based talk shows may offer opportunities for publicizing your issue and are usually easy to access. Become familiar with local radio talk show hosts and their styles.

However, you may wish to reconsider whether to appear on a radio talk show that plans to feature your issue in an on-air debate format, particularly if you represent a status quo position. If you represent the status quo— that is, if you are seeking the no vote before the government body that will decide your issue—you may automatically find yourself in a defensive posture. No matter how well you explain your side of the issue, the audience is likely to see you as the debate's loser because you are the defender. This is the reason that we rarely see incumbent candidates for office clamoring to debate their opponents; it always happens the other way around.

Radio station news staffs are comprised of even fewer personnel than those at TV stations. Typically, if the station is serious about the news, a news director is on the staff, along with two or three reporters. Most radio stations don't have news-gathering operations. They rely on wire services and newspapers for the vast majority of news they report. A copywriter will boil down a 10-inch newspaper story into a 10-second broadcast report, and an on-air personality will read it.

Radio station deadlines are less stringent, but do not call a station with a story 10 minutes before the hour or half-hour.

Many radio stations advertise news hot lines. Research the hot line numbers for all of the stations in your area.

Concentrate your radio campaign efforts on the two or three stations that are serious about news coverage. Do not be surprised if the news story you placed with station WXYZ turns up on another station 30 minutes later. Radio people also monitor each other for story ideas.

How the Media Work: Newspapers

The newspaper industry is changing dramatically. In 1967, 73 percent of Americans read a newspaper each day. By 1990, that number had shrunk to 51 percent. The numbers for 2000 are even slimmer. Nonetheless, newspapers are an important news source and remarkably important to issue campaigners.

The importance of newspaper coverage to campaign public relations people is that the printed word is powerful, credible, and insightful. It has a life of days, weeks, months, or years. Newspaper coverage gives your story authority. If you can get your story placed in the newspaper, there is an excellent chance that TV and radio will pick it up. Public relations professionals maintain that you stand a much better chance of receiving fair and complete coverage from newspaper than from television or radio, if you do a good job of packaging and selling your news. The reason for this is that newspapers are in the news business, as opposed to the entertainment industry. They deal in facts and much less in glamour and flash than their broadcast news counterparts.

Who's Who at Newspapers

The following are the key news management personnel at most newspapers:

- *Editor.* This job varies, depending on the size of the paper. He or she is ultimately responsible for all editorial content—everything except the advertising. At big papers, the editor may be only an administrator and a public figure.
- *Managing editor.* The managing editor is in charge of what gets covered and who covers it. He or she decides on the "angle," the general editorial direction stories will take. The editor provides guidance on how much space each story is assigned.
- *City editor.* The city editor is responsible for local, city, and county news. At some papers, this editor has input on what state and national issues receive coverage.
- *State editor.* Many papers have editors on staff who manage the news-gathering operations for state news. The state house correspondent or correspondents typically report to the state editor.

- *Editorial page editor.* This person coordinates the paper's positions on the issues. The editorial page editor selects and edits opinion columns and typically chairs the editorial board, a committee that decides what positions the newspaper takes on various issues.

These people are the key news executives. Above them are the management staff, and most important among management are the owner and the publisher. They set the basic editorial policy. These people can greatly influence editorial positions and the coverage of issue-related topics. When attempting to affect a newspaper's position on an issue, there is usually no substitute for going to the top. Make contact with people who have influence with the newspaper's management to arrange an introduction and to help you to influence the paper's editorial slant. A major advertiser or a personal friend of the owner or publisher can work wonders.

Editorial Page

While the editorial page is one of the least read segments of most newspapers, as many as 60 percent of the readers will often glance at the editorial page. Fully 98 percent of community leaders—particularly elected and other public officials—carefully read the editorial page. They believe that what they see on the editorial page reflects the voters' sentiments. In reality, the editorial page usually reflects little more than the views of the owner, publisher, or editorial page staff.

The importance of receiving editorial page support for your issue is to make photocopies of editorials to circulate to offices of the public officials whom you are attempting to influence. *Always* ask permission to reprint anything that appears in a newspaper. Reprinting editorials can also be useful in motivating your own public to generate constituent contacts to officials. Finally, editorial endorsement of your position permits you to cite the supporting newspapers among your list of supporters in campaign literature.

You can often receive editorial support for your issue if you simply ask for it. As a general rule, set up meetings with editorial boards as early as possible. Take in a delegation of knowledgeable spokespeople and ask for support—you will be surprised at how many times you will get a favorable editorial if you have done a good job of laying out your position and have remembered to close the sale by asking for support.

The real beauty of these editorial board meetings is that you will likely have the entire complement of news executives in the same room. You may be able to find out which reporter or reporters will be covering your story as your campaign unfolds. You will have an opportunity to get your message before all the managers who can have impact on your story.

Bad Press

The goal of the typical media campaign is not to generate positive press: With all the potentially bad things that can happen as a result of newspaper, TV, and radio reporting on your issue, wouldn't you be better off if the media were to simply let you take your story to public officials with no interference?

The goal of most media campaigns is to neutralize the other side's opportunity for favorable coverage. If you get favorable coverage, consider it icing on the cake; you've won if you can keep the media from plugging your opponent's position.

Avoid negative campaigning, though. If you have to rely on knocking your opponent's position, you may leave media people with bad opinions about you. Concentrate on the positive aspects of your issue. If you do a better job of promoting your side of the argument than your opponent does, you will win every time.

Developing Materials to Tell Your Story

If you want your story told correctly, provide extensive support materials to the media; do not rely on a reporter's note taking or memory. Offer news releases, sample editorials, art, fact sheets, and other materials throughout the campaign. By helping the reporter do his or her job, you will develop a sound working relationship. Reporters will come to trust your word on matters relating to your issue.

News Releases

News releases should be developed and issued at intervals during your campaign. A schedule of releases should be created early in the campaign; events, press conferences, and other newsworthy events should be planned weeks or months ahead of time to highlight the three to five themes on which your campaign is based. Think of the various angles that help to support your campaign themes and issue releases accordingly. You should strive to issue at least one release each week. See Exhibit 4.1 for a sample release that incorporates the major points of release writing and layout.

A news release is a prime tool of the media campaign. It tells the most important part of the story. Never try to cram too much information into a news release. If your story is newsworthy, you will be able to tell the story in 2 double-spaced pages, about 500 words. Never go beyond 3 pages. If you are unable to pique the interest of the editor or reporter in that space, your story probably is not being well told. If your story is told in 500 to 750 words, do not be surprised that subsequent interviews will result in a printed or aired story of much more substantial duration.

EXHIBIT 4.1   Sample News Release

For Immediate Release
  Contact: Sue Sharp
(419) 555-5555
E-mail—ssharp@wxyz.org

Conservationists Seek
Funding for Wildlife

Sacramento—California wildlife and generations of citizens to come will be the big winners if the California legislature enacts AB 123, which will funnel over a half billion dollars of state oil tax dollars into acquiring and maintaining habitat. The measure was introduced today by Assemblywoman Charlotte Web (D-San Jose).

The bill, which has been referred to the Assembly Committee on Natural Resources, earmarks some $600 million for the Department of Game and Fish's programs to ensure wildlife abundance in the state. The money will be generated by increasing the state tax on crude oil producers from 25 cents per barrel to 75 cents per barrel.

The measure is being backed by the California Natural Resources Coalition, a group of conservation organizations that represents over 500,000 individual conservationists. Members of the coalition include the California Conservation Federation, The League of Anglers and Hunters and the Golden State Outdoor Recreation League.

Wildlife Funding 2-2-2

"Wildlife is too important to Californians to allow shrinking habitat to endanger the future of wild animal populations," said Joe Bleuw, chairman of the Coalition and a Redding timber company executive.

"AB 123 will ensure that wildlife in our state continues to flourish."

Bleuw said that suitable tule elk habitat has diminished from millions of acres at the turn of the century to less than a half million acres today. The state's wetlands, prime wintering grounds for a host of migratory waterfowl, is less than half of its original acreage.

The oil tax was conceived to maximize the amount of available revenue, while minimizing economic hardship to local communities and corporations.

For more information about AB 123 and its benefits to California, contact The California Conservation Coalition, 4567 Buzzard Drive, Sacramento, CA, 99921. Phone (419) 555-5555.

The most important element of the release is the lead. It is the first sentence or two sentences, which tell the who, what, when, where, and why of your story. The lead must grab the attention of the editor and the public. Try to answer the age-old public relations question "What's in it for me?" in the lead.

The other key to writing a news release to be used by media outlets is to prepare the release in inverted pyramid style. That means that you should prioritize all of the information in the release and prepare it so that the most important information appears near the top. Expose all subsequent information in descending order of importance. The greatest enemies of editors and producers are time and space. Because of the intense deadlines of the news business, it is much simpler and quicker for them to trim for time and space from the bottom of the release. By writing your release in inverted pyramid style, you will stand the greatest chance of having the most important information covered—if something gets cut, it will be of lesser importance.

The release should receive wide circulation. Send it to news directors, assignment editors, and reporters who have been identified as interested in your story at TV stations. Get your release in the hands of news directors at radio stations. Send your release to at least three people at newspapers. Exhibit 4.2 is a chart with suggestions for which personnel might receive your release at newspapers.

Follow up on your release with key media. Telephone or drop in on the reporters, editors, and producers you have identified as important to your effort. Explain the issue and ask them to do a story based on your release. More times than not, this personal attention makes the difference in getting your release used. (See Exhibit 4.3 for a complete list of tips on writing a news release.)

Media Kits

At the outset of the campaign, prepare and distribute a comprehensive media kit to all the media serving the constituents of public policy officials

EXHIBIT 4.2 News Release Distribution, Newspapers

	Kind of news				
Send release to:	National	Local	State	Local Rallies	Events
Editor		X	X	X	X
Managing editor		X	X	X	X
Editorial page	X	X	X	X	
City editor		X		X	
State editor				X	
National editor (Editor of Washington Bureau)		X			
Community calendar					X
Specialty writer (e.g., environmental reporter)	X	X	X		

EXHIBIT 4.3   Tips for Writing a News Release

- For best results, hand-deliver as many releases as practical.
- Copy releases on clean, white 8 1/2-inch by 11-inch paper.
- When mailing, send releases by first-class postage. When publicizing an upcoming event, mail the release at least 10 days before.
- Identification: Print the name, address, and phone number of the media relations coordinator at the upper left of the release.
- Type releases on campaign letterhead.
- Release date: most releases should be "For Immediate Release." This means that the news is timely if printed or aired the day it is received.
- Margins and spacing: use wide margins and double-spacing, so that editors can edit.
- Headline: make it short and simple. Tell the story in five or six words.
- Style: use short, punchy sentences, with active verbs. Check and double-check grammar and spelling.
- End: at the end of the release, type "End" or "-30-."

---

whom your campaign is working to influence. The kit should be bound in a pocket folder, the cover of which should identify your campaign. All materials should be double-spaced and typed in an easy-to-read type font. The kit should include a number of items, including the following:

- A news release summarizing your issue.
- Two or three sample editorials. These are editorial-style essays, 750 to 1,000 words in length, that focus on the top messages of your campaign.
- A copy of the fact book prepared as the guidepost for your media relations staff.
- Any photographs, charts, or graphs that might visually illustrate your case to the public. Use color slides, or use videotape for television outlets.

You might also prepare a 2,000- to 3,000-word feature article that goes into more detail than your news release or editorial.

Include in the media kit a listing of the officers of your campaign, as well as media contact information. These data could be included in a cover letter that asks the media to contact you directly for further information and that offers to extend any help necessary to the media outlet in covering your campaign.

The kit should be mailed to three people at newspapers (editor, managing editor, editorial page editor). It should be mailed to news directors at television and radio stations.

Starting Your Campaign's Public Relations Effort

The time to start your public relations program is long before you go before the legislature or other governmental body. Media relations, when done to the optimum, is little more than parlaying contacts you've already made with reporters and media decision makers into favorable coverage for your issue.

Personnel

The nation's major media centers—Hollywood; Washington, DC; New York; and others—all feature a host of firms that offer media relations services. These PR firms are in place 365 days a year for the simple purpose of enabling clients to have immediate, good working relationships with players in the media. The firms' staffs spend their time cultivating these relationships and pitch their clients' stories on a fee basis. Of course, you can spend tens of thousands or millions of dollars for this kind of access. Doesn't it make more sense, especially when operating in your own backyard, to take time to develop these relationships yourself?

Someone on your campaign should be assigned the role of media relations coordinator. This should be a member of your staff or perhaps a local consultant who has a background or flair for public relations (there are many one and two-person shops in state capitols across the nation who will represent you on specific issues much less expensively than the major media firms). An exceptionally well-versed volunteer might be considered, but the role should be treated as a full-time position for the duration of the campaign. The media coordinator should be an excellent writer with a talent for boiling down complicated concepts into easy-to-understand, compelling terms.

Information and Lists

The media relations coordinator should make an audit of your issue, identifying the three to five points that are most compelling. Then, extensive background information should be researched and compiled to enable your spokesperson to provide detailed answers to the most complex questions on your issue. This information should be compiled in a well-catalogued fact book, your campaign's primary information reference. All data should be catalogued, by source, in sections corresponding to your main campaign messages.

Your staff should develop lists of media people—editors, reporters, producers, and management personnel—with whom you will work to develop coverage. A number of resources are available to help you to initially identify the media sources serving constituents in the area in which your campaign will operate. These resources include *Editors and Publishers Yearbook* for newspaper, wire service, and certain other periodicals and *Broadcaster and Cable Guide* for radio and television sources. These publications list media by state and feature listings of news managers and other leadership. The directories are likely to be available through local public libraries.

The public relations campaign's first job is to make initial contact, either through a media tour, during which you meet media contacts at their offices, via news conferences, or through a series of phone calls. Then, you must mail comprehensive media kits to ensure that all the background information on your issue is available to the press and broadcast media. The rest of the job, throughout the duration of the campaign, is to continue to feed information to the media on specific elements of your message and to answer questions, do interviews, and always put your best foot forward.

Anatomy of a Media Campaign

A public relations campaign has a beginning, a middle, and an end. The media campaign's anatomy is very similar to that of your direct lobbying or grassroots campaign.

Campaign's Kick-Off

Step 1 is the announcement of your campaign. This is done by mailing your media kit and conducting the series of editorial board and other decision-maker visits. At television and radio stations, meet with management, news directors, and reporters covering your issue. At newspapers, meet editorial boards. Meet with the news directors of the radio stations that are serious about news coverage.

Many campaigns kick off with a news conference for the reporters who will be covering the issue in the coming weeks or months. For statewide policy issues, news conferences are usually conducted for state capitol press corps and for local newspaper and broadcast outlets.

Phase 2: Maintaining the Message

The next phase of the campaign entails carrying out your campaign goal of feeding a series of news items to the media at regular intervals. The goal is to keep your story before the public on a weekly basis. During the campaign, various media people are likely to have their own ideas as to how to cover your issue. They may have story ideas that actually interfere with your message or communications goals. Your media relations coordinator must be sufficiently nimble to keep reporters from straying from the three to five main campaign themes.

This is an extremely important point and one with which most novice media relations personnel lay media have extreme difficulty. *Never* feel compelled to say anything to a reporter that does not fulfill your campaign objectives. A print or broadcast reporter may ask a question or series of questions intending to elicit from your spokesperson an intended response. If you are led into such a line of questioning, you must be quick on your feet to steer your answer back to your campaign theme.

If put on the spot, think of a way to redirect, or "bump and run" with your answer to the place you want to go. Hang tough. The reporter can print or air only what comes out of your mouth. Sticking to your campaign themes, even with a response that does not directly address the reporter's question, is vastly preferable to saying something that could damage your campaign and its members' interests.

Campaign's End

Win or lose, *you* should be in charge of how your story is told by the media in the aftermath of your campaign. As soon as possible, distribute to the press corps and other media a news release that tells the victory or loss story from your perspective. Be a gracious winner and, if you lose, be very careful about how you characterize your defeat. It is usually inadvisable to declare a moral victory in the face of defeat. By the same token, it is not a good idea to state that your campaign is giving up on your proposal, either. You and your people might change your minds in subsequent weeks.

Many losing campaigns characterize their effort as "the first step in what we knew would be a long, hard road when we began." Leave your options open. Do not proffer excuses or blame government officials for the loss. A statement such as "The Speaker of the House sold us out!" will markedly impede your chances for success the next time you decide to take your issue to the legislature.

Credit all the major players who helped in the effort, win or lose. Thank helpful legislative or administrative officials for their leadership. Report on the vote count and include a listing of the vote roll call as an addendum to your release.

Conclusion

In sum, the keys to mounting a winning media campaign are to identify your audience, frame your message in compelling terms and deliver the messages in a well-regulated manner.

Media relations alone will not win a legislative campaign, but can provide a deciding leg-up in a public policy debate. When coordinated with direct lobbying and grassroots lobbying campaigns, a sound media effort can make the difference between victory and defeat.

Developing Partnerships for Greater Success

ROBERT K. GOODWIN

Introduction

The intangible assets possessed by many, if not most, nonprofit organizations can be harnessed and managed in ways that lead to the accumulation or protection of real assets. This is particularly true when seeking to influence legislators. There is an old adage often used by fund-raisers that "three make a row," meaning that lining up more than two patrons in support of a program or goal demonstrates enough support to shape a compelling reason for others to join in. Likewise, two or more nonprofit organizations can represent a significant force, or "make a row." By blending their assets and the power of their constituencies, they can more effectively accomplish their respective goals.

Organizational alliances take many forms and are increasingly popular in both the for-profit and not-for-profit world. In the commercial space, two or more companies can coalesce their resources and, in so doing, fill gaps in capacities, create efficiencies, and deepen expertise in ways that create more competitive advantage in the marketplace. Gaining more results while expending less of the invested commodity than would otherwise be required is always the most efficient way to spend currency, whether that currency is measured in terms of capital, influence, or energy.

Increased Recognition and Power That Partnering Produces

Two words most frequently used in the world of commerce and industry describe the benefits of partnering to influence elected officials to support a goal of a not-for-profit or a coalition of not-for-profits, *leverage* and *synergy*. Leverage suggests the ability to magnify the effort expended and the impact made by one group by enlisting effort and drawing on the resources from other sources. Synergy results in a new resource being created or unleashed when two or more assets are combined. Not-for-profits are learning from this experience and finding new ways to reach their own goals by magnifying the impact of their own vital resources.

One frequently undervalued asset of many not-for-profits is the ability to mobilize their constituents by stirring their passions when the organization's interests seem to be threatened or when its goals can be advanced by broad endorsement or additional support. In that respect, not-for-profits have an advantage equal to or greater than most corporations or political actions committees (PACs) because they have the power to reach people where they live and work with messages that inspire action.

This chapter is designed to help not-for-profit leaders understand how to make "two plus two equal six." We will look at some basic rules that govern the creation and effective use of partnerships to accomplish mutual legislative goals by influencing members of Congress and other legislative representatives. Whether working at the federal level or with a local jurisdiction (we will be focusing on how to deal with Congress, although the rules generally apply to any legislative body), there are some fundamental questions that must be answered before your partnership objectives can be implemented successfully:

- How do you balance the desired goal(s) of the partnership with the mission and integrity of the individual organizations?
- What makes organizations compatible?
- How important are personal relationships between the individual organizations' leaders in developing effective partnerships?
- How do you keep partners focused on their primary objective if the respective organizations have competing interests?
- What's the best way to build effective partnerships when neither organization has had any experience partnering with each other or at all?
- Once the partnerships are formed, how do you best communicate the power of the network with legislators?
- What are some of the critical messages you must deliver to legislators?
- Which legislators do you target to deliver those messages?

We'll try to answer these questions and others like them to help you leverage the greatest legislative results and find true synergy through collaboration.

Legislators' Views of Various Forms of Coalitions

Inherent in the legislators' role is their ability to create new regulations, authorities, funding capacities, and laws that, in their view, are consistent with the interpretation of the Constitution and will advance the welfare of the citizenry. But lawmakers depend on the input of those they represent to aid in their own interpretation of what constitutes or serves the common good. At minimum, they will support something if they know that's what their constituents want. Thus, constituents have tremendous power to affect the position of their elected representatives on issues of great importance to them.

When an official knows that many people are speaking with a single voice regarding a particular issue, they certainly listen and most often respond.

In simplest terms, the more people who express support for or opposition to a specific legislative initiative, the more interested elected officials will likely be in that position. This is true because elected officials typically follow their own simple axiom—seek to satisfy the interests of the greatest number of and/or the most influential constituents. These constituents are the same people who can extend, perpetuate, or end a political career.

However, if legislators are moved by the pragmatic reasons for responding to their constituents, they are equally influenced by the philosophical relationship between citizen voice and legislative action. Understanding these philosophical underpinnings is as important as understanding how to organize your constituents effectively. Most legislators know that nonprofit coalitions merit their attention and responsiveness when their members organize around any particular issue because of at least three realities:

1. Rights granted under the Constitution
2. Expectations flowing from the civil society
3. Symbiotic relationship between government and not-for-profits

First, there is the fundamental right to petition their government for redress that all citizens enjoy and the freedom to state their views without governmental interference as provided by the Constitution. Every elected official knows that citizen voice is not to be merely tolerated but sought and affirmed. When citizens organize themselves around a legislative agenda, they provide a service to those elected to serve them because they signal priorities and direction that helps shape the officials' own agenda.

The term *special interest group,* like the word *lobbyist,* has in recent years attracted a kind of reprobation that is undeserved. Despite the rhetoric of individual activists or some media pundits who decry the legitimacy of special interest groups, most legislators recognize that there is not an American today who is not represented (whether he or she knows it or not) by at least a dozen special interest groups. Ethnic minorities, consumers, teachers, aliens, pro-choice advocates, gun control advocates, salespeople, people with disabilities, exporters—all have special interests whose views deserve to be recognized. It is these individuals and the natural groups they compose that are the grassroots of the American political process.

Many legislators will confirm that not-for-profits can help organize some response to their own legislative interests by their grassroots membership and, in so doing, are really helping to maintain the vibrancy of the democracy.[1] The late Senator John Heinz said, "For too long, active lobbying has been confined to highly paid professionals. These employees of big business have dominated the Washington lobbying scene. The growth of the citizen lobby, however, has been a useful, even essential, counterbalance to narrow-interest influence peddlers. Without citizen lobbies I doubt we would have been able to pass many of the civil rights, environmental, and even foreign policy measures that have established this country as the social conscience of the world. Certainly, the heavily financed professional lobbies are still powerful in Washington, but to the extent citizens groups wish to participate in the legislative process, it builds the kind of representative democracy intended by the framers of the Constitution."

Second, there is a growing appreciation for the efficacy of the civil society or the[2] "ideas, ideals, and social arrangements by which people find their voice and mobilize themselves for public good." Without respect to any particular legislative initiative, legislators tend to recognize and appreciate the fact that most not-for-profits exist in order to pursue some goal(s) intended to improve the quality of life for a subset of the population.

James Joseph, former CEO of the Council of Foundations, says he sees optimism[3] "in the emergence of a civic culture that seeks to preserve and promote the idea of an intermediate space between government and the individual, a space in which voluntary energy can be spontaneously generated and deployed." Related to this notion is what he calls the idea of a "good society [that] depends as much on the actions of committed individuals as it does on the soundness of government and the fairness of law. Nonprofit organizations all have their genesis in this intermediate civil space. They are reflections of positive social values and vehicles for affirming, supporting, and maintaining those values. On the one hand, they are valuable as vital instruments for civic participation, and for solving serious social problems. But they also support the affirmation and retention of the values of a civil society."

Third, nonprofit coalitions can have an elevated level of importance in the realm of the civil society because, increasingly, the relationship between government and nonprofit organizations can be described as symbiotic. Government fosters and promotes not-for-profits through a variety of devices. Not-for-profits are encouraged to grow and provide impact through mechanisms ranging from tax exemptions and deductions for donors to special mailing privileges. With the move toward privatization of government services, not-for-profits are true partners in government's goal of delivery of services to the citizenry through grants and contracts. And not-for-profits are often involved in public advocacy, trying to influence public policy and government programs in response to the needs of the members, clients, and constituents of societal groups and coalitions.

Never has the mutual dependence and the need for not-for-profits to balance government control of the relationship and the array of issues been greater. And never has the need for nonprofit managers to manage successfully this strategic dimension of their external environment from advocacy to contracted services been more important to the performance of their organizations.

Finally, lawmakers tend to have their own views about the effectiveness of the strategies of nonprofits that are most successful at affecting public

policy. A survey conducted in the summer of 1997 by the Aspen Institute resulted in a total of 98 nonprofits being named as highly effective advocates
in national public policy debates by members of Congress. While there
were many organizations among them that had large budgets, high public
visability, and large memberships, many were smaller, less well known organizations that, in addition to other methods, used strategies of collaboration and partnership to effectively pursue their legislative goals.

[4]The case studies discussed in the Aspen report illustrate it is important to:

1. Deliberately reach out to both Democrats and Republicans.
2. Maintain sub-national chapters or offices to impact state policy and
   facilitate member training and activity.
3. Work in coalitions, especially "strange bedfellow" alliances.
4. Focus resources on one or two top policy priorities.
5. Train members on everything from how a bill becomes a law to
   campaign management and coalition-building.
6. Publicize your issue and demand candidates' positions during
   election campaigns.
7. Convince high-profile organizations to take on your issue as a
   priority or special project.
8. Unify grassroots action around themes that send a national
   message.
9. Involve policy makers with others on study commissions that
   make policy recommendations.

While getting constituents to work to influence Congress takes coordinated and purposeful action (at times proactively and at times reactively),
organizational leaders can capitalize on the fact that most people, and thus
most constituents, want to be where the action is. They want to influence
and help to shape the forces of change. This means that paid staff and volunteers have important roles to play. Increasingly, volunteers are expressing the belief that nonprofit agencies not only have an obligation to give
service of the highest quality but also have a responsibility to witness, to be
advocates, and to speak out affirmatively, even militantly, on issues that affect their constituencies.

Clearly, not-for-profits face some restraints when operating in the political arena. The inability to make campaign contributions or spend too large
a percentage of their annual budget on lobbying are perhaps the most obvious. However, as Bob Smucker points out in[5] *The Nonprofit Lobbying Guide:
Advocating Your Cause and Getting Results,* power is linked to the strength
that a not-for-profit can gather behind a particular public policy proposal,
particularly if that strength is buoyed by a strong grassroots campaign.

Philosophically, legislators need to see themselves as accountable to the
people who put them in office. But going from the philosophy of citizen

voice to the effective practice of accomplishing some legislative goal means considering the most effective way(s) to translate the interest of a coalition in terms that are understood and respected by lawmakers.

This chapter is about developing and communicating that *unified* voice to the elected official(s) who are in the best position to exert their own influence in the legislative process so as to reach your desired goal. While you might assume, then, that the way to accomplish your legislative goals is simply to let the elected officials know that a lot of people favor them, there are some basic guidelines to follow to be most effective in reaching your ends. Targeted contacts are indispensable in interpreting the depth of interest by a mobilized constituency. We can assume that some form of personal contacts is essential in elevating an issue above the many others that compete for a legislator's attention and support. It is also a safe assumption that strong positive relationships developed with members of Congress will only aid in the ability to educate them regarding your issue. Thus, good interpersonal skills are a prerequisite for successful transmission of your message. However, beyond effective, targeted communication the following are some of the basic do's and don'ts when seeking to influence legislators to work for your goal(s):

Don't

- Be inconsistent with your message.
- Create coalitions simply for the sake of political leverage.
- Base your strategy on the strength of "headquarters" or the national office position.
- Threaten to withhold support.
- Provide biased data or information.
- Send high-priced counsel to deliver the position of your message.
- Promote at the expense of other initiatives.
- Politicize by making suggestions that the initiative is needlessly partisan.

Do

- Develop a rationale for why your goal is a reflection of your mission and will benefit the community, then articulate this position in the most passionate and effective manner possible.
- Seek to illustrate how your goal comports with the interest of the legislator.
- Form and work within coalitions which can continue to foster cooperation among their members once the legislative goal(s) are obtained.
- Secure support from someone who has the ear and trust of legislator(s).

- Suggest the ability to provide support for the cooperative legislator once the goal is reached.
- Do homework on the legislator's background.
- Present your message through the eyes and voice of the local constituent by using that local constituent.

Let's look at this list of don'ts and do's as a basis for understanding the best ways to construct and unleash the power of effective partnerships.

Be Sure Your Position Is Consistent with Your Mission

First, be sure the position you take is totally consistent with your mission and/or your strategic objectives. In order to be influential, you must be credible. In order to be credible, the position you seek to influence must not be seen as arbitrary or self-serving. It must be cast in the light of helping to fulfill, advance, or bolster your mission.

While there may be instances when groups with widely divergent interests come together around one particular issue, the legislator needs to be able to understand what the principle motivation or perspective is of each group. The more people from different viewpoints, communities, or demographics within a community who favor a particular end, the easier it is for the legislator to support the specific initiative. Even if different groups support (or oppose) the same initiative for different reasons, the legislator should be in the position of understanding the rationale for each interest group. He or she may then be able to build a case for the appropriateness of their position and that of those they can influence because of the many voices raised in support for or opposition to the legislative goal.

Therefore, don't seek to mobilize people without taking into consideration the need for consistency of the message, at least from the viewpoint of your constituency. To do so will ultimately weaken your overall position because the legislators may see that they cannot articulate a single position before their peers, thus weakening their ability to attract support for the overall legislative goal. Your position needs to be clear and consistent.

Present Your Message through the Eyes and Voice of Local Constituents

Don't build the case for your position on the basis of how it affects the "home office." Former Speaker of the House of Representatives Tip O'Neil was well known for his articulation of the most basic of axioms, that "all politics is local." The relevance of this idea to this discussion is that you must seek to get local voices to articulate positions of support for (or opposition to) a legislative goal. This must be at the heart of any effective strategy. While the aggregate result of many local voices may represent a resounding chorus (even national) singing a particular song, any elected official is going to be most interested in the voice of the tenors or sopranos from his or her town or district.

Try to Work with Others Once Your Legislative Goal Is Accomplished

Third, try to work with people and groups that can continue to work together once the legislative goal is achieved. History has provided ample examples of coalitions that span historical differences between their members in order to support or oppose an issue that links them for different economic or ideological reasons. But elected officials will be most attentive to those who they know will, in all likelihood, still have contact with each other and be working together at election time, not just when a particular issue is under legislative consideration. An elected official will be less likely influenced by a coalition if he or she feels that there will be so many other issues to preoccupy the individual members of the coalition by the time the official needs to raise support for reelection. In short, the power of the coalition is lost if it is dissipated or fractured. The official may feel that he or she will have other opportunities to satisfy the interests of individual coalition members, despite the intensity of interest around one issue. But a coalition remains powerful and a force to be reckoned with if the members continue to work together once the legislative issue is resolved.

Express Your Support for the Legislator

It is far more motivating to an elected official to know that by working in behalf of a particular coalition on an issue of importance to that coalition the official can expect support for when he or she needs it—at election time. Don't expect that you will influence the official to adopt your goal by making threats. Support is generally easier to quantify than opposition. People who are appreciative of the work of an elected official on a particular issue are often prepared to demonstrate that appreciation in concrete ways. Motivated voters can influence other voters in a myriad of ways; making donations to the representative, working at the precinct level to get out the vote, and seeking to influence friends and contacts on behalf of the official are the most obvious.

While people who threaten to work against an elected official because of his or her position on any issue can withhold support and influence others to do the same, such threats usually lose their intensity with time. Elected officials will always try to effect a balance, such that they can be supported by more people who think they are doing the right thing overall than opponents who feel they are taking positions that run counter to the will of the people. Often, the elected official will work to gain the support loss because of a stand taken on one issue by their stand on other issues of importance to the same constituents.

Understand How Your Goal Corresponds with the Legislator's Interest

If Congress is your target, members of Congress themselves can be your greatest source of support. Besides their ability to vote on your side of the issue, members of Congress have an inherent potential influence with their peers, which, if understood and used properly, can be among your most important assets. Congressmen can be extremely effective in reaching other members through a variety of techniques available only to them. Thus, as you target key members, you are not only trying to influence their position but that of other key members through them.

Some issues are more rooted in partisan philosophy and strategy than others. In those instances, members of Congress are less susceptible to the voices of local constituents because they are being influenced by the party leadership. That leadership draws a distinction between its position and the other party's position, which makes it more difficult for individual members to take an independent stand. Even in those instances, effective coalitions can effect minor changes in a particular bill that advances their interests but allows the sponsors to remain faithful to the primary partisan objectives.

Because of the sheer volume and complexity of issues members of Congress must consider, they depend on the feedback of their constituents to isolate specific elements of legislative proposals and to suggest parallels between those issues and the philosophical or pragmatic interests of the legislator. That's why lobbying is a process of education. Your goal is to educate each member about the consistency of your position with the member's values and commitments.

The ideal circumstance is when the member of Congress you can most reasonably reach through the influence of local constituents is also influential among his or her peers on the issue in question. You can then leverage your own influence through that of the targeted member.

Process for Developing Partners

While there are occasions when two or more organizations come together for a very specific legislative goal and only for the time necessary to work on that goal, this chapter is about creating and sustaining partnerships over a longer time span. Such partnerships require some basic prerequisites in order to succeed. They are not unlike the requirements for any two people to work well together over an extended period of time:

- Common interests or objectives
- Flexible styles or personalities
- The willingness to occasionally subordinate your own interests to the broader interests of the partners

- Egos that are malleable enough not to be impediments
- Willingness to contribute equally to achieve the common goals

Just as leaders of nation-states do not wake up one morning with an unexplained urge to collaborate, neither do nonprofit leaders. Collaboration is not a natural act. In the absence of a compelling reason, both steer their own course and avoid entangling alliances. Something has to drive them to collaborate with others, typically, an external threat or a compelling opportunity that can be addressed only with the help of others.

Successful partnerships (even those that are created for a very short-term and limited goals) require a significant expenditure of time and effort. Therefore, organizations seldom seek to develop them without a programmatic or philosophical congruence. Whether or not there is a sufficient degree of congruence to justify the investment necessary to form and grow the collaboration is the question each party must answer. As long as alliances are viewed as relationships to be constantly and patiently improved on, the level of commitment such alliances enjoy from their partners can be gradually increased.

Most not-for-profits share some aspect of their mission and public policy interests with other, and often many other, organizations. How, then, do you decide to partner with a particular organization when there may be many to choose from may be influenced by many variables? Common funders—private or public—overlapping memberships or constituencies, and shared volunteer leaders might be the more obvious connections. Likewise, two or more organizations may have similar goals but have different programmatic or organizational strengths. They may recognize their ability to complement one another or fill the voids left by each one's lack of coverage in some particular area.

Are You Good Partnership Material?

Before you can successfully undertake the necessary steps to form a partnership, you must be sure you are good partnership material. The first requirement in developing a sound partnership is to examine yourself to see if you have the kind of personality, sense of personal security, and self-confidence that will enable you and your organization to partner effectively.

As in any good marriage or business relationship, nonprofit partnerships that pursue legislative goals effectively require mutuality, flexibility, and an ability to subordinate parochial or individual goals to the combined interests of the partnership. What is true for individuals is also true for organizations. Institutional ego is as real as personal ego. When either party in a partnership manifests too strong an institutional ego or when the leader of either organization is too egocentric, dogmatic, aggressive, or inflexible, the partnership will almost always suffer or fail. This is pertinent because, while it may not be flattering to admit, your need for institutional recognition may be greater than your need to accomplish your legislative goal(s), in which case, neither you nor your organization is good partnership material.

While few leaders will admit to being so egotistical, they may admit to being inflexible. But the best partnerships are those in which each partner is willing to go more than halfway to reach the goals of their respective organizations. This is harder than it may appear. The fact is that most living species aren't conditioned to partner. Doing so somehow runs counter to instinct or conditioning. From our earliest years of socialization, we have to be taught to share, to play well together on the playground. This carries over to the adult need to work cooperatively for common goals.

While still targeting specific members of Congress, some lobbying campaigns spend a great deal of time and effort attempting to get as many groups as possible to endorse their positions. Although endorsements are worthwhile, they are often overrated. A long list of organizations supporting your position can be impressive and gives a certain amount of credibility to your cause; however, unless the groups endorsing you are also willing to do active lobbying, you cannot expect their names to carry the day. It is better to have three groups that will give you time, effort and money than 30 that will merely lend you the use of their names. Given limited resources, you should spend much more time attempting to convince people to work with you than to merely approve of what you're saying.

Nevertheless, a long list of endorsing organizations can be helpful, particularly in areas where you are not especially strong. In seeking endorsements, you should make it very clear to the groups contacted that you want to use their names publicly. It can be devastating if a group, which you claim has endorsed your position, subsequently repudiates the endorsement. This can usually be avoided by good communication from the outset. You should also keep the leaders of any group that endorses you aware of the manner in which you use its name, making sure that you send the group copies of all documents in which its name appears.

Communication is key—not just letter writing, on which not-for-profits often rely too much, but telephone calls, testimony, and personal visitations as well. Communication must include feedback and record keeping, so you know a policymaker's stand on a given issue.

What Makes Organizations Compatible?

The presumptive measure of compatibility, in the context of this discussion, is a shared legislative objective that advances the mission of the respective organizations. However, since every organization has its own reputation publicly linking with another organization raises the possibility of taking on both the negative and positive public impressions of that organization. You must be prepared to ask if such an association will bring with it any unintended negatives. This is particularly worrisome if you are considering partnering with an organization around a legislative goal but can scarcely imagine partnering around a programmatic goal. The greater the similarity of mission, the greater the degree of compatibility.

The fit becomes even more appealing, however, if each organization has strengths that truly complement the other. Different constituencies or scope of reach into communities, staff experience or competencies, and budget size are some of the assets that two or more organizations can have that produce synergy. It is also best if there is no recent history of conflict or tension between the organizations, which would serve as a distraction among their stakeholders while in the midst of a campaign for a common goal.

How Important Are Personal Relationships?

When the personal relationship is strong between the leaders of the partnering organizations, their joint legislative goals can only be pursued with greater efficiency and impact. The mission or legislative goal must always be more important than the relationship of the leaders. However, since organizations are composed of their stakeholders, and reflect the personalities of their leaders, personal relationships cannot be minimized when working on organizational goals. Respect, trust, open communication, and mutual accountability are desirable organizational attributes but are most often exemplified in the leaders of the organizations.

Thus, organizational leaders have an inordinate influence in making and maintaining the commitments from which trust grows, maintaining open communication and monitoring accountability measures. Leaders bring varying degrees of social skills or adeptness at inducing desirable response in others to the partnership enterprise. When leaders are visionary and strategic, they use their ability to influence others to work across internal and external boundaries. Whether working with the staff, board, or constituents of the partner organization or with Congress, those who are most adept at working with others can use those skills to advance common goals. Effective leaders initiate and manage change because they inspire and guide individuals and groups. As good communicators, they listen openly and send convincing messages. They foster cooperation because they build nurturing relationships.

How Do You Keep the Partner Focused?

Even the most compatible organizations compete at some level at some time for contracts, grants, staff, donors and even publicity. There may even be instances when they have different legislative goals in one area while partnering on another. The first step in ensuring a sufficient level of focus on the shared agenda is the acknowledgment that one particular goal is important enough to overshadow any other likely differences. You must weigh the potential cost of partnership while you consider the potential gain. If both your board and executive leadership agree that the gain outweighs the loss, your partnership plans can be assessed, implemented, and evaluated.

When it is tempting to deviate from the plan, the leader's role is to elevate the original goal in the minds of the team and enable team members to screen out the competing motivations, agenda, and dynamics in lieu of the larger objective. In short, it is the leader's role to keep everyone's eyes on the prize.

Know Your Partner

Allies don't just happen; they must be sought out and cultivated. There is hardly an issue in Washington that does not attract or repel numbers of groups for widely different reasons. Your chances of succeeding in a lobbying campaign will be enormously enhanced if you join with other groups that share your aims. In the nation's capital, you are likely to find them in the most unlikely places even among groups that have traditionally opposed you. In seeking allies, keep your eye on the ultimate objective of the lobbying campaign, not the positions or personalities of your allies. Few political objectives worth achieving can be gained without allies.

You must also know your prospective partner well if you are going to be effective in your joint legislative agenda. You must know if your partner's record or reputation would in any way jeopardize your goals. You must also know the person well enough to properly understand and capitalize on his or her assets. Partners may agree on how they will create value, but this is insufficient for success. They must answer other questions: How compatible are we? How will we agree on value creation priorities? How will each of us contribute to the success of the alliance? How can we overcome our natural rivalries?

To sustain successful cooperation, partners typically need to understand five key areas: the environment in which the alliance will operate, the tasks to be performed, the process of collaboration, the partner's skills, and their intended and emerging goals. To make an alliance more robust in the face of uncertainty and more resilient to changing circumstances, partners benefit from learning together about their alliance's current environment and about its likely future environment. The alternative, each partner making its own observations, drawing its own conclusions, and making its own predictions is bound to push the partners further apart. A joint effort at learning about the competitive, technological, and market environment helps partners to develop mutual trust and shared understanding and reduces the risk of straining the terms of the partnership in the future because of widely divergent or conflicting interests.

Document Clear Philosophical Agreement with the Boards

The impetus to form partnerships can come from a variety of places. Generally, however, it is the job of the CEOs or board leaders to take the initial steps. Key staff and board members need to be involved in understanding and shaping the rationale for the partnership, the strategies to be used, and the steps for implementation. If you succeed in gaining the alliance of another group, you should establish the ground rules very carefully. You will avoid all sorts of potential problems if your relationship with your allies is spelled out in detail before you undertake substantive confrontations and misunderstandings and can work together. These should be specified in a memorandum of understanding, which incorporates at least the following factors:

1. A clear statement of the ultimate objective (e.g., passage or defeat of a particular piece of legislation)
2. A list of individuals from each group who will be participating in the lobbying campaign
3. A statement of responsibility for the preparation of position papers, resource books and all other written material to be used in the campaign
4. Procedures by which contacts, error correction, and so on, will be implemented
5. A review committee for editing materials to be used in the campaign

Confrontation often arises when allies think up different ways to accomplish the same objective. The group you're working with can probably draw on different strengths than those available to your group. You should not insist that the other group merely adopt your methods: rather, give them the freedom to take advantage of their strengths. Although you may be somewhat uncomfortable with some of their arguments, as long as those postions cannot be challenged on the basis of accuracy you should let it go. The only danger here is inconsistent arguments, but these can usually be worked out when editing the memorandum of understanding. The goals and procedures worked out early in your relationship should be reviewed on a regular basis.

As the partnership develops, it's important to keep your board informed and involved. Not only do they have the ultimate responsibility for shaping the goals of the partnership, but, most often, they will have their own sphere of influence that is an asset in working with elected officials. The more influential the board member, the more potentially effective he or she will be in his or her own direct contact with legislators. Board members should be seen as one of the vital organizational assets when working to influence legislators.

Create Joint Plans

Many groups may want to join you particularly if it appears you are going to be successful in your lobbying efforts, but you should be sure that all parties shoulder their share of the burden. It is one thing to work with allies, but another to carry them. You must be sure they do their part. Each partner will need to develop specific plans in order to unleash the power of his or her respective constituency. This includes analyzing where you have the most direct route to particular legislators. You may determine that the best method for demonstrating broad support for your goal is to have constituents write, call, or visit the targeted legislators. You may determine that key constituents can be most influential if they are slated to testify before an appropriate committee hearing. You may determine that you want some members to receive high-level attention from influential constituents that are sympathetic to your goal. You may determine that you want to synchronize the contacts coming from your constituents with the contacts coming from the constituents of your partner organizations. In any case, there must be a coordinated plan.

Specifically, make sure your friends keep their promises and abide by the same standards of credibility and integrity you set for yourself. Announce in writing the specific goals and projects that each group will be expected to perform. Make sure that you keep your part of the deal and they keep theirs.

Examples of Effective Partnerships

The Corporation of National Service (CNS) and the Points of Light Foundation (POLF)

The epitome of an effective partnership is a good marriage between two loving people. Couples who love and respect each other want what's best for their mates, even more than they want for themselves. Thus, for partnerships to work in the nonprofit world, you must aim for the kind of reciprocity that places at least as high a priority on your partner organization's goal(s) as on your own. When the CNS and the POLF, along with many other organizations, successfully partnered to get Congress to reauthorize the National Community Service Act of 1993, they provided a blueprint for partnering to accomplish a legislative goal benefiting many organizations.

The CNS administers a broad array of programs that use federal funds to subsidize workers—such as Volunteers in Service to America (VISTA); Senior Volunteer Programs (such as Foster Grandparents and Retired Seniors Volunteers Program); and President Clinton's pet domestic programs, Americorps and Learn and Serve. The POLF provides technical assistance, training, model program development, and advocacy for many for-profit and not-for-profit organizations thought to be comprising the traditional volunteer workforce. Since stipended service has been a major domestic emphasis of the Clinton administration and traditional volunteer service was heavily promoted during the Bush administration, there was a need to find common ground as soon as President Clinton was elected and his own service initiative was unveiled. While neither organization considers itself to have a partisan agenda, many in Congress and many citizens associate each organization with the respective president and his party. Both CNS and POLF was able to speak directly to influential members of Congress through its constituents with sufficient effectiveness to help overcome the natural opposition to the act by those who were seeking to defeat the pet domestic program of the incumbent president.

With nearly 500 volunteer centers and 300 corporate members, the POLF has been able to speak directly to most members of Congress through the voices of local organizations that are known and respected by the individual members of Congress. Likewise, the CNS has its own diverse constituency because it champions the ideal of national service for large numbers of the nation's youth, among others, and because it provides funding and leadership to hundreds of local not-for-profits that use stipended volunteers to help accomplish their direct service objectives. It also provides funding to hundreds of school districts and universities that operate service learning programs. Together, these two organizations have tremendous influence through the number of communities they touch, directly or indirectly.

While every member of a legislative body such as Congress has a role in shaping or passing legislation, some members have special influence because of their membership or leadership on key committees. In the case of the National Community Service Act reauthorization, the relevant committees were the Health, Education, Labor, and Pension Committee in the Senate and the Education and the Workforce Committee in the House of Representatives.

As reviewed in Chapter 2, Congress, like most legislative bodies, operates through a committee structure. The committee has power because it is given the responsibility of thoroughly reviewing prospective legislation and making its recommendation to the full legislative body. And the chair people and minority leaders of each committee have tremendous influence in setting the agenda for and consideration of specific legislative initiatives. They can exact inordinate influence by control of the calendar when legislation is considered, trade off their support for initiatives that are important to other members of the committee, and shape the "floor" (minimal authorizing, regulatory, or appropriations) or "ceiling" (maximum considerations) of regulation or appropriation.

Once it was clear that passage of the National Community Service Act was in the best interest of each organization and its many constituents, mounting a campaign to influence members of Congress to vote for the act was straightforward. First, leaders from each organization identified the key members of Congress we wanted to influence. We arranged to have influential and representative constituents testify at hearing conducted by both committees. We coordinated the appearances of those who could speak credibly about the benefits of the legislation from their respective areas of influence, such as business, leading not-for-profit organizations, and educational institutions. We specifically included leaders from those organizations that were known to have raised issues about the possible conflict with their goals, such as trade unions and not-for-profits that relied on traditional volunteers.

Generations United (GU)

The time to form a coalition is when you don't need to. A good example of this principle in action is found in the work of Generations United (GU). This Washington, DC - based organization was formed in order to develop strategies around the common interests of four organizations that would appear to have competing public policy interests: The Children's Defense Fund (CDF), The American Association for Retired Persons (AARP), the Child Welfare League of America (CWLA), and the National Council on the Aging (NCA). Since GU's founding and early work, more than 100 organizations have been recruited as members. The original supposition was that these organizations that represent children's issues were often in direct competition with those that represent the interests of the elderly. Outside forces tried to create an either/or dichotomy to create conflict among the advocates for children, youth, and the elderly instead of supporting the importance of both generations. Rather than see those interests as competitive, the leaders of the organizations determined to find common public policy ground and to work toward legislative goals that would help the country's most vulnerable citizens—the young and the old.

GU is an organization whose sole reason for existing is to further the missions of its members by shaping an effective coalition. An outgrowth of its mission is to isolate and promote public policies and programs that have an intergenerational focus. Before GU was started, the founding organizations were often pitted against one another as they sought federal funding and policy changes that would benefit their respective constituencies. One journal went so far as to picture on its cover a young person and an old person, back-to-back in battle fatigues with guns ready to pace off, turn, and shoot. The message was that the country could not meet the needs of both generations, and the quickest and most able to harm the other would survive.

Over the years, those organizations came to realize that they could accomplish goals important to them individually through leverage and synergy. They found that the same rationale for providing support for the very young was true for providing support for the elderly. They also found that programs designed to benefit one group could be appropriated in ways that would benefit the other. Forming a coalition enabled the organizations to look through an intergenerational filter for the unique intergenerational intersection in current policy discussions.

The GU board of directors is composed of executives from each of the founding partner organizations and of a representative number of leaders from organizations that have since been recruited. Several members of the corporate community have been added as well. By reviewing issues from a global perspective, the board sets the vision for the coalition. Working groups composed of other staff from the member organizations delve further into specific issues that arise and establish prospective positions, which are reviewed at the board level and which then result in the embrace of specific strategies that can be pursued through vigorous lobbying by teams of coalition members. Fact sheets and a written public policy agenda are developed and distributed to support the positions of the coalition.

The 106th Congress presented several opportunities for the coalition to make its influence felt. Relationships were formed with the leadership of the Older Americans Caucus and the Children's Caucus. Together, these key caucuses sponsored intergenerational briefings on specific policy concerns of GU members. The co-chairs of both caucuses then signed a letter, which they sent to the other members of Congress, along with a copy of the GU public policy agenda extolling the importance of an intergenerational approach to public policy. Through these and other activities, they were able to shift the dialogue from competition between the two ends of the chronological spectrum to common needs and the possibilities for reciprocity and mutual support. The result has been the creation of a caucus partnership that is working to create a larger social compact, which looks at public policy that benefits all ages.

Other successful outcomes of the work of this coalition have been to focus attention on why efforts to eliminate child poverty are also important to older people and how older people can be resources to deliver services that help to retard poverty among youth. For example, legislation that expands the subsidy for childcare can include provisions to train older people as childcare workers. The result is more trained childcare professionals to help working poor families and a program that helps the elderly, opening up employment opportunities for those who need their own income subsidy. Seniors who remain vital and energetic are also able to increase their own sense of fulfillment by playing a critical role in the development of children, who benefit from the nurturing and direction the elderly can uniquely provide.

One major current issue that has united the advocates for younger and older people is that of the growing number of grandparents raising grandchildren. Together the groups work to ensure that the benefits and subsidies intended for parents and foster parents are extended to grandparents who are primary care providers. Family supports help to protect the older caregivers and the children to whom they are giving care.

These examples of the Corporation for National Service, the Points of Light Foundation and Generations United provide insight into some fundamental principles, which must exist to undergird any successful coalition. Chief among them is the commitment to finding the commonality that supports your mission and the mission of the partnering organization. The common ground is created and nourished by actions, which are clearly seen in these successful coalitions.

In addition to the specific agenda of the partnership, you must be prepared to offer support for the legislative goals of your partner(s), even if the direct link to your own interest is not evident. In return your partner must be prepared to do the same.

You must stay constructively engaged in ongoing dialogue in order to build and preserve trust among partnering organizations, which can sustain them during those difficult times when creativity and compromise are required. Given the challenges most alliances face, partners must fully appreciate all the benefits they can expect from the alliance, so they do not lose their sense of purpose when confronted with unexpected setbacks.

You must also constantly look for the goal or goals that you can embrace that, while not necessarily a top priority for your organization, can form the basis of collective action to further the important mission of the coalition. The more frequently the chief executive provides information to the board members about the contracting relationship, the more active board members will be facilitators, political advocates, buffers, and values guardians. Board members often work hard as political advocates to maintain and expand the benefits that not-for-profits derive from government. The political advocacy role incorporates specific actions by individual board members, such as telephoning legislators on behalf of the not-for-profit they serve, as well as more general political pressures applied by the board as a group.

Alliances must be formed with other citizen groups. Unlike the institutional side of our national life, which has become increasingly monolithic, citizen action expresses itself through innumberable channels. New citizen groups sprout like blades of grass after a spring rain. But the ability of the groups to shape and influence legislation will be severely limited if they do magnify their clout by observing the principles discussed in this and other chapters of this book.

Endnotes

[1]DeKieffer, Donald, *How to Lobby Congress,* Dodd, Mead & Company, 1981, p. xiii.

[2]Boris, Elizabeth, T. *Nonprofit Management & Leadership Volume 4 Number 1 Fall 1993,* Jossey-Bass Publishers "An Interview With James A. Joseph" page 108.

[3]Boris, Elizabeth, T. *Nonprofit Management & Leadership Volume 4 Number 1 Fall 1993,* Jossey-Bass Publishers "An Interview With James A. Joseph" page 107.

[4]Rees, Susan, *Nonprofit Sector Research Fund, Effective Nonprofit Advocacy Working Paper Series,* Autumn 1998, The Aspen Institute—Executive Summary—p. 3.

[5]Rees, Susan, *Nonprofit Sector Research Fund, Effective Nonprofit Advocacy Working Paper Series,* Autumn 1998, The Aspen Institute; Smucker, Bob, *The Nonprofit Lobbying Guide: Advocating Your Cause—and Getting Results,* The Independent Sector, Jossey-Bass: San Francisco, 1991.

The Use of Outside Legislative Consultants: When and How to Hire a Lobbyist

JOHN CHWAT

Introduction

Whatever term best describes lobbyists, such as legislative consultant or public affairs specialist, they exist at every level of government—local, state, and federal. These individuals have studied and practiced the profession of lobbying and are experts at influencing the legislative and executive branches of government. These specialists have three characteristics that distinguish them from other consultants in the legal and accounting fields. First, they are knowledgeable on the legislative process—they know what it takes to move legislation through a city council, a state legislature, or Congress. They are familiar with their turf and are able to present their clients' views to decision makers. Second, they have spent considerable time in the system, being employed by the legislature or having jobs associated with the legislative process, so that they are experienced with the mechanics of getting things done in a legislative setting. Third, they have influential connections, which have been cultivated over the years. These connections constitute a personalized network of contacts with members and staff of the legislature and government decision makers. Lobbyists are specialists in the legislative process and possess a unique set of experiences and knowledge. Lobbyists have the ability to write and express their clients' positions concisely for presentation to policy officials and are able to present their clients' case in small-group settings and in public. The successful lobbyist is best able to deal with a wide range of personalities to achieve client objectives.

No matter what the legislative setting, hiring an outside legislative consultant or a lobbyist is a widely accepted practice by trade and professional associations, corporations, unions, and not-for-profit organizations. Indeed, at the federal level, every group in the United States has lobbyists working on its behalf either within the organization or as outside consultants.[1] All of

EXHIBIT 6.1   Selected Nonprofit Organizations and Their Outside Counsels

Nonprofit Organization	Outside Counsel
• American Association of Retired Persons	• McDermott, Will, and Emery
• Alliance of Non-Profit Mailers	• Sidley & Austin
• Defenders of Wildlife	• Chambers Associates
• Distance Education and Training Council	• J. C. Luman and Associates
• Faith and Politics Institute	• Hauser Group
• Fund for Animals	• Meyer & Glitzenstein
• International Law Institute	• Covington & Burling
• The Nature Conservancy	• Cassidy & Associates/ Miller & Chevalier
• Solid Waste Association of North America	• Baise, Miller & Freer
• Wildlife Legislative Fund of America	• Birch, Horton, Bittner & Cherot

Source: *J. Valerie Steele, ed.,* Washington Representatives 2000 *(Washington, DC: Columbia Books.) 212, 237, 366, 371, 391, 407, 451, 558, 636, 694.*

these groups recognize that, in order to compete in the legislative process and to undertake a legislative agenda, these organizations must have individuals with experience and knowledge advising them on these matters. Success in the legislative labyrinth is, therefore, directly proportional to hiring the right staff or consultants in this field.

The Right Time to Hire

The debate over retaining an outside legislative consultant can be an important step within any organization seeking to develop or expand its government relations activities. It is not necessarily true that the only time to undertake this hiring effort relates to a legislative threat or a proactive legislative initiative by the organization. Many other factors may bring the officers and members to this decision—monitoring legislation, analyzing legislation, consulting on coalition participation, or writing articles on legislative and regulatory matters affecting the membership.

The arguments against retaining an outside legislative consultant are endless. These arguments can range from economic—"We can't afford a lobbyist"—to concern over duplicating members' connections—"I'm best friends with the Speaker, and he'll take care of us." Many volunteer organizations express concern over the image problems associated with hiring a lobbyist, claiming that lobbyists are synonymous with sleaze and corruption and that, if they were to hire one, the organization would be like every

---

EXHIBIT 6.2   You Know It's Time to Hire an Outside Legislative Counsel When Your Group . . .

- Misses key votes in the legislature on your issues
- Has difficulty in arranging meetings with key legislative staff
- Is unaware of changes made to your bill in subcommittee and committee
- Does not understand the legislative process

---

other special interest. On closer examination, however, many of these arguments can be overcome. For example, the volunteer officer who knew the Speaker really just met him briefly at a dinner attended by hundreds of other guests, and the costs of hiring a lobbyist can be kept within budget and affordable to the organization through effective contract negotiations and oversight of the lobbyist's billing practices.

There is no right time to hire a lobbyist. (See Exhibit 6.2.) Many factors are involved in this decision-making process. It depends on the organization's budget, the views of the officers and board of directors, the position of the executive director, staff capabilities, and the membership's mission statements and goals. Some organizations wait until the start of a legislative session, hiring their lobbyists in the fall before the session begins. Some organizations wait until there is a defined need, usually coming in the form of a crisis.

Challenges of a Legislative Crisis

Most organizations are familiar with procedures to address a crisis affecting the membership. For instance, the executive director suddenly has a medical emergency and leaves or an audit of the organization finds irregularities in some major accounts. Perhaps membership has dropped dramatically in six months and there is little revenue to pay monthly bills. A legislative crisis brings with it a whole new and mysterious set of circumstances, which the organization must address. This type of crisis involves the legislative process—knowledge of the legislative committee or subcommittee structure, the power of the chairperson, and the leadership of the legislature. Knowing how a bill becomes law and how to access key decision makers and staff is also key.

This crisis could come in the form of an amendment attached to a larger bill without anyone watching during a late-night session of the legislature. It could be out in the open, with a legislator introducing a bill or by a savvy legislator using parliamentary tactics to change a provision in a bill while still in the committee or subcommittee. No matter what form the legislative crisis takes, this initiative directly affects the members of the organization, and, if nothing is done to meet the challenge, it could fundamentally hurt the organization.

To have an impact on the legislative process successfully, the organization must look to expertise in developing immediate steps to meet the challenges of the moment. Knowing what to do with whom and how to do it in the legislative process usually falls to a lobbyist who has been through this type of crisis before and has succeeded to overcome these challenges with other clients.

Lack of Expertise in the Organization

Many organizations simply lack expertise on the legislative process. There may be no formal legislative or public affairs committee of the board. One volunteer board member may be trying to do everything. There may be a lack of experience by the volunteer officers, the board of directors, or the members of the organization in legislative projects. They know little of how a bill becomes law or, more important, the strategies and tactics of legislative activities. In addition, the organization's staff does not have the background or experience to advise the officers on what to do to meet legislative challenges, monitor activities, and analyze what is being done in the legislature that affects the members. Seeking expertise by a lobbyist to perform these consulting services can enhance the organization's ability to become involved in the legislative process.

Difficult Membership Activation

Another key indicator to consider in retaining a lobbyist is the organization's lack of interest in legislative affairs. Organizations that are affected by legislation and government policies may find it difficult to frame the issue correctly, to provide materials to members that can be used in the legislature, and to explain how to get involved so as to activate their members—and officers.

Apathy within the organization's membership will effect any attempt to influence elected officials—letter writing, visiting officials, contacting them by telephone has proven to be a failure. An apathetic organization may be the result of not having a clearly defined legislative program, and strategy to implement this program. A lobbyist can be a significant catalyist to change the apathy mood within an organization as part of his or her services to the organization.

Size and Location of the Organization

Several other factors might be considered in retaining outside legislative counsel. The organization's size may dictate the ability to afford lobbyist fees and whether the organization's budget and resources are able to sustain legislative campaign costs throughout the legislative process, which sometimes last almost a year. The number of members also relates to the ability to network support broadly within the legislature to achieve goals and objectives. Also, organizations that are located father away from the legislature may find it difficult to participate in coalition meetings and visitations to key legislators and staff. Therefore, they must retain a lobbyist to represent their interests day-in and day-out while the legislature is in session. Fly-ins by the organization just do not take care of the ongoing legislative challenges. Even if the organization is based near the legislature, it must decide if additional support and expertise by a lobbyist is needed to supplement its visits to both the legislature and other groups in the city.

Types of Legislative Consultants to Consider

There is a wide variety of legislative consultants affiliated with an equal number of diverse types of firms available for organizations to retain on a short-term or long-term basis. Their relationships with firms span the gambit—from one-person-at-home consultants to large, international companies. Each has its own characteristics, background, and specialties.[2] Moreover, each has their own fee structure for lobbying services. Some firms maintain lobbyists with Democratic or Republican connections, having served as staff (or elected official) to these legislators. Others specialize in issues or have lobbyists assigned to areas based on their experience—health, labor, environment, and others. Further still, some lobbyists have backgrounds that lend themselves to various industries, as opposed to issues—hospitality, defense contractors, and so forth. Organizations wishing to retain outside counsel must consider many factors in their selection processes.

One-Stop Shops

The term, "one-stop shop", is commonly used within the public affairs community and is relatively new in the context of lobbying. It refers to firms that offer potential clients more than just legislative consulting. It is an effort by these firms to assist clients in a variety of ways that transcend the single service of influencing the legislature. These firms commonly provide a one-stop shop for clients in areas that include public relations (media and methods to influence the trade press, print media [newspapers], radio, TV, cable, magazines) legal services; lobbying services such as grassroots activation, coalition building, direct mail; to influence voters on policy issues. If the services are not included within these shops, they more than likely will subcontract with other companies in support of the client's needs. Most, if not all, of these one-stop shops are affiliated with large companies, and their lobbying component may include from 80 to 100 lobbyists who may also perform public relations consulting services. The larger company that owns this one-stop-shop is usually an international public relations or advertising company with many offices worldwide. It provides a shopping list of services to meet client objectives.

Mid-to-Small Boutique Firms

Another term recently used in relation to lobbying firms is *boutique,* which references a specialty or an expertise that is tailored to the client's interest. It could refer to issues the firm lobbies for or just the fact that it pays attention to what services the client wants and implements it. Many of these firms have a principal officer (president, CEO) and two of three support staff including a legislative and secretarial employee. Some firms are larger with ten or less employees considered within the lobbying community as a small company. The largest firms have 100 employees but these are less than three in Washington, DC, shops with a full spectrum of clients, as well as specialties in specific issues and industries.

Universally, these types of lobbying firms have former legislative staff involved in the ownership and day-to-day lobbying by the firm. These former legislative committee counsels or leadership staffs or former chiefs of staff to retiring legislators have the understanding of the system, and contacts to offer clients access to a changing legislative environment. For example, a key legislator becomes Speaker and some of his or her former staff set up shop to search for clients. Therefore, many of these firms change rapidly and are bought out and acquired by larger firms over the years, depending on who is in power and who is not. A small fraction of them survive for long periods of time as specialists in the legislative process, not depending on the moods of the electorate and who is in power at a particular time.

Law Firms

Law firms are positioned to provide their clients litigation services with specialties in administrative law, dealing with government and regulations. Law firms that seek to add a legislative component to their practice offer lobbying services to their clients as a specialty practice to supplement the legal part of the firm. Most legislators are attorneys, and are knowledgeable of the law, how to present themselves in public and debate issues similar to an attorney practicing in a court of law. A lawyer is familiar with legislative drafting, (knowing how and where to change the law) which is an additional service to the firm's legal clients. There is a wide variety of law firms—from the very small, one- or two-person, shop to the largest firms in the world, which maintain legislative consulting services.

Law firms might establish an office in a capital, specifically designed to provide lobbying services as a part of their litigation and regulatory services. These law firms are usually run by the headquarters firm located outside the capital, and the partners and associates involved in the lobbying services perform these functions for the entire firm, regardless of the location for all its offices. Law firms also have subject specialties—labor, health, antitrust, intellectual property, and more. They can also be affiliated with former Democratic or Republican elected officials, but the recent trend is to have on staff a mix of both party officials to offer clients a wide range of influencing both Republican and Democratic decision makers in the U.S. Congress.

Methods of Seeking the Right Lobbyist

Finding the right lobbyist for the organization may be as difficult as finding the right dentist, lawyer, or doctor. The Yellow Pages is one source, but, due to the number of names available and the lack of information on the firms, it is not reliable. Other reference works are available, but none describes how to select the lobbyist for the organization. There are more professional ways to select a legislative consultant.

Acquiring Referrals and Recommendations

The single most valuable method of obtaining names of qualified legislative consultants is through referrals and recommendations. These can come from a variety of sources, all of which will produce lobbyists who have the right match with the organization. The organizations might seek out individuals who are not only familiar with the organization's interest, but also connected to lobbyists involved in the legislature. Referrals could be made from contacts of like-minded organizations or allied industries with retained lobbyists—government officials, legislative staff, and legislators who understand the organization, observe lobbyists on a regular basis, and can make appropriate recommendations. Legislative staff are visited regularly by lobbyists and can make judgments on how the lobbyists present the views of their clients. A legislative staff person may be able to recommend based on his or her personal knowledge of one or more firms. The same is true with a legislator.

The best method of asking for a referral is to be direct and to the point—"Do you know a lobbyist whom we can talk to about representing our interests?" During the course of the discussion, the person making the recommendation will know your needs, and possibly your budget, and will think of a good match based on knowing the organization and the lobbyist.

The second source of referrals are individuals within the organization from family, friends, neighbors, and business associates who may know lobbyists who are active with the legislature.

The third source of recommendations is unsolicited contacts made by lobbyists to the organizations and unsolicited contacts made by others on behalf of a lobbyist to the organization. For example, from time to time, an organization may receive correspondence and materials from a lobbyist seeking representational services. Many lobbying firms target various organizations on their specific issues and solicit business either directly or by a third-party recommendation, explaining how they could assist the organization on legislative issues affecting their members.

Researching the Lobbyist

Aside from referrals and recommendations, another method for obtaining lobbyist names for consideration is to conduct a research campaign. One source of information is the list of registered lobbyists that is required at all levels of government.[3] These lists provide timely information on the clients who have retained particular lobbyists and permit the organization to contact references on those lobbyists. These lists also provide the names of lobbyists and their firms for review, in many cases arranged by subject matter and cross-referenced to clients. Many of these registration lists also provide a preview of lobbyists' fees. There are also many directories published that can be extremely helpful in further researching lists of lobbyists to solicit for possible consulting opportunities.

Interviewing and Selecting the Lobbyist

Some organizations do not go through a formal selection process in choosing their outside legislative consultants. They rely on recommendations and may select a lobbyist after one meeting with the organization's executive director or senior official. This process relies on possible connections within the organization that the lobbyist has, or perhaps the referral was of such high caliber there would be little point in reviewing other applicants. Moreover, some organizations seek out a particular lobbyist to represent their interest. In these cases there is no competition for their selection. This may occur when the lobbyist's reputation is known to the organization or if the lobbyist's activity in the legislature would be of immediate value to the organization.

Most organizations, however, develop a selection process, which includes a group of key officials within the organization—the executive director, the chairperson of the legislative committee, and executive committee (board) members. This select group can review the backgrounds of the applicants, conduct the interviews, and make the selection for recommendation to the board of directors. In some cases, the lobbyist candidates (usually narrowed down to two) appear before the entire board of directors for the selection. The selection committee can develop the list of services desired and, in some cases, set a request for proposals (RFP) to selected lobbyists for response by a specific date. These RFPs set out the type of firm and background being solicited, the services desired, and the date for submission of a proposal for consideration. The selection committee reviews the lobbyists' proposals and usually selects two or three for the interview. The main purpose of the interview is to see each lobbyist and the way he or she handles questions from the committee. Seeing the lobbyist can help the committee to visualize if this is the right person to represent their interests in the legislature. Questions and answers can also elicit important information on which to make a decision. Ultimately, the lobbyist is selected and the board of directors approves the choice.

Budgeting for a Lobbyist and Contracting for Services

Many times, organizations fail to budget adequately for an outside consultant. A figure is determined on what they can best afford, but they neglect to add unforeseen items, such as expenses relating to projects resulting from the lobbyist's services. These might include publications or the printing of materials for distribution to the legislative staff or membership; mailing costs or telephone expenses resulting from a lobbying campaign; and travel, room, and board for the lobbyist to board meetings in order to report on activities in the legislature. Some expenses can be limited, and each organization develops its budgeting priorities differently. Some place the lobbyist's fee and expenses in a separate line item (consultant services or legislative projects) or place them under a legislative committee budget. Still further, some budgeted items relating to materials, publications, and mailing are dispersed to other accounts. Primarily, the budget for a lobbyist includes his or her fee and related expenses that are clearly approved by the organization in advance of billing. Once the lobbyist is selected and a budget approved, the organization should draw up a contract for services, which may need a review by an attorney. Some organizations submit a letter contract to the lobbyist that outlines the services, fees, and date for starting and ending the services. (See Exhibits 6.3 and 6.4.)

Most of these letters are no more than two pages in length and usually start out "This letter will constitute a contract for services. . . ." The letter is answered by the lobbyist, in turn, with a letter back to the organization, accepting the terms of the letter-contract. Some organizations prepare a more involved contract, which lists services, fees, expenses, confidentiality provisions, insurance coverage requirements, dates of service, termination provisions for 60 or 90 days' notice, and renewal provisions. Whether the organization decides to issue a letter-contract or a contract for services to the lobbyist, it is very important to focus on the services provisions, as they list what the lobbyist must provide the organization. If the lobbyists deviates from the list of services in the contract, it will result in additional billings by the lobbyist or even a renegotiation of the contract terms, since these additional services require more time and effort by the lobbyist to undertake for the client.

EXHIBIT 6.3   Key Items to Include in a Lobbying Contract

- Specific work to be performed (services)
- Beginning and ending time frame (start and end date)
- Fees: how and when to be paid (payment)
- Expenses
- Termination notice (30 to 60 days)
- Confidentiality

EXHIBIT 6.4   Sample Letter-Contract to a Lobbyist

January 1, 2000

Mr. Joe Smith
Smith & Smith Co.
100 X Street
Washington, DC 20000

Dear Mr. Smith:

We appreciate your recent visit with our executive committee and for the time you took with your staff to review your proposal of last week to provide our XYZ Association with government relations consulting services. I am pleased to inform you that we have decided to retain your firm as our legislative consultant for the coming year and want to congratulate you on an excellent presentation and proposal.

Accordingly, this letter will constitute a contract for services, and we would appreciate your responding in kind, acknowledging the items contained in the letter and agreeing to our proposed relationship. As soon as we receive your letter, we can set a time to meet and begin our plans for the year. We intend to begin your firm's services as of January 1, 2001, for a 12-month period ending December 31, 2001, at a monthly retainer rate of $2,500, payable at the first of each month. You should expect to bill for services each month to my attention. We will pay reasonable expenses associated with your services not to exceed $500 per month, and any excess of these expenses must be approved by me prior to your incurring them. In addition, we will pay for travel, room, and board outside the Washington, DC, area, plus a per diem per day of $800, with approval necessary prior to your billing these expenses.

We would like to have your firm monitor all federal legislation in our areas of concern, recommend additional areas we should review, represent our association in matters relating to federal legislation, and write a monthly column on bills you are following for the association. In addition, you should report on a biweekly basis to me and the chairman of the legislative committee, Mr. Kind, whom you met at the interview. We, in turn, will transmit your reports to the appropriate board and committee members. You should also plan to respond to requests by my office and Mr. Kind relating to any matter relevant to federal legislation. You will be asked to report on your activities at our quarterly board of directors meetings and to brief me prior to these meetings. You should consider all information transmitted to our office as confidential unless we distribute materials to the Congress or outside the association.

We look forward to working with you and your staff in the months to come. Please contact me on receipt of this letter.

Sincerely,

Linda Byrd, Executive Director
XYZ Association

Ways to Pay for Services

Organizations are familiar with a whole host of methods of paying for consulting or professional services. Contingent fees are sometimes paid to individuals to do work contingent on being successful. Another term for this payment is *commissions*, paying a percentage amount to someone for a particular activity (e.g., introducing the client to the right person to accomplish their objectives). In many states, contingent fee contracts for lobbying services are illegal.[4] Commission payments do not lend themselves to lobbying services. Some legal fees are paid by providing the law firm with a retainer-plus arrangement. This permits the firm to draw down or take payment on the retainer paid upfront by the client through hourly billings; when that retainer is exhausted, an hourly rate is used. Retainer-plus arrangements also do not lend themselves to lobbying. There are two methods of payment for lobbyists—hourly rate and monthly retainer.

Hourly Rate

Most organizations are familiar with payment for professional services by an hourly rate. They pay their attorney fees in this manner—just as many other professionals such as plumbers, electricians, and auto mechanics, charge by the hour. Lobbyists set their hourly fees through negotiations with the client; if there is a budget, there is a limit on the number of hours to bill within that hourly rate fee. Several items are important to consider in the hourly fee arrangement. The first is called the surprise charge. This appears in the monthly billings when the lobbyist details their expenses and services. Many times, this results in conflict between the client and the lobbyist on the number of hours or half-hours billed for a particular activity. Another variation on this is the billing by hour when the lobbyist goes to a board meeting or travels away from the legislature. Unless these billings are clearly limited during the contract negotiation (e.g., flat fee when traveling to and from board meetings), there will be problems along the way, which may require a lawyer. Hourly rates vary extensively for legislative consulting. It is not unusual for a lobbyist to bill at least $100 per hour for his or her time and $75 per hour for associates. Fees in excess of $250 are not uncommon for larger lobbying firms (One-stop shops or law firms). Rates depend on the lobbyist, his or her background, the size of the firm, and many other factors, not least of which is the organization's ability to pay the fee.

It is very difficult to budget an hourly rate fee structure unless the organization early on sets out the total amount that can be billed under this arrangement. For example, using a 40-hour workweek, many clients are skeptical of the number of hours a lobbyist works on their account, especially if the lobbying firm has other clients. Hourly fees can mount up quickly. During an intense month of lobbying the legislature, if the lobbyist works half-time on one organization's account at the rate of $100 an hour, this can result in an $8,000 bill for that single month (20 hours a week × 4 weeks × $100). Expenses are billed in addition to the hourly rate and can range from the organizations's coverage of all expenses incurred (telephone, facsimile, courier, travel, room and board, etc.) to the organization's coverage of only those expenses the organization approved above a certain amount. Expenses and hourly rate fees are entirely negotiable.

Monthly Retainer

The most popular form of payment and the best for budgeting purposes is the monthly retainer fee. The fee is billed out each month, plus expenses, and both of these items are set in the letter-contract or contract for services. The organization can decide to pay for all expenses incurred, including telephone, reproduction of materials, facsimile, courier, and other costs, provided they are detailed and receipts either attached or available. Travel, room, and board expenses are also usually covered. Some lobbyists do not bill out expenses but, rather, bill only the expenses that are extraordinary, such as large reproduction of materials, entertainment of large groups, and travel. The monthly retainer fee is set by negotiation and can range be $1,000 or more. The amount of the fee rests squarely on the type of services to be undertaken for the organization. For example, the lobbyist who monitors all federal and state legislation on a regular basis, provides consulting in all areas of interest affecting the organization, and provides unlimited lobbying activity in the legislature on all issues will bill a higher monthly fee than a lobbyist who is retained for one assignment in the legislature. Expenses and monthly retainer fees are entirely negotiable.

Payment Schedules

While the method of payment to lobbyists is usually covered in the letter-contract or contract for services (on a certain date each month, for example) many organizations pay the month after receiving the invoice from the lobbyist. It is not unusual for a client to receive an invoice for services undertaken in January, billed to the client February 1, and not paid to the lobbyist until March 1—that is almost a 60-day float. Other variations of this payment scheduling include invoicing for work done and not receiving payment for 30 to 45 days.

Each organization is different. Some have very close relations with their lobbyists and pay very quickly on receipt of the invoice. It is entirely up to the organization to create its own payment schedule, but that schedule must be made clear to the lobbyist at the beginning of their relationship, so that any problems can be solved quickly. Advance payments are not unheard of, in which the lobbyist receives a month or more (up to a year) of retainer fees for work to be done. Partial upfront payments can also be arranged, in which the first two or three months are paid in advance. These schedules are entirely negotiable.

Work with Lobbyists

Once a lobbyist is retained as a consultant, he or she is under constant review by the officers, board, and members of the organization. "Are we getting what we paid for?" is a common refrain, and all eyes are on the wins and losses columns in the legislature. Therefore, it is very important at the outset for the lobbyist to have a clear understanding of his or her mission, role, responsibilities, and goals within the organization. Some lobbyists have worked with trade and professional associations or not-for-profit groups for many years and are very well versed in the mechanics of intra-association management. These seasoned veterans of association politics may bring added value to the consulting relationship.

The Working Relationship—"Who's in Charge?"

The lobbyist must be able to receive instructions and develop a close working relationship with someone (executive director, chairperson of a committee, or president) or a group of officials (legislative committee, board of directors, or executive committee) within the organization at the very beginning of the relationship. Worse still, the lobbyist will have no clear idea of who is in charge within the organization. This can result in a lack of clear policy development and can confuse the lobbyist's message to the legislature. When a crisis develops during a legislative session, there must be a clear understanding of whom the lobbyist calls first and how best to expand the information flow to the organization. Most organizations have the lobbyist work very closely with the executive director, who, in turn, develops policy with the president and executive committee. Some develop close relationships with the chairperson of a legislative committee and the executive director, depending on the structure of the organization.

The Reporting Function—"Who Receives Information?"

Information flow is often critical during a legislative session. It is especially important if the organization is in the midst of a legislative crisis. The lobbyist's intelligence-gathering and monitoring functions, therefore, become a lifeblood of information to the key decision makers in the organization, and the lobbyist's ability to get this information to those decision makers quickly is a value-added service. Information can also be submitted through reports on projects or the provision of materials or testimony during a hearing. There is an endless list of types of information available to the lobbyist for transmission to the organization.

As previously mentioned, in the beginning of the relationship, it is important for there to be clear lines of authority as to who receives information within the organization. Some lobbyists submit memoranda, reports, and other information to the executive director; to the executive committee;

and, if applicable, to a legislative committee. In other lobbying firms, the entire board of directors receives information. In others, even state association executive directors and presidents are added to this list, depending on the size of the organization. In these days of e-mail, it is very simple for lobbyists to communicate quickly to an entire board of directors. The lobbyist's reporting of information also involves policy decisions that may have an impact on the budget for the lobbyist—does the lobbyist report to the membership at the annual meetings or at each board meeting? Does the lobbyist write articles for the organization's publications on a regular basis? These reporting functions are critical in providing services to the organization, fulfilling contract items for the lobbyist and in setting the legislative agenda for the organization.

Policy Decision Making—"What Can I Say?"

Each organization needs to establish at the outset what is the mission and goals of its legislative agenda. Only in this way will the lobbyist clearly understand the policy decisions under which he or she operates in his or her activities on behalf of the organization in the legislative environment. Many organizations do not have board of director–approved policy statements. Still others have not developed mission statements for their legislative committees. Internally, the organization should have very-well-defined objectives for the lobbyist to undertake—introducing bills, passing amendments, monitoring special issues, preventing legislation that is adverse to the membership from passing, securing witnesses at a public hearing, and so on. These objectives can be laid out in the letter-contract or contract for services.

It is also important to determine what lobbyists can say on behalf of the organization in their representational services. Some organizations permit wide latitude for the lobbyist to interact with staff and members of the legislature on their behalf. Others do not permit lobbyists to meet with legislative staff but, rather, attend all meetings with the lobbyist and fall back on the lobbyist's consulting role for the organization to implement or not, at the organization's discretion. Developing clear guidelines by the organization on policy presentation for the lobbyist will greatly assist the organization evaluate the lobbyist's services via the contract.

Evaluation of a Lobbyist's Performance

During the contract period for the lobbyist, the organization will be evaluating his or her performance with an eye toward contract renewal. There should be clear procedures within the organization for this evaluation purpose. The lobbyist, too, must have a clear sense of whether he or she is performing well or is having problems with the client. Most lobbyists know very well if they are underachieving on behalf of their clients—missed votes, poor reporting on key events, and lack of confidence by the client in decisions made or recommended. A whole host of warning bells go off when lobbyists are not meeting organization's goals, which were not only established in the letter-contract or contract for services but are repeated by the organization's officers to the lobbyists during the year. Evaluating the lobbyist can also be of great importance in hiring another lobbyist for the next legislative session, in the event the first lobbyist does not work out. The organization that must go through the process a second time is familiar with the lobbyist's problems in serving the client and will be obtained only from a thorough evaluation and reflection by the organization.

Acquiring Information on the Lobbyist's Work

One way to evaluate whether a consultant is doing his or her job is to hear from others on the lobbyist's performance. Information from staff and members of the legislature is vital in this regard. Perhaps a member of the organization meets with a legislator and asks the question "How did our lobbyist do on our issue with you and your staff? Was she helpful? What's your opinion of the lobbyist?" Obviously, if the lobbyist never met with that member or helped the staff after being told this was a key legislator with whom to work, the answer will not encourage the organization to re-hire that lobbyist for the next session. Another way to receive information on the lobbyist work is to ask individuals involved in similar subject areas of the organization—such as allied associations or like-minded groups. If the organization is involved in coalitions, then ask one of the coalition partners his or her opinion. Views can also be expressed by members of the organization in an internal review: "Was the lobbyist responsive to your requests for information? How did the lobbyist work with that key board member or chairperson of a committee? Did the lobbyist take direction well?" Finally, the lobbyist's direct supervisor within the organization—the executive director or president or board members—can evaluate the lobbyist's performance.

Winning and Losing

It is hard to evaluate a lobbyist based solely on whether he or she has won the organization's vote in the legislature or not. Did the lobbyist get 100 co-sponsors on the bill or not? Did the lobbyist lose more votes for the organization? Unfortunately, many organizations do evaluate their lobbyists by a win-lose factor. If they failed, more often than not they were replaced. If they did not try to overcome the odds and work hard against a bill and still failed, they were replaced. If they failed to live up to expectations by getting a bill introduced or doing something they had said they could do, they were replaced.

Winning, of course, is a tremendous boost to lobbyists, and their support within the organization is assured—at least as long as the winning continues. The losses, on the other hand, do create credibility problems within the organization and for the lobbyists. The only way for lobbyists to overcome the negative impacts of these losses on the organization is to do the best job (and most viable) possible in trying to stop the adverse legislative action. The best position lobbyists want to be in is when the president of the organization says, "We lost the vote, but, due to the lobbyist's help, we did all we could do. We will try again next year!"

Linking Goals to Services

Another method of evaluating the lobbyist's performance is to link the organization's goals to the lobbyist's services during the contract period. If these goals were very specific, such as listing the legislative actions the lobbyist is required to implement, then the review process as to whether the lobbyist performed satisfactorily can be determined by the organization. Other factors in this linkage process can be included that may not be listed in the organizations goals, such as the lobbyist's ability to keep key officials informed on legislative developments, the lobbyist's working relationship and personality interaction with the executive director, president, and board members; and the types of materials the lobbyist prepared for the organization. The bottom line is did the lobbyist do the job she or he was contracted for? If the answer is yes, then a decision on renewal of the contract, if desired, is a little less complicated. If no, then the decision may mean looking to hire a new lobbyist.

Conclusion

All organizations at one time or another become involved in the legislative process and may consider hiring outside legislative consultants. This chapter provided a guide to this process. It is a commonly accepted practice by all organizations to retain lobbyists with special expertise to advise the organizations of the legislative initiatives that affect their members. The chapter reviewed the right time for organizations to consider hiring lobbyists and the types of lobbying consultants to consider. In addition, the chapter surveyed the methods of seeking out and selecting the right lobbyist for the organization, and it outlined the various ways to pay for the services of these lobbyists. Once a lobbyist has been selected and retained, there are various ways to work with the lobbyist and evaluate his or her performance, so that the organization can decide whether to retain the lobbyist's services for another year. This chapter sought to unlock some of the mysteries behind hiring lobbyists and to assist organizations in making a determination as to whether they should embark on this hiring process.[5]

Endnotes

[1]J. Valerie Steele, ed., *Washington Representatives 2000* (Washington, DC: Columbia Books, 2000) 1–1277.

[2]John L. Zorak, *The Lobbying Handbook* (Washington, DC: John L. Zorak, 1990) 51–79.

[3]On a federal level, for example, further information regarding lobbying registration requirements and procedures may be obtained from Senate Office of Public Records, 232 Senate Hart Office Building, Washington, DC, 20510, phone 202-224-0758, and House Legislative Resource Center, 1036 Longworth House Office Building, Washington, DC, 20515, phone 202-225-1300.

[4]For example, the State of Illinois prohibits lobbyist compensation in the form of contingent fees; see Chapter 15, *Illinois State Law*, section 15.32, "Prohibited Practices/Principles." A complete review of other state prohibitions on contingency fees can be found in Peter C. Christianson et al., *Lobbying, PACs, and Campaign Finance 50 State Handbook* (St. Paul, MN: West Group, 2000), 1065.

[5]For further information on this subject, see Robert L. Guyer, *Guide to State Legislative Lobbying* (Gainesville, FL: Engineering THE LAW, Inc., 1999) 48–67; Michael E. Kastner, ed., *Creating and Managing an Association Government Relations Program*, (Washington, DC: American Society of Association Executives, 1998), 49–60; and Jerald A. Jacobs, *Association Law Handbook*, 3rd ed. (Washington, DC: American Society of Association Executives, 1996), 94–96.

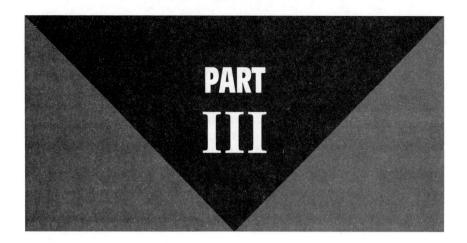

PART III

THE LEGAL ASPECTS OF GOVERNMENT AFFAIRS AND LOBBYING

WALTER P. PIDGEON, JR.

Part 2 highlighted the major methods that can be used to create a successful government affairs program, including creating a strong grassroots appeal and using a political action committee (PAC) to gain actual and perceived power. It also discussed significantly increasing your communications programs to gain visibility, forming partnerships with other organizations to gain greater attention from legislators and using consultants to widen your professional arsenal.

Part 3 contains one chapter, yet it is one of the most important subjects in the book. Chapter 7 is authored by Bruce Hopkins of Polsinelli, Shalton & White. Bruce is a well-known writer on the subject of law and the not-for-profit. This chapter provides an opportunity to review the legal aspects of government affairs and lobbying.

A complete review of the legal aspects of government affairs, as it relates to a not-for-profit, is a must for those who wish to protect and enhance the government affairs function. Throughout the book, we have discussed the opportunities for most not-for-profits to engage in the government affairs function. While there are many opportunities out there, you need to know the boundaries. Some not-for-profits can do more than others.

This chapter will discuss the differences between direct lobbying and grassroots lobbying and who can do what; ways to communicate properly with members; budget limitations; the measurement of allowable lobbying; work with affiliated groups; recordkeeping rules; and a variety of other areas that pertain to legal aspects of a sound government affairs function.

The Legal Aspects of Government Affairs and Lobbying

BRUCE R. HOPKINS

Introduction

Nonprofit organizations, to qualify as charitable entities, are required to meet several basic criteria, one of which, as stated in the Internal Revenue Code, is that "no substantial part of the activities" of the organizations may constitute "carrying on propaganda, or otherwise attempting, to influence legislation." Consequently, it is a fundamental principle of U.S. tax law that, to be tax-exempt and to be eligible to receive deductible charitable contributions, a charitable organization may not engage in a significant amount of effort to influence legislation, or *lobbying.*

Despite this limiting criterion, the charitable community can do far more in the way of lobbying than is generally realized. In general, however, there is much misunderstanding as to the scope of this prohibition, with many organizations believing the boundaries as to allowable lobbying to be far more restrictive than they actually are. Many forms of lobbying by charitable organizations are permissible, and some activities that are considered lobbying are, in reality, either the carrying out of exempt program functions or fund-raising. Generally, moreover, lobbying of the executive branch departments and agencies is not restricted by a general ban on lobbying by charitable groups.

Contemporary federal tax law provides three sets of rules concerning lobbying by charitable organizations:

1. The rules applicable to organizations that do not make or have revoked election of the elective rules (termed the *substantial part test*)
2. The elective rules (the *expenditure test*)
3. The rules for private foundations (lobbying is essentially prohibited)

These two tests are discussed below.

General Legislative History

The provision generally prohibiting legislative activities by tax-exempt charitable organizations was added to the federal tax law in 1934, without benefit of congressional hearings, in the form of a floor amendment in the Senate. Nonetheless, much statutory law has been added, since 1934, in the realm of legislative activities by charitable organizations. In 1969, Congress adopted special rules pertaining to legislative activities by private foundations. In 1976, Congress enacted so-called *elective* rules for eligible public charities. In 1987, Congress enacted law to introduce a system of taxes as penalties on charitable organizations (and sometimes their managers) for engaging in excessive lobbying.

Generally, a contribution to a charitable organization results in a charitable contribution deduction. However, where a charitable organization receives a contribution that is earmarked for use in influencing specific legislation, the contribution is not deductible as a charitable gift.

Definition of *Legislation*

An analysis of the rules concerning legislative activities by charitable organizations is best commenced with a discussion as to what constitutes *legislation* under the federal tax laws.

Substantial Part Test

The term *legislation,* as defined for purposes of the substantial part test, has several manifestations—principally, action by Congress, a state legislative body, a local council or similar governing body, and the general public in a referendum, an initiative, a constitutional amendment, or a similar procedure. *Legislation* generally does not include action by an executive branch of government, such as the promulgation of rules and regulations, nor does it include action by independent regulatory agencies. This is the case even where the support of a legislator is sought.

It is assumed that appropriations bills are items of legislation for federal tax purposes, although the term *legislation* is a derivative of the word *law,* which generally refers to rules of human conduct. By contrast, the enactment of an appropriations measure merely amounts to the establishment of budget authority—basically, authority in the executive branch to obligate and expend funds. Also, the term *legislation* includes proposals for the making of laws in countries other than the United States.

It is the view of the IRS that an attempt to influence the confirmation, by the U.S. Senate, of a federal judicial nominee constitutes, for these purposes, an attempt to influence legislation. This position is based on the definition of the term *legislation* found in the expenditure test, where the term is defined to include "resolutions" and "similar items."

Expenditure Test

The term *legislation,* as defined in the Internal Revenue Code, includes "action with respect to Acts, bills, resolutions, or similar items by the Congress, any State legislature, any local council, or similar governing body, or by the public in a referendum, initiative, constitutional amendment, or similar procedure." The term *legislation* also includes a proposed treaty required to be submitted by the president to the Senate for its advice and consent from the time the president's representative begins to negotiate its position with the prospective parties to the proposed treaty.

The position of the IRS that an attempt to influence the confirmation, by the U.S. Senate, of a federal judicial nominee constitutes an attempt to influence legislation is reflected in the expenditure test, in examples in the regulations.

Legislative Activities

It is essentially irrelevant, for purposes of classification of an organization as a charitable entity under federal tax law, that the legislation advocated would advance the charitable purposes for which the organization was created to promote. (Nonetheless, an important exception to this general rule are the activities sheltered by virtue of the *self-defense exception.*) This position should be contrasted with the state of the law prior to enactment of the Revenue Act of 1934.

Substantial Part Test

Although legislative activities take many forms, the law basically differentiates between *direct* lobbying and *grassroots* lobbying. Direct lobbying includes the presentation of testimony at public hearings held by legislative committees, in correspondence and conferences with legislators and their staffs, and in the publication of documents advocating specific legislative action. Grassroots lobbying consists of appeals to the general public to contact legislators or take other specific action on legislative matters.

Under the general rules, an organization is, according to the tax regulations, regarded as attempting to influence legislation if it "(1) contacts, or urges the public to contact, members of a legislative body for the purpose of proposing, supporting, or opposing legislation; or (2) advocates the adoption or rejection of legislation." Under these general rules, the charitable organization involved may be denominated an *action* organization and, hence, cannot qualify as a tax-exempt charitable entity.

There are two types of action organizations in the legislative activities context:

1. An organization as to which a "substantial part of its activities is attempting to influence legislation by propaganda or otherwise"
2. An organization as to which its "main or primary objective or objectives (as distinguished from its incidental or secondary objectives) may be attained only by legislation or a defeat of proposed legislation," and "it advocates, or campaigns for, the attainment of such main or primary objective or objectives as distinguished from engaging in nonpartisan analysis, study or research and making the results thereof available to the public"

For an organization to be denied or lose tax-exempt status because of lobbying activity, the legislative activities must be undertaken as an act of the organization itself. Thus, for example, the IRS has recognized that the legislative activities of a student newspaper are not attributable to the sponsoring university. Similarly, during the course of the anti–Vietnam War efforts on many college and university campuses, which included legislative activities, the principle was established that the activities by students and faculty were not official acts of the particular institution.

As noted in the following section on the substantial part test, legislative activities undertaken by a charitable organization at the written invitation of a legislative body or committee (but not an individual legislator) are not regarded as lobbying for these purposes. The same is true with respect to activities that constitute nonpartisan analysis, study, and research.

Expenditure Test

Under the expenditure test, as previously noted, the definition of *legislation* includes the term *action*. The term *action* is "limited to the introduction, amendment, enactment, defeat, or repeal of Acts, bills, resolutions, or similar items."

Definition of Influencing Legislation

These rules, as provided in the regulations, define the term *influencing legislation* in two ways:

1. Any attempt to influence any legislation through communication with any member or employee of a legislative body or with any other governmental official or employee who may participate in the formulation of the legislation (a *direct lobbying communication*)
2. Any attempt to influence any legislation through an attempt to affect the opinions of the general public or any segment of the public (a *grassroots lobbying communication*)

A charitable organization's lobbying expenditures for a year are the sum of its expenditures during that year for direct lobbying communications (*direct lobbying expenditures*) and for grassroots lobbying communications (*grassroots expenditures*).

Direct Lobbying

A communication with a legislator or government official, or an employee of either, is a direct lobbying communication only where the communication refers to *specific legislation* and reflects a view on the legislation. In addition, where the communication is with a government official or employee, the communication is a direct lobbying communication only where the principal purpose of the communication is to influence legislation.

The term *specific legislation*, as stated in tax regulations, means "legislation that has already been introduced in a legislative body and a specific legislative proposal that an organization either supports or opposes." In the case of a referendum, a ballot initiative, a constitutional amendment, or another measure that is placed on the ballot by petitions signed by a required number or percentage of voters, an item becomes specific legislation when the petition is first circulated among the voters for signature.

Where a communication refers to and reflects a view on a measure that is the subject of a referendum, ballot initiative, or similar procedure and is made to the members of the general public in the jurisdiction where the vote will occur, the communication is generally a direct lobbying communication. This is because the members of the general public are, for this purpose, considered legislators. Nonetheless, it is possible that this type of communication will be exempted from classification as a direct lobbying communication on the ground that it is nonpartisan analysis, study, or research.

Grassroots Lobbying

A communication is regarded as a grassroots communication only where the communication refers to specific legislation, reflects a view on the legislation, and encourages the recipient of the communication to take action with respect to the legislation. The IRS considers this definition to be "very lenient," because it "will permit many clear advocacy communications to be treated as NONlobbying." The IRS commentary on this definition adds: "This is part of the Service's attempt to maintain a careful balance between the statutory limits on electing public charities' lobbying expenditures and the desire of those organizations to involve themselves in the public policy making process to the greatest extent consistent with those statutory limits." There is no question that many charitable organizations can engage in advocacy efforts without, by reason of these rules, crossing the line whereby the efforts would be considered grassroots lobbying. One of the principal ways in which advocacy efforts can avoid classification as grassroots lobbying is to refrain from including in the communication a *"call to action."* As the following examples illustrate, a charitable organization can easily engage in what may be called generic grassroots lobbying, without having the effort classified as grassroots lobbying for tax purposes, by using means of communication about the organization's stance on issues and pending legislation that only the most unconscious among its constituency will fail to understand. Simply put, it is not very difficult for an organization to communicate its views on legislative matters to the general public, while sidestepping the snare of the requisite call to action.

As previously noted, the term *specific legislation* is legislation that has already been introduced in a legislative body and a specific legislative proposal that the organization supports or opposes. Also, as previously noted, in the case of a referendum, a ballot initiative, a constitutional amendment, or another measure that is placed on the ballot by petitions, an item becomes specific legislation when the petition is first circulated among the voters for signature.

The scope of the concept of grassroots lobbying is constrained not only by the definition of the term *specific legislation* but also by the phrase "encouraging the recipient . . . to take action." Encouraging a recipient to take action with respect to legislation means that the communication does at least one of the following:

1. States that the recipient should contact a legislator or an employee of a legislative body or should contact any other governmental official or employee who may participate in the formulation of legislation
2. States the address, telephone number, or similar information about a legislator or an employee of a legislative body
3. Provides a petition, tear-off postcard, or similar material for the recipient to communicate with a legislator or an employee of a legislative body or with any other government official or employee who may participate in the formulation of legislation
4. Specifically identifies one or more legislators who will vote on the legislation as opposing the communication's view with respect to the legislation, being undecided with respect to the legislation, being the recipient's representative in the legislature, or being a member of the legislative committee or subcommittee that will consider the legislation

With respect to the fourth category, a communication specifically identifying one or more legislators who will vote on the legislation as supporting the communication's view with respect to the legislation is not a grassroots lobbying communication as long as the communication does not otherwise specifically identify (as previously defined) the legislator and/or is not otherwise a grassroots lobbying communication because it is classified in one or more of the other three categories. Also, as to this fourth category, encouraging the recipient to take action does not include naming the main sponsor(s) of the legislation for purposes of identifying the legislation.

Communications described in one or more of the first three categories not only encourage but also directly encourage the recipient to take action with respect to legislation. Communications described in the fourth category, however, do not directly encourage the recipient to take action with respect to legislation. Thus, a communication would encourage the recipient to take action with respect to legislation but not directly encourage the action, if the communication does no more than identify one or more legislators who will vote on the legislation as opposing the communication's view with respect to the legislation, being undecided with respect to the legislation, being the recipient's representative in the legislature, or being a member of the legislative committee or subcommittee that will consider the legislation. Communications that encourage the recipient to take action with respect to legislation but that do not directly encourage the recipient to take action with respect to legislation may be within the exception for *nonpartisan, study, or research* and, thus, not be grassroots lobbying communications.

Mass Media Advertising

A mass media advertisement that is not a grassroots lobbying communication under the three-part grassroots lobbying definition may nonetheless be a grassroots lobbying communication by virtue of a rule that is applicable to a limited type of paid advertisement in the mass media. For these purposes, the term *mass media* means television, radio, billboards, and general circulation newspapers and magazines. (It may also include the Internet.) General circulation newspapers and magazines do not include newspapers or magazines published by a charitable organization that has elected the expenditure test and where the election is in effect, except where the total circulation of the newspaper or magazine is greater than 100,000 and fewer than one-half of the recipients are members of the organization. Where an electing charity is itself a mass media publisher or broadcaster, all portions of that organization's mass media publications or broadcasts are treated as paid advertisements in the mass media, except the specific portions that are advertisements paid for by another person.

It is presumed that a mass media advertisement, paid for by a charitable organization, is grassroots lobbying if it (1) is made within two weeks before a vote by a legislative body, or committee (but not a subcommittee) of a legislative body, on a "highly publicized" piece of legislation; (2) reflects a view on the general subject of the legislation; and (3) either refers to the legislation or encourages the public to communicate with legislators on the general subject of the legislation. The presumption can be rebutted by demonstrating either that the charitable organization regularly makes similar mass media communications without regard to the timing of legislation (a "customary course of business" exception) or that the timing of the paid advertisement was unrelated to the upcoming vote. However, even if there is a successful rebuttal in this regard, a mass media communication is a grassroots lobbying communication if the communication would be a grassroots lobbying communication under the general rules describing that term.

Advocacy Communications

The law imposes rules concerning the situation where expenses incurred for what are initially nonlobbying communications can subsequently be characterized as grassroots lobbying expenditures where the materials or other communications are later used in a lobbying effort. For this result to occur, the materials must be "advocacy communications or research materials," which are any communications or materials that both refer to and reflect a view on specific legislation but that do not, in their initial format, contain a direct encouragement for recipients to take action with respect to legislation.

Where advocacy communications or research materials are subsequently accompanied by a direct encouragement for recipients to take action with respect to legislation, the advocacy communications or research materials themselves are treated as grassroots lobbying communications, unless the primary purpose of the organization in undertaking or preparing the communications or materials was not for use in lobbying. In the absence of this primary purpose, all expenses of preparing and distributing the advocacy communications or research materials will be treated as grassroots expenditures; in the case of subsequent distribution of the materials by another organization, however, the characterization of expenditures as grassroots lobbying expenditures under this rule applies only to expenditures paid less than six months before the first use of the advocacy communications or research materials with a direct encouragement to action.

The primary purpose of the organization in undertaking or preparing advocacy communications or research materials will not be considered to be for use in lobbying if, prior to or contemporaneously with the use of the advocacy communications or research materials with the direct encouragement to action, the organization makes a substantial nonlobbying distribution of the advocacy communications or research materials (without the direct encouragement to action). Whether a distribution is "substantial" is determined by reference to all of the facts and circumstances, including the normal distribution pattern of similar nonpartisan analyses, studies, or research by that and similar organizations. In the case of advocacy communications or research materials that are not nonpartisan analysis, study, or research, the nonlobbying distribution of them will not be considered substantial unless the distribution is at least as extensive as the lobbying distribution of them.

Where the nonlobbying distribution of advocacy communications or research materials is not substantial, all of the facts and circumstances must be weighed to determine whether the organization's primary purpose in preparing the communications or materials was for use in lobbying. While not the only factor, the extent of the organization's nonlobbying distribution of the communications or materials is particularly relevant, especially when compared with the extent of their distribution with the direct encouragement to action. Another particularly relevant factor is whether the lobbying use of the advocacy communications or research materials is by the organization that prepared the document, a related organization, or an unrelated organization. Where the subsequent lobbying distribution is made by an unrelated organization, there must be "clear and convincing" evidence (which must include evidence demonstrating cooperation or collusion between the two organizations) to establish that the primary purpose for preparing the communication was for use in lobbying.

Membership Communications

Expenditures for certain communications between a charitable organization and its members are treated more leniently than are communications to nonmembers. A person is a member of a charitable organization if the person pays dues or makes a contribution of more than a nominal amount, makes a contribution of more than a nominal amount of time, or is one of a limited number of "honorary" or "life" members who have more than a nominal connection with the organization and who have been chosen for a valid reason (such as length of service to the organization or involvement in activities forming the basis of the organization's tax exemption) unrelated to the organization's dissemination of information to its members. A person who is not a member of an organization by reason of the foregoing definition may be nonetheless treated as a member if the organization demonstrates to the satisfaction of the IRS that there is a good reason for the fact that its membership requirements do not meet the terms of this definition and that its membership requirements do not operate to permit an abuse of these rules.

A person who is a member of a charitable organization that is a member of an "affiliated group of organizations" is treated as a member of each of the organizations in the affiliated group. A person who is a member of an organization that is a member of a limited affiliated group of organizations is treated as a member of each organization in the limited affiliated group, but only to the extent that the communication relates to a *national legislative issue*. A *limited affiliated group* is, as discussed below, one where there are no interlocking boards or where members do not bind other members on legislative issues, other than national legislative issues.

Expenditures for a communication that refers to, and reflects a view on, specific legislation are not lobbying expenditures if the communication satisfies each of the following requirements:

1. The communication is directed only to members of the organization.
2. The specific legislation to which the communication refers, and on which it reflects a view, is of direct interest to the organization and its members.

3. The communication does not directly encourage the member to engage in direct lobbying (whether individually or through the organization).
4. The communication does not directly encourage the member to engage in grassroots lobbying (whether individually or through the organization).

A communication between an organization and a member of the organization made to directly encourage the member to engage in direct lobbying is itself considered direct lobbying. Thus, expenditures for a communication that refers to, and reflects a view on, specific legislation and that satisfies the first, second, and fourth of the requirements, but not the third, are treated as expenditures for direct lobbying. A communication between an organization and a member of the organization made to directly encourage the member to urge persons other than members to engage in direct or grassroots lobbying is considered grassroots lobbying. Thus, expenditures for a communication that refers to, and reflects a view on, specific legislation, and that satisfies the first and second of the listed requirements, but not the fourth, are treated as grassroots lobbying expenditures (irrespective of whether the third of these requirements is satisfied).

Expenditures for any written communication that is designed primarily for members of an organization (but not directed only to members) and that refers to, and reflects a view on, specific legislation of direct interest to the organization and its members are treated as expenditures for direct or grassroots lobbying, depending on the type of lobbying that the communication encourages. If this type of communication directly encourages readers to engage individually or through the organization in direct lobbying but does not directly encourage them to engage in grassroots lobbying, the cost of the communication is allocated between expenditures for direct lobbying and grassroots expenditures. The portion of the cost to be allocated includes all costs of preparing all the material with respect to which readers are urged to engage in direct lobbying, plus the mechanical and distribution costs attributable to the lineage devoted to this material. The amount allocable as a grassroots expenditure for this type of communication is the amount calculated under the rules for communications where only direct lobbying is directly encouraged multiplied by the sum of the nonmember subscribers percentage and the "all other distribution percentage." For these purposes, the nonmember subscribers percentage is treated as zero unless it is greater than 15 percent of total distribution.

Earmarking

A transfer is a grassroots expenditure to the extent it is earmarked for grassroots lobbying purposes and is not a particular type of transfer that is not an exempt purpose expenditure. A transfer, including a grant or payment of dues, is earmarked for a specific purpose

1. To the extent that the transferor directs the transferee to add the amount transferred to a fund established to accomplish the purpose or
2. To the extent of the amount transferred or, if less, the amount agreed on to be expended to accomplish the purpose, if there exists an agreement, oral or written, whereby the transferor may cause the transferee to expend amounts to accomplish the purpose or whereby the transferee agrees to expend an amount to accomplish the purpose.

A transfer that is earmarked for direct lobbying purposes, or for direct lobbying and grassroots lobbying purposes, is regarded as a grassroots expenditure in full, unless the transferor can demonstrate that all or part of the amounts transferred were expended for direct lobbying purposes, in which case the part of the amounts transferred is a direct lobbying expenditure by the transferor. The regulations provide rules for treating as a lobbying (direct or grassroots) expenditure transfers for less than fair market value from a public charity, which has elected the expenditure test, to any noncharity that makes lobbying expenditures.

Allocation Rules

The regulations provide allocation rules for communications that have a lobbying and a nonlobbying purpose. These rules differentiate costs of a communication that may be considered direct lobbying, grassroots lobbying, or a nonlobbying expenditure. Expenditures for either type of lobbying (*lobbying expenditures*) include amounts paid or incurred as current or deferred compensation for an employee's services attributable to lobbying, and the allocable portion of administrative, overhead, and other general expenditures attributable to lobbying, such as expenditures for researching, drafting, reviewing, copying, publishing, and mailing a direct or grassroots lobbying communication, as well as an allocable share of overhead expenses.

One rule requires that the allocation between the amount expended for the lobbying purpose and the amount expended for the nonlobbying purpose be reasonable. This rule applies to a charitable organization's lobbying communication that also has a bona fide nonlobbying purpose and that is sent only or primarily to its members. A charitable organization that includes as a lobbying expenditure only the amount expended for a specific sentence or sentences that encourage the recipient to take action with respect to legislation is not considered to have made a reasonable allocation.

The other allocation rule is for nonmembership communications. Where a nonmembership lobbying communication also has a bona fide nonlobbying purpose, an organization must include as lobbying expenditures all costs attributable to the parts of the communication that are on the same specific subject as the lobbying message. Whether or not a portion of a communication is on the same specific subject as the lobbying message depends on the surrounding facts and circumstances. In general, a portion of a communication is on the same specific subject as the lobbying message if that portion discusses an activity or a specific issue that would be directly affected by the specific legislation that is the subject of the lobbying message. Thus, for the expenditure to be a lobbying one in these circumstances, the activity or issue involved must be affected by legislation referenced in the message, and the legislation must be "specific"; otherwise, the portion of the communication is not lobbying. Discussion of the background or consequences of the specific legislation, or discussion of the background or consequences of an activity or a specific issue affected by the specific legislation, is also considered to be on the same specific subject as the lobbying communication.

If a communication (other than to an organization's members) is both a direct lobbying communication and a grassroots lobbying communication, the communication is treated as a grassroots lobbying communication, unless the charitable organization is able to demonstrate that the communication was made primarily for direct lobbying purposes, in which case a reasonable allocation between the direct and grassroots lobbying purposes is permitted.

Exceptions to Lobbying Activities

Notwithstanding the foregoing rules, certain activities, that may be related to lobbying, are not regarded as lobbying activities for tax purposes. More of the true exceptions are those available as part of the expenditure test.

Substantial Part Test

There are no statutory exceptions to the substantial part test, except to the extent an activity is regarded as a program activity by reason of the operational test. That is, if an activity qualifies as charitable, educational, scientific, religious, or the like, it almost certainly is not a lobbying activity.

Nonpartisan Activities

It is from this perspective that the law has developed an exception, from the substantial part test, for activities that constitute making available the results of nonpartisan analysis, study, or research. This exception is much like the one provided in the context of the expenditure test.

An organization may engage in nonpartisan analysis, study, and research and publish the results (much of which is charitable, educational, and/or scientific activity), where some of the plans and policies formulated can be carried out only through legislative enactments, without being an action organization, as long as it does not advocate the adoption of legislation or legislative action to implement its findings. That is, an organization may evaluate a subject of proposed legislation or a pending item of legislation and present to the public an objective analysis of it as long as it does not participate in the presentation of suggested bills to the legislature and does not engage in any campaign to secure the enactment of the legislation. However, if the organization's primary objective can be attained only by legislative action, it is an action organization and cannot be tax-exempt as a charitable entity. In general, promoting activism instead of promoting charitable, educational, scientific, religious, and like activities can deny an organization classification as a charitable entity.

As for the specific connotation of the term *propaganda*, it appears clear that the term is not as expansive as merely spreading particular beliefs, opinions, or doctrines. Rather, the word connotes public address with selfish or ulterior purpose and characterized by the coloring or distortion of facts.

Until the rules are accorded additional clarification, it is inadvisable to borrow too heavily from the expenditure test rules in interpreting the substantial part rules. Still, it seems fair to observe that the exception for nonpartisan analysis, study, and research is substantively the same in both settings.

Analysis of Broad Social, Economic, and Similar Problems

While the expenditure test contains an exception for the analysis of broad social, economic, and similar problems, there is no such specific exception that is an element of the substantial part test. Much of this type of analysis, however, falls within the scope of what is generally regarded as charitable, educational, scientific, religious, and like activity and, to that extent, can be regarded as an exception to the substantial part test definition of *legislative activities*.

Membership Communications

While the expenditure test contains an exception for membership communications, there is no such exception that is an element of the substantial part test. Much of this type of analysis, however, falls within the scope of what is generally regarded as charitable, educational, scientific, religious, and like activity and, to that extent, can be regarded as an exception to the substantial part test definition of *legislative activities*.

Again, where the activity is one of monitoring legislation, rather than attempting to influence the legislative process, the activity is not likely to be considered lobbying. This is particularly the case where the persons receiving the information are members of the organization.

Requests for Technical Advice

While the expenditure test contains an exception for certain requests for technical advice, there is no such statutory exception that is an element of the substantial part test.

Nonetheless, the IRS has conceded that a charitable organization that does not initiate any action with respect to pending legislation but merely responds to a request from a legislative committee to testify is not, solely because of the activity, an action organization. To sustain this exception, the IRS has stated that (1) proscribed attempts to influence legislation "imply an affirmative act and require something more than a mere passive response to a Committee invitation" and (2) "it is unlikely that Congress, in framing the language of this provision, intended to deny itself access to the best technical expertise available on any matter with which it concerns itself."

Thus, while some of the details may be different, both the substantial part test and the expenditure test involve exceptions for the provision of technical advice to legislative bodies.

Self-Defense Communications

While the expenditure test contains an exception for certain self-defense communications, there is no such statutory exception that is an element of the substantial part test.

It is possible, however, that this type of communication would be exempted by the exceptions for nonpartisan analysis, membership communications, or provision of technical advice. Further, First Amendment considerations would be most compelling in this context.

Expenditure Test

Six categories of activities are excluded from the term *influencing legislation* for purposes of the expenditure test:

1. Making available the results of nonpartisan analysis, study, or research
2. Providing technical advice or assistance to a governmental body or legislative committee in response to a written request by the body or committee
3. Appearances before, or communications to, any legislative body with respect to a possible decision of that body that might affect the existence of the organization, its powers and duties, its tax-exempt status, or the deduction of contributions to it (the *self-defense exception*)
4. Communications between the organization and its bona fide members with respect to legislation or proposed legislation of direct interest to it and them, unless the communications directly encourage the members to influence legislation or directly encourage the members to urge nonmembers to influence legislation

5. Routine communications with government officials or employees

6. Examinations and discussions of broad social, economic, and similar problems, even if the problems are of the type with which government would be expected to deal ultimately

Nonpartisan Activities

Activities constituting *nonpartisan analysis, study,* or *research* are neither direct lobbying communications nor grassroots lobbying communications.

For the purpose of this exception, "nonpartisan analysis, study, or research" means an independent and objective exposition of a particular subject matter, including any activity that is *educational* for federal tax purposes. Thus, nonpartisan analysis, study, or research may advocate a particular position or viewpoint as long as there is a "sufficiently full and fair exposition of the pertinent facts to enable the public or an individual to form an independent opinion or conclusion." The mere presentation of unsupported opinion, however, does not qualify as nonpartisan analysis, study, or research.

Normally, a determination as to whether a publication or broadcast qualifies as nonpartisan analysis, study, or research is undertaken on a presentation-by-presentation basis. If a publication or broadcast is one of a series prepared or supported by an electing organization and the series as a whole qualifies as nonpartisan analysis, study, or research, then any individual publication or broadcast within the series is not a direct or grassroots lobbying communication, even though an individual broadcast or publication does not, by itself, meet the standards of the exception. While the determination of a broadcast or publication as part of a series ordinarily depends on all of the facts and circumstances of each situation, with respect to broadcast activities, all broadcasts within any period of six consecutive months ordinarily is eligible to be considered part of a series.

Organizations, however, must exercise caution when relying on this series portion of the exception. This is because if an electing organization times or channels a part of this type of a series in a manner designed to influence the general public or the action of a legislative body with respect to a specific legislative proposal, the expenses of preparing and distributing the part of the analysis, study, or research will be treated as expenditures for a direct or grassroots lobbying communication, as the case may be.

An organization may choose any suitable means, including oral or written presentations, to distribute the results of its nonpartisan analysis, study, or research, with or without charge. These means include the distribution of reprints of speeches, articles, and reports; the presentation of information through conferences, meetings, and discussions; dissemination to the news media, including radio, television, and newspapers; and the use of other public forums.

Once again, however, this aspect of this exception must be used cautiously, in that the IRS has created a rule that potentially erodes this aspect of the exception. That is, for these purposes, the communications may not be limited to, or directed toward, persons who are interested solely in one side of a particular issue. It does not require much elaboration of the point to speculate how an organization is to divine the scope of persons' "interests" for this purpose.

There is a third difficulty with respect to this exception for nonpartisan analysis, study, or research. This is the fact that, even though certain analysis, study, or research is initially within the exception, subsequent use of the analysis, study, or research for grassroots lobbying may cause the activity to be treated as a grassroots lobbying communication that is not within this exception. (This rule does not cause any analysis, study, or research to be considered a direct lobbying communication.)

Moreover, a communication that reflects a view on specific legislation is not within the realm of this exception if the communication directly encourages the recipient to take action with respect to the legislation. The rules as to when a communication directly encourages the recipient to take action with respect to legislation are discussed. A communication encourages the recipient to take action with respect to legislation, but not directly encourage action, if the communication does no more than specifically identify one or more legislators who will vote on the legislation as opposing the view of the communication with respect to the legislation, as being undecided with respect to the legislation, as being the recipient's representative in the legislature, or as being a member of the legislative committee or subcommittee that will consider the legislation.

Membership Communications

The rules concerning membership communications are significant, as previously discussed. Expenditures for a communication that refers to, and reflects a view on, specific legislation are not lobbying expenditures if the communication satisfies the following requirements: (1) the communication is directed only to members of the organization; (2) the specific legislation the communication refers to, and reflects a view on, is of direct interest to the organization and its members; (3) the communication does not directly encourage the members to engage in direct lobbying; and (4) the communication does not directly encourage the members to engage in grassroots lobbying. An expenditure that meets the first, second, and fourth requirements is treated as an expenditure for direct lobbying. An expenditure that satisfies the first, second, and third requirements is treated as an expenditure for grassroots lobbying. The regulations provide rules by which expenditures for any written communication that is designed primarily for members of an organization, and that refers to, and reflects a view on, specific legislation of direct interest to the organization and its members are treated as expenditures for direct or grassroots lobbying.

Analysis of Broad Social, Economic, and Similar Problems

Examinations and discussions of broad social, economic, and similar problems are neither direct lobbying communications nor grassroots lobbying communications, even if the problems are of the type with which government would be expected to deal ultimately. Thus, lobbying communications do not include public discussion or communications with members of legislative bodies or governmental employees, the general subject of which is also the subject of legislation before a legislative body, as long as the discussion does not address the merits of a specific legislative proposal and as long as the discussion does not directly encourage recipients to take action with respect to legislation. For example, this exception excludes from grassroots lobbying an organization's discussions of problems, such as environmental pollution or population growth, that are being considered by Congress and various state legislatures, but only where the discussions are not directly addressed to specific legislation being considered and only where the discussions do not directly encourage recipients of the communication to contact a legislator, an employee of a legislative body, or a government official or employee who may participate in the formulation of legislation.

Requests for Technical Advice

A communication is not a direct lobbying communication if the communication is the provision of technical advice or assistance to a governmental body, a governmental committee, or a subdivision of either in response to a written request by the body, committee, or subcommittee. The request for assistance or advice must be made in the name of the requesting body, committee, or subdivision rather than an individual member of one or more of these entities. Similarly, the response to one of these requests must be available to every member of the requesting entity. For example, in the case of a written response to a request for technical advice or assistance from a congressional committee, the response will be considered available to every member of the requesting committee if the response is submitted to the person making the request in the name of the committee and it is made clear that the response is for the use of all of the members of the committee.

Technical advice or assistance may be given as a result of knowledge or skill in a given area. Because the advice or assistance may be given only at the express request of a governmental body, committee, or subdivision, the oral or written presentation of the assistance or advice need not qualify as nonpartisan analysis, study, or research. The offering of opinions or recommendations ordinarily qualify under this exception only if the opinions or recommendations are specifically requested by the governmental body, committee, or subdivision or are directly related to the materials so requested.

Self-Defense Communications

A communication is not a direct lobbying communication if

1. The communication is an appearance before, or communication with, any legislative body with respect to a possible action by the body that might affect the existence of the electing public charity, its powers and duties, its tax-exempt status, or the deductibility of contributions to the organization.

2. The communication is by a member of an affiliated group of organizations and is an appearance before, or communication with, a legislative body with respect to a possible action by the body that might affect the existence of any other member of the group, its powers and duties, its tax-exempt status, or the deductibility of contributions to it.

3. The communication is by an electing public charity, more than 75 percent of the members of which are other charitable organizations, and is an appearance before, or communication with, any legislative body with respect to a possible action by the body that might affect the existence of one or more of the charitable member organizations, their powers, duties, or tax-exempt status or the deductibility, as charitable gifts, of contributions to one or more of the charitable member organizations, but only if the principal purpose of the appearance or communication is to defend the charitable member organizations (rather than the noncharitable member organizations).

4. The communication is by an electing public charity that is a member of a limited group of organizations and is an appearance before, or communication with, the Congress of the United States with respect to a possible action by the Congress that might affect the existence of any member of the limited affiliated group, its powers and duties, its tax-exempt status, or the deductibility of contributions to it.

Under any of the four elements of this exception, a charitable organization may communicate with the entire legislative body, committees, or sub-committees of the body, individual legislators, members of their staffs, or representatives of the executive branch who are involved in the legislative process, if the communication is limited to the prescribed subjects. Similarly, under this exception, an organization may make expenditures in order to initiate legislation if the legislation concerns only matters that might affect the existence of the organization, its powers and duties, its tax-exempt status, or the deductibility of contributions to it.

Measurement of Allowable Lobbying

The federal tax rules concerning limitations on legislative activities by charitable organizations, other than private foundations, contain three essential elements: the meaning of the term *legislation,* the meaning of the term *influencing* legislation, and—the most significant of these elements—the concept of a *substantial* part of a charitable organization's activities.

Substantial Part Test

A determination as to whether a specific activity or category of activities of a charitable organization is, for these purposes, *substantial* must basically be a factual one. Indeed, until enactment of the expenditure test, discussed in the following paragraphs, the law offered no formula for computing substantial or insubstantial legislative undertakings. Thus, the Senate Finance Committee, in its report accompanying the Tax Reform Act of 1969, said that "the standards as to the permissible level of [legislative] activities under the present law are so vague as to encourage subjective application of the sanction. In its report accompanying the Tax Reform Act of 1976, the Senate Finance Committee portrayed the dilemma this way: "Many believe that the standards as to the permissible level of [legislative] activities under present law are too vague and thereby tend to encourage subjective and selective enforcement.

One approach to attempting to measure substantiality in this context is to determine what percentage of an organization's spending is devoted on an annual basis to efforts to influence legislation. (This is essentially the approach underlying the expenditure test.) However, the limitation on influencing legislation involves more than simply a curb on expenditures or diversions of funds; it includes restrictions on certain levels of activity as well. A portion of an organization's efforts and activities devoted to legislative activities may well be regarded as more important than the organization's expenditures for the purpose.

Thus, it is clear that the meaning of the term *substantial* in this setting is unknown. (That is largely why the expenditure test was established.) Still, it is not reckless speculation to assert that 10 percent or less of something is insubstantial. *Insubstantial* is probably synonymous with *slight; substantial* is the same as *ample* or *considerable.*

The tax law frequently uses terms such as *exclusively* and *primarily. Exclusively* literally means "all," or 100 percent. *Primarily* means more than one-half, probably 65 percent. In the tax-exempt organizations context, *substantially all* has often been defined to mean at least 85 percent. Thus, *insubstantial* is probably in the range of no more than 10 or 15 percent. For some, defining *insubstantiality* as up to 15 percent of expenditures or activities may seem too aggressive. But certainly a 10 percent ceiling is not unreasonable, with 15 percent perhaps used as a warning level. When lobbying expenditures are deemed by the management of a charitable organization, which is attempting to operate within the substantial part test, to be approaching a level that is "too high," the organization generally has three options: (1) discontinue lobbying activities that take the organization beyond the boundary of insubstantiality; (2) elect the expenditure test (if that would alleviate the problem); or (3) place the lobbying activities in a separate, affiliated organization.

In the context of activities, however, a percentage standard may be of less utility. An exempt organization enjoying considerable prestige and influence might be considered as having a substantial impact on the legislative process solely on the basis of a single official position statement, an activity considered negligible when measured according to a percentage standard of time expended. A standard such as this, however, would tend to place undue emphasis on whether or not a particular legislative effort was successful.

In 1972, the U.S. Court of Appeals for the Tenth Circuit gave a new dimension to the concept of "attempting to influence legislation," when it upheld the revocation of tax exemption of a ministry organization. The court, after holding that the pertinent income tax regulations properly interpret the intent of Congress (before enactment of the expenditure test), found the following substantial legislative activities: articles constituting appeals to the public to react to certain issues, support or opposition to specific terms of legislation and enactments, and efforts to cause members of the public to contact members of Congress on various matters. Of particular consequence was the court's explicit rejection of a percentage test in determining substantiality, which was dismissed as obscuring the "complexity of balancing the organization's activities in relation to its objectives and circumstances." Said the court: "The political [i.e., legislative] activities of an organization must be balanced in the context of the objectives and circumstances of the organization to determine whether a substantial part of its activities was to influence or attempt to influence legislation."

Expenditure Test

Because of the considerable and continuing uncertainty as to the meaning and scope of the rules proscribing legislative activities by charitable organizations, Congress, in enacting the Tax Reform Act of 1976, sought to clarify and amplify the proscription. While the difficulties of compliance with the legislative activities limitation have been manifold, perhaps the greatest dilemma has been in relation to ascertainment of the method by which substantial activities are determined—that is, whether such activities are a function of time expended, funds spent, or another criterion.

Mechanical Test

The expenditure test involves an attempt to use a mechanical test for measuring permissible and impermissible ranges of lobbying expenditures by eligible charitable organizations and does so, as noted, in terms of the expenditure of funds and a sliding scale of percentages. (Technically, the basic concept that legislative activities cannot be a substantial portion of the undertakings of a charitable organization was not altered by enactment of the expenditure test.)

Exempt Purpose Expenditures

These standards to allowable lobbying expenditures are formulated in terms of declining percentages of total *exempt purpose expenditures*. In general, an expenditure is an exempt purpose expenditure for a tax year if it is paid or incurred by an electing public charity to accomplish the organization's exempt purposes. These expenditures include the following:

1. Those paid or incurred to accomplish one or more charitable purposes, including most grants made for charitable ends
2. Amounts paid or incurred as employee compensation (current or deferred) in furtherance of a charitable purpose
3. The portion of administrative expenses allocable to a charitable purpose
4. All lobbying expenditures
5. Amounts expended for nonpartisan analysis, study, or research
6. Amounts expended for examinations of broad social, economic, and similar problems
7. Amounts expended in response to requests for technical advice
8. Amounts expended pursuant to the self-defense exception
9. Amounts expended for communications to members that are not lobbying expenditures
10. A reasonable allowance for straight-line depreciation or amortization of charitable assets
11. Certain fund-raising expenditures

A charitable organization's transfer is treated as an exempt function expenditure if it is one of two types. One of these types of transfers is a transfer that is made to a charitable organization in furtherance of the transferor's exempt purposes and that is not earmarked for a noncharitable purpose. For example, a payment of dues by a local or state organization to a state or national charitable organization, respectively, is an exempt purpose expenditure of the transferor to the extent it is not otherwise earmarked. The second type of transfer is a controlled grant, but only to the extent of the amounts that are paid or incurred by the transferee that would be exempt purpose expenditures if paid or incurred by the transferor. There are certain types of transfers that are not regarded as exempt function expenditures.

The term *exempt function expenditure* does not include the following:

1. Amounts paid or incurred that are not for purposes described in the preceding first through nine, and eleven, items
2. The amount of transfers to members of an affiliated group, made to artificially inflate the amount of exempt function expenditures, or to certain noncharitable organizations
3. Amounts paid to or incurred for a *separate fund-raising unit* of the organization or to an affiliated organization
4. Amounts paid to or incurred for any person who is not an employee or any organization that is not an affiliated organization, if paid or incurred primarily for fund-raising, but only if the person or organization engages in fund-raising, fund-raising counseling, or the provision of similar advice or services
5. Amounts paid or incurred that are properly chargeable to a capital account with respect to an unrelated trade or business
6. Amounts paid or incurred for a tax that is not imposed in connection with the organization's efforts to accomplish charitable purposes (such as the unrelated business income tax)
7. Amounts paid or incurred for the production of income, where the income-producing activity is not substantially related to exempt functions (such as the costs of maintaining an endowment)

An organization's transfer is not an exempt function expenditure if it is one of three types. First, a transfer is not an exempt function expenditure if it is made to a member of any affiliated group of which the transferor is a member. Second, transfer is not an exempt function expenditure if the IRS determines that the transfer artificially inflates the amount of the transferor's or transferee's exempt function expenditures. In general, the IRS will make that determination if a substantial purpose of a transfer is to inflate those exempt function expenditures. A transfer of this type is generally not considered an exempt function expenditure of the transferor; however, this type of transfer is an exempt function expenditure of the transferee to the extent that the transferee expends the transferred amount in the active conduct of its charitable activities or attempts to influence legislation. Third, a transfer is not an exempt function expenditure if it is not a controlled grant and is made to a noncharitable organization that does not attempt to influence legislation.

Fund-Raising Expenses

For these purposes, the term *fund-raising* includes three practices:

1. The solicitation of dues or contributions from members of the organization, from persons whose dues are in arrears, or from the general public

2. The solicitation of gifts from businesses or gifts or grants from other organizations, including charitable organizations

3. The solicitation of grants from a governmental unit or any agency or instrumentality of the unit

A *separate fund-raising unit* of an organization, as provided in tax regulations, "must consist of either two or more individuals, a majority of whose time is spent on fundraising for the organization, or any separate accounting unit of the organization that is devoted to fundraising." Also, the tax regulations provide that "amounts paid to or incurred for a separate fundraising unit include all amounts incurred for the creation, production, copying, and distribution of the fundraising portion of a separate fundraising unit's communication."

The Computing of Lobbying Amounts

The basic permitted annual level of expenditures for legislative efforts (the *lobbying nontaxable amount*) is determined by using a sliding scale percentage of the organization's exempt function expenditures, as follows: 20 percent of the first $500,000 of an organization's expenditures for an exempt function, plus 15 percent of the next $500,000, 10 percent of the next $500,000, and 5 percent of any remaining expenditures. The total amount spent for legislative activities in any one year by an eligible charitable organization, however, may not exceed $1 million. A separate limitation—amounting to 25 percent of the foregoing amounts—is imposed on attempts to influence the general public on legislative matters (the *grassroots nontaxable amount*).

A charitable organization that has elected the expenditure test and that exceeds either or both of these limitations becomes subject to an excise tax in the amount of 25 percent of the excess lobbying expenditures. As respects these two limitations, the tax falls on the greater of the two excesses. If an electing organization's lobbying expenditures normally (that is, on average over a four-year period) exceed 150 percent of either limitation (the *lobbying ceiling amount* or the *grassroots ceiling amount*), it will lose its tax-exempt status as a charitable entity. A charitable organization in this circumstance is not able to convert to a tax-exempt social welfare organization.

There is a special exception with respect to the first, second, or third consecutive determination year for which an organization's first expenditure test election is in effect. Pursuant to this exception, a determination as to the organization's ongoing tax-exempt status because of lobbying activities is not required if, taking into account as base years only those years for which the expenditure test election is in effect, (1) the sum of the organization's lobbying expenditures for the base years does not exceed 150 percent of the sum of its lobbying nontaxable amounts for the same base years and (2) the sum of the organization's grassroots expenditures for these base years does not exceed 150 percent of the sum of its grassroots nontaxable amounts for the base years. Where the standards of this special exception are not satisfied, the rules as to loss of tax exemption because of excessive lobbying apply.

Affiliated Organizations

The expenditure test contains bases for aggregating the expenditures of related organizations, so as to forestall the creation of numerous organizations for the purpose of avoiding the limitations on lobbying expenditures imposed by the test. Generally, members of an affiliated group are treated as a single organization for purposes of measuring both lobbying expenditures and permitted lobbying expenditures.

Where two or more charitable organizations are members of an affiliated group and at least one of the members has elected the expenditure test, the calculations of lobbying and exempt function expenditures must be made by taking into account the expenditures of the group. If these expenditures exceed the permitted limits, each of the electing member organizations must pay a proportionate share of the penalty excise tax, with the nonelecting members treated under the substantial part test. There are two ways two organizations are deemed affiliated for these purposes:

1. Where the governing instrument of one of the organizations requires it to be bound by decisions of the other on legislative issues
2. Where the governing board of one of the organizations includes persons who
   a. Are specifically designated representatives of the other organization or are members of the governing board, officers, or paid executive staff members of the other organization and,
   b. By aggregating their votes, have sufficient voting power to cause or prevent action on legislative issues by the first organization

The ability of the controlling organization to control action on legislative issues by the controlled organization is sufficient to establish that the organizations are affiliated; it is not necessary that the control be exercised. Two organizations, neither of which is regarded as a tax-exempt charitable organization, are affiliated only if there exists at least one charitable organization that is affiliated with both organizations.

For these purposes, the phrase *action on legislative issues* includes taking a position in an organization's name on legislation, authorizing any person to take a position in the organization's name on legislation or authorizing any lobbying expenditures. The phrase does not include actions taken merely to correct unauthorized actions taken in the organization's name. There are separate rules for members of a limited affiliated group of organizations, which generally are organizations that are affiliated solely by reason of governing instrument provisions that extend control solely with respect to national legislation.

Definition of *Affiliation*

As previously noted, two charitable organizations are deemed affiliated when the governing board of one of the organizations includes persons who (1) are specifically designated representatives of the other organization or are members of the governing board, officers, or paid executive staff members of the other organization and, (2) by aggregating their votes, have sufficient voting power to cause or prevent action on legislative issues by the first organization.

Interlocking Directorates

Two organizations have interlocking governing boards if one organization (the controlling organization) has a sufficient number of representatives on the governing board of the second organization (the controlled organization), so that, by aggregating their votes, the representatives of the controlling organization can cause or prevent action on legislative issues by the controlled organization. If two organizations have interlocking governing boards, the organizations are affiliated without regard to how or whether the representatives of the controlling organization vote on any particular matter.

Generally, the number of representatives of an organization (the controlling organization) who are members of the governing board of a second organization (the controlled organization) are presumed sufficient to cause or prevent action on legislative issues by the controlled organization if that number either constitutes a majority of incumbents on the governing board or constitutes a quorum, or is sufficient to prevent a quorum, for acting on legislative issues. However, if, under the governing documents of an organization (the controlled organization), it can be determined that a lesser number of votes than the number described in the preceding sentence is necessary or sufficient to cause or to prevent action on legislative issues, the number of representatives of the controlling organization who are members of the governing board of the controlled organization will be considered sufficient to cause or prevent action on legislative issues if it equals or exceeds that number. But, notwithstanding either of the preceding sentences, if the number of representatives of one organization is less than 15 percent of the incumbents on the governing board of a second organization, the two organizations are not affiliated by reason of interlocking governing boards.

There are rules describing members of the governing board of one organization (the controlled organization) who are considered representatives of a second organization (the controlling organization). A member of the governing board of a controlled organization may be a representative of more than one controlling organization. A person with no authority to vote on any issue being considered by the governing board is not a representative of any organization.

A board member of one organization (the controlled organization) is a representative of a second organization (the controlling organization) if the controlling organization has specifically designated that person to be a board member of the controlled organization. A board member of the controlled organization is specifically designated by the controlling organization if the board member is selected by virtue of the right of the controlling organization, under the governing instruments of the controlled organization, either to designate a person to be a member of the controlled organization's governing board or to select a person for a position that entitles the holder of that position to be a member of the controlled organization's governing board.

A board member of one organization who is specifically designated by a second organization, a majority of the governing board of which is made up of representatives of a third organization, is a representative of the third organization as well as being a representative of the second organization pursuant to the rules in the preceding paragraph. A board member of one organization who is also a member of the governing board of a second organization is a representative of the second organization.

A board member of one organization who is an officer or a paid executive staff member of a second organization is a representative of the second organization. Although titles are significant in determining whether a person is a member of the executive staff of an organization, any employee of an organization who possesses authority commonly exercised by an executive is considered an executive staff member for these purposes.

Governance of Instrument Requirements

One organization (the controlling organization) is affiliated with a second organization (the controlled organization) by reason of the governing instruments of the controlled organization if the governing instruments of the controlled organization limit the independent action of the controlled organization on legislative issues by requiring it to be bound by decisions of the other organization on legislative issues.

If a controlling organization is affiliated with each of two or more controlled organizations, then the controlled organizations are affiliated with each other. If one organization is a controlling organization with respect to a second organization and that second organization is a controlling organization with respect to a third organization, then the first organization is affiliated with the third organization.

An affiliated group of organizations is a group of organizations,

1. Each of which is affiliated with every other member for at least 30 days of the tax year of the affiliated group (determine without regard to the election discussed in the following paragraphs)
2. Each of which is an organization eligible to make the expenditure test election
3. At least one of which is an electing member organization (as defined in the following paragraphs)

Each organization in a group of organizations that satisfies the foregoing requirements is a member of the affiliated group of organizations for the tax year of the affiliated group. For any tax year of an organization, it may be a member of two or more affiliated groups of organizations. If all members of an affiliated group have the same tax year, that tax year is the tax year of the affiliated group. If the members of an affiliated group do not all have the same tax year, the tax year of the affiliated group is the calendar year, unless a special election is made.

For these purposes, an *electing member organization* is an organization to which the expenditure test election applies on at least one day of the tax year of the affiliated group of which it is a member. The expenditure test is not considered to apply to the organization on any day before the date on which it makes the election.

The tax year of an affiliated group may be determined according to the rule of this paragraph if all of the members of the affiliated group so elect. Each member organization must apply the expenditure test rules, by treating its own tax year as the tax year of the affiliated group. The election may be made by an electing member organization by attaching to its annual return a statement from itself and every other member of the affiliated group that contains the organization's name, address, and employer identification number, as well as its signed consent to the election. The election must be made no later than the due date of the first annual return of any electing member for its tax year for which the member is liable for the expenditure test tax. The election may not be made or revoked after the due date of the return, except on such terms and conditions as the IRS may prescribe.

Excess Lobbying Expenditures of Affiliated Group

There are rules concerning the exempt function expenditures, lobbying expenditures, and grassroots expenditures of an affiliated group of organizations, as well as the application of the tax on the excess lobbying expenditures of the group. An affiliated group of organizations is treated as a single organization for purposes of the tax on excess lobbying expenditures. For any tax year of the affiliated group, the group's lobbying expenditures, grassroots expenditures, and exempt function expenditures are equal to the sum of the lobbying expenditures, grassroots expenditures, and exempt function expenditures, respectively, paid or incurred by each member during the tax year of the affiliated group. The lobbying and grassroots nontaxable amounts for the affiliated group for a tax year are determined under the general rules and are based on the sum of the exempt function expenditures described in the preceding sentence. The lobbying and grassroots ceiling amounts for the affiliated group for a tax year are calculated under the general rules based on the nontaxable amounts determined pursuant to the same sentence.

The tax on excess lobbying expenditures is imposed for a tax year of an affiliated group if the group has expenditures of this nature. For any tax year of an affiliated group, the group's excess lobbying expenditures are the greater of (1) the amount by which the group's lobbying expenditures exceed the group's lobbying nontaxable amount or (2) the amount by which the group's grassroots expenditures exceed the group's grassroots nontaxable amount.

An electing member organization is liable for all or a portion of the tax on the excess lobbying expenditures of an affiliated group of organizations. An organization that is liable under this rule is not liable for any tax based on its own excess lobbying expenditures. A member of the affiliated group that is not an electing member organization is not liable for any portion of the tax that is imposed with respect to the affiliated group.

If the tax imposed on the excess lobbying expenditures of an affiliated group of organizations is based on the amount described in the rule concerning the group's lobbying taxable amount, and at least one electing member has made lobbying expenditures, each electing member organization is liable for its allocable portion of the tax, on the basis of its share of the lobbying expenditures of all of the electing members of the group. The same rule applies with respect to the group's grassroots expenditures. If the tax on the excess lobbying expenditures of an affiliated group of organizations is based on the amount derived from application of the rule concerning the group's grassroots expenditures, and if the rules described in the preceding two sentences do not apply because no electing organization has made lobbying or grassroots expenditures, each electing member organization is liable for its allocable portion of the tax, on the basis of its share of the exempt function expenditures of all of the electing members of the group.

An electing member organization that is liable for all or a portion of the tax on the excess lobbying expenditures of an affiliated group of organizations is liable for the tax as if the tax were imposed for its tax year with which or within which ends the tax year of the affiliated group. If an organization is liable for its tax year for two or more taxes imposed on the excess lobbying expenditures of two or more affiliated groups, then the organization is liable for only the greater of the two or more taxes.

An electing member organization that ceases to be a member of an affiliated group of organizations, the tax year of which is different from its own, must thereafter determine its liability for the tax on excess lobbying expenditures as if its tax year were the tax year of the affiliated group of which it was formerly a member. An organization to which this rule applies that is liable for the tax is liable for the tax as if the tax were imposed for its tax year within which ends the tax year of the affiliated group of which it was formerly a member. The IRS may, at its discretion, permit an organization to disregard this rule and to determine any liability for the tax on excess lobbying expenditures on the basis of its own tax year.

Application of Election Limitations to Affiliated Groups of Organizations

There are rules concerning the application of the limitations of the expenditure test limitations to members of an affiliated group of organizations. For each tax year of an affiliated group of organizations, the calculations fall under the rules where tax exemption is lost when lobbying or grassroots expenditures for the base years exceed 150 percent of lobbying or when grassroots nontaxable amounts must be made, the basis of expenditures of the group. If, for a tax year of an affiliated group, it is determined that the sum of the affiliated group's lobbying or grassroots expenditures for the group's base years exceeds 150 percent of the sum of the group's corresponding nontaxable amounts for the base years, then, under the expenditure test, each member organization that is an electing member organization at any time in the tax year of the affiliated group will be denied federal tax exemption, beginning with its first tax year beginning after the end of such tax year of the affiliated group. Thereafter, tax exemption will be denied unless, pursuant to the rule concerning reapplication for recognition of exemption, the organization reapplies for exemption and is recognized by the IRS as exempt as a charitable organization. For these purposes, the term *base years* generally means the tax year of the affiliated group for which a determination is made and the group's three preceding tax years. Base years, however, do not include any year preceding the first year in which at least one member of the group was treated as a charitable entity.

An organization that is a member of an affiliated group of organizations but that is not an electing member organization remains subject to the substantial part test with respect to its activities involving attempts to influence legislation.

The filing requirements under these rules apply to each member of an affiliated group of organizations for the member's tax year with which, or within which, ends the tax year of the affiliated group. Each member of an affiliated group of organizations must provide to every other member of the group, before the first day of the second month following the close of the affiliated group's tax year, its name, its identification number, and the information required under the reporting rules for its expenditures during the group's tax year and for prior tax years of the group that are base years. For groups that make the special election to have each member file information with respect to the group based on its tax year, each member must provide the information required pursuant to the rule described in the preceding sentence by treating each tax year of any group member as a tax year for the group. In addition to the information required under the reporting rules, each member of an affiliated group of organizations must provide on its annual information return the group's tax year and, if the special election is made, the name, identification number, and tax year identifying the return with which its consent to the election was filed.

Moreover, each electing member organization must provide on its annual information return (1) the name and identification number of each member of the group and (2) the appropriate calculation of excess lobbying expenditures of the group if the organization is an electing member organization liable for all or any portion of the tax imposed on excess lobbying expenditures.

Members of a Limited Affiliated Group of Organizations

There are additional rules for members of a limited affiliated group of organizations, which generally are organizations that are affiliated solely by reason of provisions of their governing instruments that extend control only with respect to national legislation. Generally, the rules concerning excess lobbying expenditures of an affiliated group and concerning application of the expenditure test to affiliated groups of organizations do not apply to members of a limited affiliated group. Thus, the expenditure test applies individually to electing members of a limited affiliated group. Generally, members of a limited affiliated group that are not electing organizations are subject to the substantial part test.

A limited affiliated group consists of two or more organizations that meet the following requirements:

1. Each organization is a member of an affiliated group of organizations.
2. No two members of this affiliated group are affiliated by reason of interlocking governing boards.
3. No member of this affiliated group is, under its governing instruments, bound by decisions of one or more of the other members on legislative issues other than national legislative issues.

For these purposes, the term *national legislative issue* means legislation, limited to action by the Congress of the United States or by the public in any national procedure. If an issue is both national and local, it is characterized as a national legislative issue if the contemplated legislation is congressional legislation. Each organization in a group of organizations that satisfies these requirements is a member of the limited affiliated group.

There are rules that apply to a controlling member organization that has the expenditure test election in effect for its tax year. These rules apply whether or not the organization is also a controlled member organization. In determining a controlling member organization's expenditures, no expenditure may be counted twice.

A member of a limited affiliated group is a controlling member organization if it controls one or more of the other members of the limited affiliated group, and a member of a limited affiliated group is a controlled member organization if it is controlled by one or more of the other members of the limited affiliated group. Whether an organization controls a second organization is determined by whether the second organization is bound, under its governing instruments, by actions taken by the first organization on national legislative issues.

A controlling member organization for which the expenditure test election is in effect must include in its direct lobbying expenditures for its tax year the direct lobbying expenditures paid or incurred with respect to national legislative issues during the year by each organization that is a member of the limited affiliated group and is controlled by the controlling member organization. A like rule requires the attribution of grassroots expenditures to a controlling member organization. The exempt function expenditures of a controlling member organization do not include the exempt function expenditures (other than the previously referenced lobbying expenditures) of any organization that is a controlled member organization with respect to it.

A controlled member organization that is an electing organization but that does not control any organization in the limited affiliated group must apply the expenditure test without regard to the expenditures of any other member of the limited affiliated group.

In addition to the information required by the general reporting rules, each controlling member organization for which the expenditure test election is in effect must provide on its annual information return the name and identification number of each member of the limited affiliated group. Each controlling member organization for which an expenditure test election is in effect must notify each member that it controls of its tax year in order for the controlled organization to disseminate information, as discussed in the last sentence of this paragraph. This notification must be made before the beginning of the second month after the close of each tax year of the controlling member for which the election is in effect. Every controlled member organization (whether or not the expenditure test election is in effect with respect to it) must provide to each member of the limited affiliated group that controls it, before the first day of the second month following the close of the tax year of each controlling organization, its name, its identification number, and the lobbying expenditures and grassroots expenditures on national legislative issues incurred by the controlled member organization.

Recordkeeping Rules

Substantial Part Test

There are no specific recordkeeping rules under the substantial part test. Of course, the burden is always on a charitable organization to prove (usually to the IRS) that it is not engaging in substantial lobbying activities. Thus, the prudent charitable organization operating under the substantial part test will maintain whatever records are necessary to allow it to satisfy this burden of proof.

As previously discussed, the emphasis of the substantial part test is on *activities.* Therefore, the organization attempting to adhere to this test should keep a record of its legislative activities, not just its expenditures for legislative activities. Thus, for example, the *value* of volunteer time associated with legislative activities must be determined.

Nonetheless, in connection with the substantial part test, the record-keeping obligations must focus largely on expenditures. At a minimum, it is the place for the charitable organization using the test to start. These records should include the following:

1. The portion of amounts paid or incurred as compensation for an employee's services for lobbying
2. The amounts paid to or incurred by consultants and other independent contractors for services for lobbying
3. Amounts paid or incurred for other expenses in connection with lobbying activities (such as travel, postage, computer, facsimile, and publication costs)
4. The allocable portion of administration, overhead, and other general expenditures attributable to lobbying
5. Any other expenditures for direct or grassroots lobbying

An organization endeavoring to comply with the substantial part test should seek the services of an accountant to determine the extent to which costs should be allocated and to institute a system for keeping track of these costs. This effort is not unlike the exercise charitable organizations often go through in determining fund-raising costs.

Of course, in determining the value of legislative activities in connection with the substantial part test, a charitable organization should not include the value of legislative activities that are excluded from treatment as lobbying.

Expenditure Test

An electing public charity must keep a record of its lobbying expenditures for a tax year. These records must include the following:

1. Expenditures for direct lobbying
2. The portion of amounts paid or incurred as compensation for an employee's services for direct lobbying
3. Amounts paid for out-of-pocket expenditures incurred on behalf of the organization and for direct lobbying
4. The allocable portion of administration, overhead, and other general expenditures attributable to direct lobbying

5. Expenditures for publications or for communications with members to the extent that the expenditures are treated as expenditures for direct lobbying

Identical recordkeeping requirements apply with respect to grassroots expenditures.

Reporting Rules

Substantial Part Test

A charitable organization that is operating under the substantial part test is obligated to report some information on its legislative activities to the IRS, as part of the process of filing its annual information return. In this regard, there are two sets of information that an organization operating under this test is expected to provide:

1. An answer to the following question: During the year, has the organization attempted to influence national, state, or local legislation, including any attempt to influence public opinion on a legislative matter or referendum? If the answer is yes, the organization is requested to provide the total expenses paid or incurred in connection with the legislative activities.
2. A statement attached to the return, giving a detailed description of the legislative activities and a classified schedule of the expenses paid or incurred.

There is no guidance as to what is meant by a *detailed description* or a *classified schedule*. Consequently, an organization can provide a narrative description of its legislative activities, perhaps accompanying this description with exhibits (such as copies of testimony and correspondence). If these activities are excluded from consideration as lobbying activities, they should be prominently identified as such. The classified schedule would presumably be along the lines of the list of the 5 items provided above as suggested recordkeeping obligations.

Whatever this range of information is, it is considerably less onerous than that required as part of the expenditure test. For one thing, the substantial part test reporting requirements do not obligate the charitable organizations involved to differentiate between direct lobbying and grassroots lobbying activities. For another thing, the substantial part test reporting requirements do not contain anything akin to the requirement under the expenditure test of computing the year's lobbying nontaxable amount and grassroots nontaxable amount. The expenditure test reporting requirements mandate the computation of the direct and grassroots lobbying nontaxable amount, the direct and grassroots lobbying ceiling amount, and the total direct and grassroots lobbying amounts. Moreover, the substantial part test has nothing equivalent to the affiliated group rules.

The IRS is well aware of this disparity in reporting obligations. There is talk of efforts at the IRS to clarify the reporting responsibilities of charitable organizations operating under the substantial part test. It may be anticipated that any such clarification will not result in an easing of these responsibilities.

Expenditure Test

In order to make information about the legislative activities of electing charitable organizations obtainable by the public, the required contents of the annual information returns filed by these organizations are expanded in relation to what must be reported by an organization operating under the substantial part test. Thus, an electing organization must disclose in its information return the following:

1. The amount of its direct lobbying expenditures
2. The amount of its grassroots lobbying expenditures
3. Other and total exempt function expenditures
4. The amount that it could have spent for direct lobbying purposes without becoming subject to the 25 percent excise tax (the lobbying nontaxable amount)
5. The amount that it could have spent for grassroots lobbying purposes without becoming subject to the tax (the grassroots nontaxable amount)
6. The lobbying nontaxable amount for each year in the four-year averaging period
7. The lobbying ceiling amount for each of these four years
8. Total direct lobbying expenses for each of these four years
9. The grassroots nontaxable amount for each of these four years
10. The grassroots ceiling amount for each of these four years
11. Total grassroots lobbying expenses for each of these four years

An electing organization that is a member of an affiliated group must provide this information with respect to both itself and the entire group.

Other Aspects of the Expenditure Test

An eligible charitable organization that desires to avail itself of the expenditure test must elect to come within these standards and can do so on a year-to-year basis.

The Election

This election is effective with the beginning of the tax year in which the election is made. For example, if an eligible organization, the tax year of which is the calendar year, makes the election on December 31, 2000, the organization is governed by the expenditure test for its tax year beginning January 1, 2000. Once made, the expenditure test election is effective (without again making the election) for each succeeding tax year for which the organization is an eligible organization and that begins before a notice of revocation is filed.

Charitable organizations that may not or that choose not to make the election are governed by the substantial part test. Churches, conventions or associations of churches, integrated auxiliaries of churches, certain supporting organizations of noncharitable entities, and private foundations may not elect to come under these rules—private foundations having been made subject to stringent regulation in this regard. Consequently, the types of organizations that are eligible to elect the expenditure test are educational institutions, hospitals, medical research organizations, organizations supporting government schools, publicly supported charitable organizations, and supporting organizations of public charities.

If a charitable organization is denied tax exemption for a tax year by reason of the expenditure test and thereafter is again recognized as an exempt charitable organization, it may again elect the expenditure test. An organization that is denied tax exemption by reason of the expenditure test may apply for recognition of exemption as a charitable organization for any tax year following the first tax year for which exemption was denied. An application of this type must demonstrate that the organization would not be denied tax exemption by reason of the expenditure test if the expenditure test election had been in effect for all of its previous tax year.

A newly created organization may make the expenditure test election before it is recognized by the IRS as a tax-exempt charitable organization (and determined to be an organization eligible to make the election), and the organization may submit the form by which the election is made at the time that it submits its application for recognition of exemption. If the newly created organization is determined to be an eligible organization, the election will be effective with the beginning of the tax year in which the organization makes the election. However, if a newly created organization is determined by the IRS not to be an eligible organization, the organization's election will not be effective, and the substantial part test will apply from the date the organization was recognized as a charitable organization.

Voluntary Revocation of Election

An organization may voluntarily revoke an expenditure test election by filing a notice of voluntary revocation with the appropriate IRS center. A voluntary revocation of this election is effective with the beginning of the first tax year after the tax year in which the notice is filed. If an organization voluntarily revokes its election, the substantial part test will apply with respect to the organization's activities in attempting to influence legislation, beginning with the tax year for which the voluntary revocation is effective.

Just as the matter of election of the expenditure test should be the product of a thoughtful decision, so, too, should a voluntary revocation of this test. The IRS is likely to assume that an organization that cannot satisfy the expenditure test also cannot satisfy the substantial part test. Thus, a voluntary revocation of the expenditure test could lead to an IRS examination of the organization's ongoing eligibility for tax exemption as a charitable entity.

Any such assumption by the IRS would be based on its view that the expenditure test is generous. This line of thinking is predicated on the thought that 20 percent of an organization's expenditures is more than *insubstantial*. While there is considerable validity to this thought, the conclusions that flow from it may not apply in every instance. For example, an organization may find that all of its attempts to influence legislation constitute grassroots lobbying. If this type of lobbying represents 9 percent of the organization's expenditures, it may be lobbying that is too extensive for the expenditure test but not for the substantial part test.

An organization that is contemplating voluntary revocation of the expenditure test should consider adding to the notice of revocation an explanation as to why the notice is being filed. This type of explanation could thwart any IRS follow-up action.

Re-election of Expenditure Test

If a charitable organization's expenditure test election is voluntarily revoked, the organization may again make the expenditure test election, effective no earlier than for the tax year following the first tax year for which the revocation is effective.

Involuntary Revocation of Expenditure Test

While an election of the expenditure test by an eligible organization is in effect, if the organization ceases to be an eligible organization, its election is automatically revoked. The revocation is effective with the beginning of the first full tax year for which it is determined that the organization is not an eligible organization.

If an organization's expenditure test election is involuntarily revoked under this rule but the organization continues to be a charitable entity, the substantial part test will apply with respect to the organization's activities in attempting to influence legislation, beginning with the first tax year for which the voluntary revocation is effective. If the organization thereafter becomes an eligible organization, it may, if it desires, elect the expenditure part test, in accordance with the foregoing rules.

This rule is, of course, different from the rule that causes an organization to lose its recognition as a tax-exempt charitable organization because of excessive lobbying under the expenditure test. Even when that occurs, however, a charitable organization may become re-eligible for recognition as a tax-exempt charitable organization.

Reapplication for Exemption

As previously noted, an organization that is denied exemption from taxation by reason of one or more transgressions of the expenditure test may apply for recognition of tax exemption as a charitable entity for any tax year following the first tax year for which the exemption is denied. This type of application for recognition of tax exemption must demonstrate that the organization would not be denied exemption from taxation by reason of the expenditure test if the expenditure test election had been in effect for all of its previous tax year ending before the application is made. This is done by providing the calculations as to its direct and grassroots lobbying expenditures or, if applicable, these lobbying expenditures for an affiliated group that would have applied for that year. This is a somewhat unfair requirement, in that it applies even when the applicant organization is not making the expenditure test election at the time of application for recognition of exemption.

This application must also include information that demonstrates to the satisfaction of the IRS that the organization will not knowingly operate in a manner that would disqualify it for tax exemption as a charitable entity by reason of attempting to influence legislation. Thus, this type of application must contain information to convince the IRS that the applicant charity will satisfy both the substantial part test and the expenditure test—a burdensome requirement that is inconsistent with the concept of having alternative tests. These requirements unneccessarily penalize the charitable organization that, having lost its tax exemption because of excessive lobbying, has remedied that aspect of its operations and is reapplying for recognition of exemption.

Timing of the Election

A charitable organization (which is not a private foundation) may attempt to influence the legislative process as long as the organization stays within the bounds of insubstantiality (or, perhaps, substantiality). Thus, a charitable organization desiring to engage in legislative activities must, in assessing *insubstantiality*, decide whether to use the substantial part test or elect the expenditure test and must determine whether one or more exceptions provided by either test are available. In an optimum situation, a charitable organization can expend 20 percent or more of its total expenditures on attempts to influence legislation.

There are many variables to consider when deciding whether to elect the expenditure test. Principally, a charitable organization must assess the type or types of lobbying in which it is engaged or will be engaged, assign an amount and percentage of expenditures to the lobbying activity or activities, and determine the limitations imposed under both tests. For example, a charitable organization that seeks to engage entirely in grassroots lobbying is best advised not to make the election because the limitation on that type of lobbying is probably more stringent under the expenditure test than under the substantial part test. In contrast, if all lobbying is direct lobbying and exceeds 10 percent of total expenditures, the election is probably advisable.

Those who advocate the expenditure test stress the certainty of the rules that it provides. This test provides crisper definitions of what is, and what is allowable, lobbying. It provides an opportunity to become alerted to excessive lobbying before imposition of the sanction of loss of exemption, in part by means of the four-year averaging mechanism and in part because of the 25 percent warning tax.

Those who caution against the expenditure test warn of the complexity of the rules, the cost of compliance, the fact that an organization is affirmatively electing to become subject to taxes, the higher profile that may result from the election (greater identification of the organization as a lobbying entity), and the possibility that making the election will appear to highlight a tax exemption problem and trigger an IRS audit. (Representatives of the IRS insist, however, that the making of the election does not cause the organization to become "audit bait." Indeed, there have been suggestions that an audit may be more likely in the case of a nonelecting organization.)

Other factors an organization should consider, in determining whether to elect the expenditure test, are the following:

1. The possibility that the IRS may begin enforcing the substantial part test using one or more standards other than the volume of legislative activity
2. The fact that the time expended by volunteers for lobbying is taken into account for purposes of the substantial part test and is disregarded for purposes of the expenditure test
3. The fact that lobbying is assessed annually pursuant to the substantial part test and over a four-year average under the expenditure test
4. The potential impact of the affiliation rules in the expenditure test
5. The additional recordkeeping responsibilities imposed by the expenditure test
6. The additional reporting responsibilities imposed by the expenditure test
7. The potential of applicability of the taxes enacted in 1987
8. The difficulties posed by the expenditure test in establishing a related lobbying organization

Finally, a nonelecting charitable organization desiring to engage in a substantial amount of lobbying can convert to a social welfare organization to pursue those activities.

There is reason to believe that the IRS will be more closely examining the legislative activities of charitable organizations that have not elected the expenditure test. This is in part because the IRS is anxious for lobbying charitable organizations to make the election, so as to increase the flow of data to the IRS about legislative activities of charitable organizations that is stimulated by the increased reporting requirement. It is not unreasonable to expect the IRS to narrowly interpret the scope of the insubstantiality exception contained in the substantial part test, perhaps by resurrecting the doctrine that substantiality need not be measured in terms of activities or expenditures but can be a function of general influence, determined with hindsight. It will be interesting to see what definitions and other interpretations of the substantial part test the IRS develops, inasmuch as the IRS is not supposed to use the expenditure test rules in developing and applying the substantial part test.

Lobbying Expenditures and Taxes

If a charitable organization loses its tax exemption because of attempts to influence legislation, a tax in the amount of 5 percent of the *lobbying expenditures* is to be imposed on the organization for the year of loss of exemption. (This tax does not apply to any organization that has elected to use the expenditure test or that is ineligible to make that election.) A lobbying expenditure is any amount paid or incurred by a charitable organization in carrying on propaganda or otherwise attempting to influence legislation.

A separate tax is applicable to each of the organization's managers (basically, its officers, directors, and key employees) who agreed to the making of the lobbying expenditures (knowing that they were likely to result in revocation of its tax exemption), unless the agreement was not willful and due to reasonable cause. This tax is also an amount equal to 5 percent of the lobbying expenditures and can be imposed only where the tax on the organization is imposed. If more than one person is liable for this tax on management, all of the persons involved are jointly and severally liable for the tax.

Constitutional Law Considerations

It has been asserted that the proscription on substantial legislative activities imposed on charitable organizations violates constitutional law principles. While the issues have been repeatedly presented to the courts, until 1982 none of the litigants had been successful in securing a decision finding that this provision is constitutionally deficient.

Representative of these decisions was one handed down in 1979. The issues involved were the following: does this tax limitation on legislative activities (1) impose an unconstitutional condition on the exercise of First Amendment rights (that is, the right to engage in legislative activity); (2) restrict the exercise of First Amendment rights as being a discriminatory denial of tax exemption for engaging in speech; (3) deny restricted organizations the equal protection of the laws in violation of the Fifth Amendment; and/or (4) lack a compelling governmental interest, which would justify the restrictions on First Amendment rights?

The courts' approach on the First Amendment question has been to recognize that the lobbying of legislators constitutes an exercise of the First Amendment right of petition and, thus, that the amendment protects legislative activities. Often cited in this context is the Supreme Court declaration that the general advocacy of ideas is constitutionally protected as part of this nation's "profound national commitment to the principle that debate on public issues should be uninhibited, robust, and wide-open." However, the courts inevitably go on to observe that this tax law limitation does not violate First Amendment rights because it does not, on its face, prohibit organizations from engaging in substantial efforts to influence legislation.

This position is based on a 1959 Supreme Court pronouncement upholding the constitutionality of a regulation that excluded from deduction as business expenses amounts expended for the promotion or defeat of legislation. There, the Court stated that the "petitioners are not being denied a tax deduction because they engage in constitutionally protected activities, but are simply being required to pay for these activities entirely out of their own pocketbook, as everyone else engaging in similar activities is required to do under the provisions of the Internal Revenue Code." Thus, when it comes to substantial legislative activities, charitable organizations are required to fund these efforts from their own resources, and this result is not regarded as a denial of a deduction or an exemption for engaging in constitutionally protected activities.

As regards the second aspect of the First Amendment question, this argument is premised on the fact that several categories of tax-exempt organizations are free to lobby and that certain types of outlays by business corporations for lobbying are deductible. Thus, the proposition is that the lobbying condition on charitable groups is a discriminatory denial of a tax exemption for engaging in speech. The courts hold that this principle relates to legislative efforts "aimed at the suppression of dangerous ideas," not to denials or revocation of tax exemptions for charitable organizations.

Similar short shrift has been given to the equal protection challenge, which is based on the fact that similarly situated (that is, tax-exempt) organizations are accorded different treatment with respect to lobbying activities. The courts usually concede that this involves a classification that accords differing treatment to classes but that it is permissible, since the classification does not affect a "fundamental" right or involve a "suspect" class. The applicable standard of scrutiny—which this statutory limitation has been repeatedly ruled to satisfy—is whether the challenged classification is reasonably related to a legitimate governmental purpose. This standard is also deemed met where the courts evaluate the constitutionality of the proscription on legislative activity as respects legislative activities in relation to the requirement that it be rationally related to a legitimate government purpose. Several of these purposes are usually found served: "assurance of governmental neutrality with respect to the lobbying activities of charitable organizations; prevention of abuse of charitable lobbying by private interests; and preservation of a balance between the lobbying activities of charitable organizations and those of non-charitable organizations and individuals."

Thus, until 1982, all of the courts that considered the matter had made it clear that there is no constitutional imperfection in the federal tax antilobbying clause. In that year, however, the U.S. Court of Appeals for the District of Columbia Circuit changed the complexion of the constitutional law concerning the antilobbying rule applicable to charitable organizations. The appellate court agreed that this restriction on legislative activities does not violate free speech (First Amendment) rights but—after concluding that an organization that acquires tax exemption and charitable donee status is thereby receiving a government subsidy—held that this subsidy cannot constitutionally be accorded on a discriminatory basis and that to do so violates equal protection (Fifth Amendment) rights. Therefore, the court held, the fact that charitable organizations are required to limit their lobbying to an insubstantial extent, while certain other organizations—such as veterans' organizations—can lobby without such limits, is an unconstitutionally discriminatory allocation of this government subsidy.

This appellate court held that "by subsidizing the lobbying activities of veterans' organizations while failing to subsidize the lobbying of . . . charitable groups, Congress has violated the equal protection guarantees of the Constitution." While the court decided that the challenge to the lobbying restriction is weak if based solely on free speech claims and equal protection claims, it concluded that "the whole of . . . [the] argument well exceeds the sum of its parts" and that a "First Amendment concern must inform the equal protection analysis in this case."

As a prelude to its findings, this court concluded that a "high level of scrutiny is required" because the lobbying restriction on charitable organizations "constitutes a limitation on protected First Amendment activity" and because the equal protection argument involves "what is clearly a fundamental right." Under law, this scrutiny requires a determination as to whether "a substantial governmental interest supports the classification." The court based its conclusion on the premise that nonprofit organizations that embody both features of tax exemption and eligibility to attract tax-deductible contributions are essentially alike. Inasmuch as the court was not persuaded that there is a valid governmental interest to be served by treating charitable groups and veterans' groups differently on the matter of lobbying, the court ruled that the distinctions between the two classes of entities are "post hoc rationales" that are "constitutionally illegitimate." Hence, the court found an unconstitutional denial of equal protection rights.

The remedy desired by the plaintiff in this 1982 case was the invalidation of the lobbying restrictions on charitable organizations, which the court was not inclined to do. First, it wrote that unfettered lobbying by charitable organizations would increase the likelihood of "selfish" contributions made solely to advance the donors' personal legislative interests. Second, the court concluded that Congress believes that the public interest requires limitations on lobbying by charitable organizations and that "even when they attempt to remedy constitutional violations, courts must resist ordering relief that clearly exceeds the legitimate expectations of Congress." The reverse approach—to place the same restrictions on veterans' groups as are presently imposed on charitable groups—was far more appealing to the court and received serious consideration. But the court hesitated to strike down what it termed the "preferential treatment now accorded the lobbying of veterans' organizations," since veterans' groups were not parties to the litigation. Instead, the case was ordered remanded to the district court "with the instruction that it cure the constitutionally invalid operation of Section 501(c) after inviting veterans' organizations to participate in framing the relief." However, before the remand could occur, the decision was appealed to the U.S. Supreme Court.

The Supreme Court reacted swiftly, hearing arguments in March 1983 and on May 23, 1983, unanimously reversing the court of appeals. In so holding, the Court reiterated its position that the lobbying restriction on charitable organizations does not infringe First Amendment rights or regulate any First Amendment activity, that Congress did not violate the equal protection doctrine in the Fifth Amendment, and that Congress acted rationally in subsidizing (by means of tax exemption and charitable deductions) lobbying by veterans' organizations while not subsidizing lobbying by charitable organizations generally. As to the free speech issue, the Court held that the federal tax law "does not deny . . . [a charitable organization] the right to receive deductible contributions to support its nonlobbying activity, nor does it deny . . . [a charitable organization] any independent benefit on account of its intention to lobby" but that "Congress has merely refused to pay for the lobbying out of public moneys."

Noting that "legislatures have especially broad latitude in creating classifications and distinctions in tax statutes," the Court concluded that the distinctions in the lobbying context that Congress made between charitable and veterans' organizations do not use any "suspect classification," are not violative of equal protection principles, and are "within Congress' broad power in this area." Moreover, the Court accepted the views that "Congress was concerned that exempt [charitable] organizations might use tax-deductible contributions to lobby to promote the private interests of their members" and that "our country has a long standing policy of compensating veterans for their past contributions by providing them with numerous advantages." Consequently, it appears that the proscription on substantial legislative activities by charitable organizations, contained in the federal tax rules, is beyond further challenge in the courts.

It is unlikely that the enactment of the expenditure test in 1976, and the finalization of its regulations in 1990, will stem the flow of comment and proposed legislation on the subject. In fact, a call for further legislative action in this area appeared within days of adoption of the 1976 tax act. This aspect of the law of tax-exempt organizations has always been a fertile field for the commentators and is likely to remain so.

Nontax Rules

Bodies of law other than federal taxation may pertain to lobbying done by or for nonprofit organizations. The principal law outside the federal tax context is the Federal Regulation of Lobbying Act. Most individuals who lobby for compensation must register with and report to the Clerk of the House of Representatives and the Secretary of the Senate.

There are other rules. The *Byrd Amendment* prohibits the use of federal funds received as grants, contracts, and loans or pursuant to cooperative agreements for attempts to influence an officer or employee of a governmental agency in connection with the awarding, obtaining, or making of any federal contract, grant, loan, or cooperative agreement. Regulations published by the U.S. Office of Management and Budget provide that costs associated with most forms of lobbying activities do not qualify for reimbursement by the federal government. Most states also have laws regulating lobbying by nonprofit and other organizations.

Conclusion

Although charitable organizations are permitted to engage in lobbying—and can do more of it than is generally realized—the rules as to the

measurement of allowable lobbying are intricate. Every charitable organization that is eligible to make the election should make a determination as to whether to remain under the substantial part test or elect to
adhere to the rules of the expenditure test. Often, the exceptions to the
lobbying rules are significant. Even where the organization navigates
the federal tax law requirements, there may be other federal and state
rules to confront.

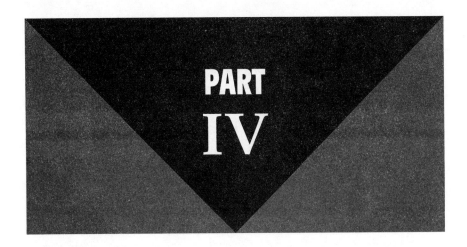

PART IV

DEVELOPING A STRATEGIC PLAN FOR A NOT-FOR-PROFIT

WALTER P. PIDGEON, JR.

Throughout the past three parts of the book, you have had the opportunity to become acquainted with the various aspects of how the government affairs process works. By now, you have thought about the ways to use these materials to start or refine your government affairs program.

Part 4 gives you an opportunity to examine various ways to implement a program that fulfills your short- and long-term goals. Before you begin to read Chapter 8, you should quickly review the first three parts of the book to determine

1. What are the goals of your current or proposed government affairs program?
2. Will you need state coverage, federal coverage, or both?
3. What kind of grassroots network can your organizations achieve?
4. What would be the ideal communication outcome?
5. What kind of partnerships can you form now? What kind do you need to form?
6. Can you do it alone or will you need outside help?

7. What are the legal aspects of a government affairs program and how do you deal with them?
8. What will you need to underwrite the cost of your government affairs plan and how can you procure these funds?

The most basic question to ask is "What are my goals?" Only you and your key leadership can answer it. The answer to this question will determine the size and dimension of your program. Remember, you do not have to have a full-blown program right from the start. You might never need a full-blown program. Base your program on need.

Most not-for-profits find themselves involved in both state and national issues. If you are a small, local organization, for example, certain issues, such as postal rates and unrelated business income tax (UBIT), can have a profound effect. The same is true for a large, national organization. A local bill may infringe on your mission, or it may set a dangerous precedent. Be careful how you set your parameters.

Most not-for-profits need to have a grassroots network to function. In the government affairs arena, this is your perceived power and your best weapon. In most cases, don't begin the government affairs process if you haven't developed a grassroots network.

Obtaining the visibility you need to function well in the government relations arena is vital. It is also a sound strategic move to achieve awareness goals for your overall organization.

The first rule of thumb is that very few organizations can do it all alone. Not-for-profits need to be constantly partnering with other entities to gain the size and strength they need to be noticed. If you think you have enough partners, you are wrong. You never have enough. AARP (explained in Chapter 8), one of the most powerful lobby groups in Washington, DC, is constantly looking for new partners. Maybe your organization could be one of them. Always look for new partners. It is one of the keys to keeping your organization vital, visible, and strong.

The question of capacity is also something to consider. Do you have a large enough or an experienced enough staff to conduct a government affairs program? If not, you will need outside help. Even in an association whose primary mission is government affairs must seek outside help to obtain this kind of expertise. Don't hesitate to use outside help. In appropriate cases, it gets the job done in less time and with less money.

In Chapter 7, Bruce Hopkins provided an in-depth review of the legal aspects of government affairs and how it relates to your not-for-profit IRS status. This provides you with a starting point, but it is important that you consult with your lawyer and accountant before you embark on your government affairs plan. These experts will make sure that your plan does not exceed the IRS limits set for your not-for-profit. In addition, you should have your attorney and accountant review your plan annually to make sure that you are still within the limits.

The most important aspect of all, like it or not, is the financial needs of your government affairs program. It is important that you settle on a realistic plan based on funding projections. Remember, this is a different kind of fund-raising process than most not-for-profit leaders are accustomed to, yet most of the fund-raising principles apply. You will also find that you will be able to tap additional funds from current donors. The new donors who are attracted by the existence of a government affairs function will also surprise you. In addition, if you work at it, you can transform these new government affairs donors to programmatic donors.

Now that you have envisioned a government affairs plan for your not-for-profit based on your review of the first seven chapters and your perception of need, you are now ready to begin Chapter 8. Please keep an open mind concerning the material, as it may or may not be as you expect. Remember, government affairs work is never a stagnant thing. The process moves quickly, and those who hesitate or do not have sound objectives will be plowed under or left behind. Welcome to the world of the insider's club.

A Strategic Plan for Success

WALTER P. PIDGEON, JR.

Introduction

By now, you have a basic idea of how to implement or enhance a government affairs program. It is important to understand that a well-run government affairs program can play a significant role in the success of a not-for-profit. This includes legislative success as well as a number of additional benefits, including nonrestricted revenue, new volunteers, and visibility for your cause.

Finding your niche and primary focus is vital. You cannot be all things to all people. Find the area in which you can best serve and become a leader in this area. Determine what is or what will be your geographic spread. Determine if you want to focus on the state level, federal level, or both—it will make a big difference in your approach and in your financial requirements.

Most organizations rely on volunteer support, whether they are raising funds or establishing a grassroots network. Since current funds and staff are often inadequate, it is important to determine how you can attract volunteer assistance. It is also important that you take advantage of the visibility that you receive from the government affairs function. You will often need a media campaign to push your government affairs agenda, but this can also assist you in gaining the reputation you desire for the mission of your entire organization.

A sound government affairs program also relies on partnering with other organizations to gain the strength needed to gain the advantage. Power is what it is all about. Currently, I am helping my not-for-profit, the Wildlife Legislative Fund of America (WLFA), to introduce a bill in Congress. While WLFA is recognized as one of the most powerful lobby groups in Washington, DC, with regards to its issue, we did not approach Congress alone. We formed a coalition consisting of 97 organizations that span the conservation movement. WLFA's voice is being heard, loud and clear, due to the coalition's strength and the millions of individual members and participant organizations that it represents. Coalitions simply provide a better chance of getting bills passed.

As you create your strategic plan, you will need to determine what kind of professional leadership you will need to develop and maintain your government affairs program. No matter how large your government affairs function is or will become, you will need the expertise of an outside consultant. My organization, WLFA, is in the business of providing government affairs services. While it is our fulltime mission, we have a quality array of full-time professionals who are experts in government affairs, law, communications, fund raising, and management. We use outside consultants all the time to assist at both the state and federal levels. Why do we use consultants rather than hiring more staff? Simply stated, we cannot afford to hire the expertise that consultants bring to the table and, in many cases, we need them for only short periods of time. This is particularly true for a national association that works at both the federal and state levels. Local consultants open doors and get the job done way before an outsider would even have the opportunity to assess the situation.

I have had the privilege of serving in a number of professional leadership roles in not-for-profit organizations with various missions, such as youth, health, business, and recreation. They were as diverse as you can imagine, yet they all possessed common values or traits:

1. They were all a part of the not-for-profit community.
2. They represented a defined group or constituency.
3. They were recognized as representing an important mission.
4. They all had a volunteer base—some strong, some weak.
5. They all had a dedicated staff.

Do these traits sound familiar to you? Most not-for-profits have them. It is important to take a close look at each to determine if your organization has these traits and, if so, how well they are being positively exploited.

You would think that being a part of the not-for-profit community is a given, yet the following question needs to be asked: where do you fall in the community and how do you relate to the other parts? We all know that section 501 organizations are different. Chapter 7 explained the legal differences, but we all know that (c)3 organizations talk a different language than the (c)4 or (c)6. There also seems to be the perception that a (c)3 serves a higher mission or that a (c)6 pays more, since it requires higher-quality professionals. These perceptions may be right or wrong. The point is that all not-for-profits have unique needs and goals.

In the government affairs realm, though, we need to get beyond these barriers. A sound government affairs program will take full advantage of its organization's IRS status, and, if necessary, organizations should form other not-for-profits within their structure to better serve their constituents. A sound program will also network with all facets of the not-for-profit community to best serve its members and the government affairs function.

Speaking of members or constituents, take a moment to consider if your organization can be recognized easily for whom you serve. For example, imagine an association called the Home Healthcare Provider Association.

From an outsider's point of view, this name does not describe its members well. Does this group represent nurses who specialize in home healthcare services? Does it represent people who need home healthcare providers? Perhaps the association is covering everyone in the entire home healthcare industry. In reality, very few organizations serve such a broad base. On the other hand, do not define your constituents so narrowly that you end up with no power base. Make sure that your current and targeted constituents and the general public can clearly understand whom you represent. In our example, if the group represents home care nurses, why not make the organization's name reflect it, such as The Home Healthcare Nurses Association?

Having other groups and individuals recognize your organization as *the* not-for-profit representing a certain constituency group is the highest compliment you can receive, and it is a major factor in creating a successful government affairs operation. Think of the brand names that trigger instant recognition of whom they represent:

- AARP (so recognizable that it dropped its name altogether)
- American Trucking Association
- U.S. Chamber of Commerce
- American Red Cross
- United Way of America

While some of these names convey positive images, others may not. The important thing is that the branding they have achieved has helped them to be a powerful force in the government affairs arena. Your organization may not have the same brand name identity as those listed, yet you can achieve this brand recognition if you work at it. As you may know, when organizations are formed, they often select names that reflect the founder's wishes or a name that has meaning at the time. Over the years, the name, particularly a long name, can be awkward to sell and difficult to use. AARP is a classic example. The American Association of Retired People gave way to using AARP. In 1999, it dropped its name and now simply uses AARP. Not many organizations could pull that off, however.

Most organizations that conclude that their names are a barrier either refine the name or choose a new name altogether. This is a growing trend and a healthy one. Taking egos and other factors off the table, the real purpose of a not-for-profit is to stay true to its mission. If a name refinement can help to serve your constituents better, that's a good thing. Plus, it can do wonders for the government affairs function. When the organization is being sold to legislators or powerbrokers, a brand that clearly defines and represents what is being sold can make it an easier sell. A well-thought-out name identifies you as the source for your cause and constituents.

The strength of your volunteer base can go a long way in selling your organization, both in the regular activities that you perform and in the government affairs arena. Simply stated, power is a good thing when it comes to government affairs. If your volunteers are a powerbase or, at least, are perceived as a power base, it helps. Another place to go for power is pure numbers, particularly when you can provide an impressive count of people who are actively working as volunteers. It is impressive to say, for example, that your organization has thousands of volunteers. When I was working for the Boy Scouts of America (BSA), we used the volunteer count all the time. We were able to distinguish ourselves from most other youth-serving organizations by the use of the number. BSA also had the clout factor. Top volunteers were often the who's who of the community.

Not all organizations can use the volunteer equation to push their agenda. While most organizations can emphasize that they have dedicated volunteers, they may not have the numbers or the power volunteers. If this is the case for you, make it a priority to develop a plan to recruit the top-level volunteers you need.

Obviously, this is more difficult to do than it sounds, yet top-level volunteers are available for your organization. Acquiring them takes time, but you must make it a priority. If volunteer recruitment is one of your challenges, you should develop a separate volunteer recruitment plan based on the total volunteer experience. Create a plan that focuses on both the objectives that your not-for-profit wishes to attain and the return benefits that potential volunteers may want to receive.

The government affairs function can attract powerful volunteers who seek visibility and recognition. Often, it can be a win/win situation for both the organization and the volunteer. My book *The Universal Benefits of Volunteering: A Practical Workbook for Nonprofit Organizations, Volunteers and Corporations* can assist you in developing a plan that can attract the power volunteers you seek.

What about your staff? Most not-for-profits have a group of dedicated professionals who perform a number of roles in making the organization function. Several of the functions that staff perform are similar to other not-for-profits. You should have a full-time president/CEO. Like it or not, titles count. Government affairs work dictates that the chief professional in a not-for-profit be perceived as and labeled as the CEO.

Proper titles and functional responsibilities need to be given to all staff. Your employees need the power to function. The government affairs function is a fundamental part of this. If a position is part-time, give the person in that position a title that can be used in the government affairs arena—for example, external affairs director. If the position is full-time, give the person a title such as government affairs director.

The not-for-profit staff is a key element in the government affairs program. This applies to the entire staff, not just the people in the government affairs department. Everyone from the program director to the receptionist have to know how he or she fits into the government affairs function. For example, a member calls the Washington, DC, office of a major national association at

5:59 P.M. on a Friday. The receptionist is in the process of locking the front door and stops to pick up the telephone to take a message. The message is that Monday morning at 10:00 A.M. a bill will be introduced in a committee of the California State legislature that could dramatically affect the organization's membership. What is the receptionist's role?

1. Does she leave an e-mail message and hope the government affairs director gets it in time?
2. Does she give the member a telephone number to call?
3. Does the receptionist try to contact the government affairs director?
4. All the above?

This can happen at any time. In fact, a similar situation occurred in the organization that I lead. We had a process in place to take care of the situation, and it provided our organization with a grand opportunity to display our commitment to our constituents. It also helped us to significantly increase our visibility both in California and at the national level. A government affairs process needs to be in place that:

1. Informs each staff member on the role he or she plays in the government affairs function.
2. Has contingency plans to handle all emergencies.
3. Identifies key, professional leadership on-call 24 hours a day, 7 days a week to handle these situations.

Our example could have been handled in the following manner:

1. The receptionist calls the key staff person (home phone, cell phone, pager, etc.).
2. The call is returned immediately by the assigned staff person to the member who called to get the details and map out a plan.
3. Calls to key individuals in California are conducted over the weekend.
4. If the key staff person is deemed to lead the charge, travel arrangements are made to California.
5. A strategy is created and refined over the weekend. Testimony is prepared. Key individuals are secured to testify, and arrangements are made to approach legislators before the committee hearing.
6. The use of an in-state consultant is considered:
   a. As a resource to open doors.
   b. To help to localize the approach with a familiar face to committee members.
   c. As a backup in case you are delayed for any reason or cannot make it due to other commitments.

The bottom line is that this situation, and any other, can be handled if you have a process in place and if the entire staff understand that they have a stake in the government affairs function.

Now you are getting close to the starting gate. You want to create or enhance your government affairs program, but you want to make sure that the plan is sound, that your volunteer leadership will buy into it, and that the staff will make the plan work. To accomplish this task, you will want to develop a needs assessment to make sure you are prepared.

Needs Assessment

A needs assessment will provide your organization with an overall idea of what you have and what you will need.

What Are the Best Ways to Accomplish This Task?

The best way to start this process is to have key members of your staff provide the information that you seek. The kinds of questions that are asked will be the key.

Throughout this chapter, you will see examples of how you can perform this process. This is only a guide: feel free to adapt the examples to fit your unique needs. Discovering and fulfilling your needs is an important part of the process. Start with the basic template provided and then refine it to fit your particular circumstances.

Who Should Develop the Needs Assessment?

Most of the data for your needs assessment will be provided by your staff, but there are also other places to find valuable information, including the following:

- Members
- Volunteers
- Other leaders in your organization
- Legislators
- The media

Your list may also include other groups. The important thing is that you cover all your bases, so that your plan will be comprehensive. Nothing is more disheartening than developing a plan that does not include one of your member groups. This process is also a great way for your membership to buy into the plan that you are creating.

What Are the Key Areas?

The needs assessment process affords you an opportunity to increase your awareness of the variety of needs of your organization. As you examine each area, you should be honest with yourself. This is not the time for a public relations campaign. You will be trying to find your strong areas, of course, but you also want to find all of the weak ones. The strong areas will be a little easier to determine, but the hard part will be discovering how you can exploit them.

The weak areas are a bit more difficult to determine. You may be able to correct or improve some of them, but the remaining ones may be a lost cause or beyond your control. That means that your once perfect plan will need to be adapted to fit your overall assessment.

You will need to make an overall assessment of the following:

1. Your professional requirements
2. Your volunteer requirements
3. Costs and funding issues
4. Determining the parameters
5. Determining your prime issues
6. Ways in which you will make your voice heard
7. Your desire to lead or to follow
8. Your evaluation process

We will examine these key areas in the following sections.

Assessing Your Professional Requirements

The government affairs function cannot exist without high-quality professional talent. It is important, therefore, to recognize what you have and what you need. The extent of the available talent will, in many ways, dictate the size and dimension of your government affairs function. You will need to determine the following:

1. Your organization's internal capacity
2. Your need for external help
3. The fundamental traits you need to make the process productive
4. The kind of training that may be needed

What Is Your Organization's Internal Capacity? The internal capacity that a not-for-profit organization needs to conduct a successful government affairs function varies a great deal with the type of the organization. A small social service organization may have only one employee who acts as the CEO and the government affairs director, while a large trade asso-

EXHIBIT 8.1 Guide to Assessing Internal Capacity

This guide is used to determine if current staff can assume additional government affairs duties, if they cannot, or if some current duties be dropped or reassigned.

Staff	Current Duties	Anticipated Duties	Dropped/Reassigned
CEO			
Deputy			
Government affairs			
Operations director			
Communications director			
Program director			
Field staff			
Support staff			
Others			

Conclusion

1. Current staff is adequate to meet the government affairs task. _____
2. The staff needs to be reorganized to perform the task. _____
3. The staff cannot perform the entire task. New staff is needed. _____
4. The staff cannot perform the entire task. An outside consultant is needed. _____

ciation may have an office of full-time government affairs professionals. Internal capacity depends on the culture of your organization and the amount of money that is available.

To start to assess your needs, develop a simple chart, as in Exhibit 8.1. List your current staff by title from the CEO to the receptionist. Also, list positions that may be added in the future, as well as positions you feel you will need in order to perform the government affairs role. Next, list the current duties of each position, anticipated duties within the government affairs role, and reassigned duties to make way for the anticipated government affairs duties. Your conclusions should be quite telling. The resulting chart will show you your staff needs for the government affairs function.

Recently, I received a call from an individual who runs a national healthcare association. We have been friends for several years, and we often use each other as sounding boards for the decisions that we have to make in our respective organizations. We spent a long time talking about the changes that are taking place in his association, including the strong possibility of a merger, the increasing workload of his staff, the volunteer challenges, and his struggle to find and retain quality professional talent.

Finding and retaining a high-quality staff is becoming the number one challenge for not-for-profits and it is a major issue to consider when looking at overall capacity. Consider the following questions:

- How overworked is your staff?
- Can the staff take on additional duties?
- Can part of the current functions of certain staff members be given to others? Can those functions be reduced or even dropped?

Staff evaluation is not an area to be taken lightly; it will be crucial to the success or failure of your government affairs role. For the most part, your conclusions will be one of the following:

- Your current staff is adequate for the challenge.
- Your organization needs to reorganize staff assignments and functions.
- You need to hire additional staff.
- You need to hire outside consultants to do part or all of the work.

If you feel that your staff is adequate, congratulations. You have managed to achieve the first major step toward developing your government affairs function. If you fall into one of the other categories, then you have another problem. A word of caution on both of these, though: if you feel that your staff is adequate, be sure of it. A good CEO, for example, may not be good in the government affairs role. Don't try to make your staff fill roles that they are not trained for or do not have the desire to perform. Reorganizing your staff can have a positive or negative effect. It may be the right thing to do, but, if it results only in spreading the work around, it can have an adverse effect.

Hiring a government affairs director is a major step. It will require a large outlay of money and time to search for the best candidate. It also requires a great deal of time to train the new employee. It is important that you consider the real cost of hiring such a person. For a number of organizations, this is the way to go; for others, it is not. How do you decide? Often, money is the larger factor, but the decision needs to be a little deeper than that. The question you have to ask is "would a full-time government affairs director make a big enough difference to justify the expense?"

Do You Need External Help?   As previously noted, a number of not-for-profit organizations use consultants to supplement, or completely perform, the government affairs function. You need to find out what is right for your organization. (See Exhibit 8.2.) Some of the functions of the program can or should be performed by key staff members, while other tasks take a level of expertise that your staff may not have. Examples of the kinds of areas that

EXHIBIT 8.2   Task Needs Assessment

The task needs assessment is designed to help you determine who should be assigned to the government affairs tasks—that is, current staff, new staff, or an outside consultant.

Tasks Needed	Current Staff	New Staff	Outside Consultant
Planning			
Federal representation			
State representation			
(list the states)			
Legislative tracking			
Grassroots development			
Testifying			
Writing bills, etc.			
Issue campaigning			
(list the issues)			
Networking/Alliance building			
Other areas			

may not be best for your staff include direct lobbying and work that is not geographically realistic to manage. Direct lobbying requires a great deal of time and relationship building, which most not-for-profit leaders do not have the time to perform. Also, it often does not make sense to travel hundreds of miles (or even around the block) if someone else can do the job better and more quickly.

The work that outside consultants perform in my organization has made a major difference in our success. We could not function without them. My organization's role is to represent outdoor sports enthusiasts nationwide. We are often running campaigns in 8 to 10 states at a time. While I obviously have a place in this process and we do send staff out to these states, we use a host of consultants who know our issue and are the best in their field. We also use other consultants who are experts in particular areas, such as polling, media campaigns, and fund-raising.

My organization's primary mission is government relations. We use dozens of consultants every year. I heartily recommend that consultants be used in at least part of your strategic thinking. (Chapter 6 details the use of outside consultants.)

In a nutshell, you need to know what services you desire, how to ask for the services, and how to measure the results. It sounds easy, but it isn't.

EXHIBIT 8.3   Outside Consultant Needs Assessment

1. Determine the role or roles that an outside consultant needs to perform:
   a. Government affairs
   b. Fund-raising
   c. Public relations
   d. Other (explain)

2. What is your budget for consultants?
   —Source of income:
   a. Current budget
   b. New sources
   c. Other (explain)
   d. Total income

   —What are the expected expenses?
   a. Consultant fees
   b. Communications
   c. Administrative overhead
   d. Other (explain)
   e. Total expense

3. What is the right mix of skills and personality to complement your staff and volunteers?

4. What assignments will each consultant be given?

Consultant	Function	Expected Outcome

5. Determine the method of choosing your consultants.

6. Develop a list of expected standards and compare it with possible candidates.

7. Interview the candidates and select the consultant.

8. Create an evaluation plan to keep the consultants on track.

(See Exhibit 8.3.) Once you have determined what your needs are, the search is on for the best talent at a fair price: remember that you get what you pay for and good talent is worth every penny. Don't sell your program short by trying to save a few dollars. It never works and often costs more in lost time. Finding the right talent is the biggest challenge. The following are a few suggestions:

1. Before approaching a prospective consultant, always check out the person's qualifications.

2. Ask around; if you have been networking as you should, you know other not-for-profits that have used consultants. Ask them who is worth a look.

3. Check with other organizations' leaders who are working in the same area or with organizations that have missions similar to yours.

4. Be careful to avoid selecting a consultant who is too close to a competing organization.

5. Don't be cheap, but be sure to see if the consultant's fee structure is in line with that of other consultants and that the fee structure is flexible enough to work within your budget.

6. Always develop a plan of action and an evaluation process at the beginning of the relationship.

What Fundamental Traits Make the Process Productive? Productivity is the key to assessing any staff or consultant function. The government affairs area is no exception. It is an area, however, that can be challenging to measure on a day-to-day basis. Over the long term, it is easier—that is, did we win or not? Government affairs work is a lot more than that, though. (See Exhibit 8.4.)

The fundamental question in government affairs productivity is "Has the not-for-profit increased its influence?" All of the other questions in Exhibit 8.4 help you to answer this one, yet the answer is as much a feeling as a fact. You always seem to know if you are heading up or down. The government affairs process can be complicated, and the challenge is measuring how effectively the work has been performed.

One of the keys is found in the number and quality of volunteers you are able to secure and the measured tasks that they perform. Securing the right volunteers for the right tasks, such as fund-raising and volunteer recruitment, is essential. This is far more important than acquiring great numbers of volunteers who do not fit the needed profile.

The quality and effectiveness of an organization's grassroots network are a prime concern. The assumption of any elected official is that your organization represents a body of people that could help him or her be re-elected. The questions are, is that true and are your constituent ranks increasing?

You cannot perform the government affairs role unless you raise the funds needed to make it work. Set a goal, but make sure you assess the process you have created.

Coalition building is a major way to gain visibility and power. Measure the number of coalitions that your organization has been involved with and those in which you took the lead. Also, ask yourself what did these coalitions really accomplish? Coalitions, by definition, have a beginning and an end. Your evaluation can help you determine which of those you wish to continue to be part of and which of those you wish to leave. Focus only on the coalitions that have the highest return to your organization. This will also free time to examine other opportunities.

EXHIBIT 8.4   Traits Assessment

This evaluation sheet can help your not-for-profit to determine how effective the government affairs functions has been to date.

Answer the following questions:

1. Has your not-for-profit increased its government affairs influence in the past three years? _____ (yes/no)

2. How many volunteers did you have at the end of last year? _____ Is this an increase over the year before? _____ (yes/no) How many of these volunteers assist the organization in the government affairs function? _____ Is this an increase over the year before? _____ (yes/no)

3. Do you have a grassroots lobbying effort? _____ (yes/no) If so, what is your evaluation of how effective it has been, based on a scale of 1 to 9, with 9 being the most effective? _____

4. Do you raise funds based on your government affairs activity? _____ (yes/no) If so, how much did you raise last year? _____ What sources did it come from?

Source	%
a. Individual	_____
b. Business	_____
c. Other (explain)	_____

   How did you procure these funds?

Method	%
a. Direct solicitation	_____
b. Direct mail	_____
c. Telephone calls	_____
d. Other (explain)	

   What techniques did you use?

Techniques	%
a. General solicitation	_____
b. Issues campaign promotion	_____
c. Special interest groups	_____
d. Political action committee (PAC)	_____
e. Other (explain)	_____

5. What is your organization's level of coalition involvement? _____ How many successfully fulfilled their goal last year? _____ List the coalitions that you are currently involved in and rate:

Coalition Name/Purpose	Level of Interest (High/Low)	Effectiveness (1 to 9)	Continue/Drop

EXHIBIT 8.4 Traits Assessment *(continued)*

6. Rate the staff and consultants who are involved in the government affairs function:

   <u>Name</u>   <u>Staff</u>   <u>Consultant</u>   <u>Effective Rate (1 to 9)</u>

7. List the number of contacts made and who were the most significant last year:

   <u>Contacts Made by Our Organization</u>   <u>Purpose</u>   <u>Key Contact</u>

   <u>Other Organizations Contacting Us</u>   <u>Purpose</u>   <u>Key Contact</u>

8. How many bills were authored by your organization last year? _____
   How many were successful? _____

9. What do you feel is the overall image of the organization? Rate by target audience:

   <u>Target Audience</u>   <u>Rating (1 to 9)</u>
   a. Legislators   _____
   b. Media   _____
   c. Other organizations _____
   d. Opinion makers   _____
   e. Others (explain)   _____

   What are your findings based on?
   a. Your opinion   _____
   b. Survey(s)   _____ (indicate who received the surveys)
   c. Other sources (explain) _____

10. How has the government affairs function benefited the overall organization?
    a. Has it helped raise more nongovernment affairs funds? _____ (yes/no)
       If so, how much? _____
    b. Has it attracted more members? _____ (yes/no)
       If so, how many? _____
    c. Has it increased your visibility? _____ (yes/no) If so, explain. _____
       _____
       _____
    d. Has it enhanced your programs? _____ (yes/no) If so, explain. _____
       _____
       _____
    e. Has it helped increase the quality of your staff? _____ (yes/no) If so, explain.
       _____
       _____

Do not overlook the standards you set for your staff and for your consultants. Make sure that they are in sync with your goals and aspirations. Don't assume anything. Set the standards high, expect quality service, and make sure that they receive feedback and praise when they perform. Make sure that you conduct regular evaluations as well.

Measure your contacts with outside sources. This includes legislators, other key organizations, and the media. Visibility is one of the keys to a successful government affairs function. Make sure that legislators see you as an insider, make sure that key constituents see you as the authority, and make sure that the media use you as a resource.

Legislators and their aides often do not create the language written in most proposed legislation. Lobbying groups are often the authors. The process works in two ways:

1. The organization writes the proposed bill.
2. A legislator approaches an organization to request that they author a bill. This is the real measure of the strength and power of a not-for-profit. This can provide the organization's leadership with a great deal of pride and satisfaction, although no one, except those close to the process, will ever know who authored the bill. The real reward is that you have made it to the inner circle, which pays huge dividends for the bill in question and for future relationships with that member and other legislators.

The government affairs function can and should significantly increase your image in your current circles of influence and way beyond. All of us can name organizations that have become so familiar to us that they have entered the vocabulary of our nation. That's power. These organizations run the gambit from the National Rifle Association to Planned Parenthood. No matter where your beliefs fall in the spectrum of these and other organizations, they have made a major impact within the government affairs arena.

Can your organization attain such an image? Perhaps, but most not-for-profits will never make it to that level and really don't need to in order to fulfill their missions. Keep your goals in mind and shoot for the level that fits your resources and needs.

Power, influence, and visibility all have their rewards. The rewards include the fact that your government affairs work will add value to the rest of your activities and programs including attracting volunteers, raising more money, and gaining more recognition as the authority in your field of interest. This is not a time to be shy about using your hard earned visibility and recognition to gain a significant increase in your marketing share.

What Kind of Training Is Needed?   Training can be both formal and on-the-job. Your entire staff needs to be trained in the government affairs function. Everyone plays a role. In my organization, we train everyone on what the government affairs function is and how each individual relates to the current activities.

A receptionist who doesn't know about the current government affairs agenda tells a prospective caller that the organization is not up to par. This can blow a not-for-profit's image, lose members or volunteers and, even, cost you money since a not-for-profits' life depends on how it is perceived. Bring your staff into the process at the beginning. Sell them on the concept and ask for ideas and input. You will be surprised at the enthusiasm and great ideas that can be generated by this process.

Some recommended training techniques include the following:

- A kick-off training session for all staff. Think about using an expert to walk your staff through the process and link the process to your organization's future—a future that includes a skilled staff who will be rewarded for their hard work.
- Regular government affairs briefings for the entire staff. Always create time for questions.
- A regular, updated "cheat" sheet for your staff. Try to limit it to one page and make each point short and clear.
- Quarterly or semi-annual staff reviews of the entire government affairs agenda. Review the successes in the process, as well as areas that need improvement. Always let the staff know the next steps and how they relate to the process.

Determining Your Volunteer Requirements

Volunteers are an essential part of a successful government affairs plan. Although some organizations may disagree with this statement due to the nature of their work or the size of their staff, most of us do not fall into this camp. Most organizations are eager to accept the help and guidance of volunteers. I cannot envision a plan that would exclude an element of volunteer support.

Questions to Ask about Volunteer Requirements   The first obvious question is "what is needed?" (See Exhibit 8.5.) Volunteer recruiting is an ongoing process, so the need question will evolve. It is difficult to determine the volunteer requirements of any not-for-profit, but certain types of volunteers will be in most organizational plans.

A government affairs committee is a starting point. Participants in this committee will typically be your leading volunteers who are the most interested in your program. Their function varies, depending on each organization, but they should be helping to set the agenda to be approved by the board or top governing body. They should also be the key group that,

EXHIBIT 8.5   Volunteer Needs Assessment

Volunteers are needed at all levels of the government affairs process. This assessment sheet will help to begin the process of analyzing current and future needs.

Level	Area	Positions	Current	Need
National	Organization's board	List positions in relationship to GA function		
	Government affairs committee	**a.** Chair **b.** Vice chair **c.** Members (list each by function) **d.** Issue driven		
	Pool	**a.** Testify **b.** Make calls **c.** Other (list)		
State	Government affairs committee	**a.** Chair **b.** Vice chair **c.** Members (list each by function) **d.** Issue driven		
	Pool	**a.** Testify **b.** Make calls **c.** Other (list)		
Grassroots		**a.** Members (list each function)		

through staff leadership, helps to put the plan in place. Depending on your organization's size, you may have subcommittees of the government affairs function—for example, a national association may have state committees, which fall under the national committee's jurisdiction.

Another good way of organizing is around issues. You may have a core government affairs committee, but within that structure certain volunteers are picked to lead the charge on ongoing or onetime issues.

It is also a good idea to have a pool of high-level volunteers who are willing to do special projects for you, such as testifying, visiting key legislators, and making calls to the right people at the right time.

The final thing that you will need is a structure to promote and effectively use the grassroots element of your organization. The grassroots part of a government affairs plan can be a powerful weapon. At my organization, we find a number of ways of firing-up the grassroots constituents, including the following:

EXHIBIT 8.6   Ten-Step Guide to Discovering High-Quality Volunteers

1. Find any excuse to contact your constituents.

2. Make a written evaluation of each constituent whom you meet:
   Rank each prospect's potential:

Area	Rank (1 to 9)
a. Volunteer	
b. Contributor	
c. Solicitor	
d. Other	

3. Develop a cultivation plan, based on your evaluation, and market yourself to the best prospects.

4. Create a profile of your best prospects.

5. Research who knows these prospects and whom the prospects may know.

6. Determine how the volunteer prospect can best serve the organization.

7. Select the appropriate people to ask the prospect to serve.

8. Ask the volunteer prospect to participate at the right time and in the right place.

9. Evaluate your results.

10. Determine the next step:
    a. If the prospect agrees to serve, follow up immediately to move the prospect into the proper volunteer role.
    b. If the prospect turns down the opportunity, determine the reason and see if another volunteer opportunity would better suit the prospect's interest.

- Ongoing direct-mail promotions
- An e-mail alert system
- Rallies at the grassroots level
- An in-state structure, which promotes volunteer involvement

The "do we have it" component was covered earlier in the chapter, to some extent. You need to know your volunteer resources and if you don't have what is needed, you need to discover ways to find volunteer talent.

Finding the volunteer talent takes some research, but it mostly takes a bit of shoe leather. (See Exhibit 8.6.) While current discussions and trends seem to focus on the lack of volunteer talent, quality volunteers *are* available. Today's volunteer is different, in some ways, from the volunteer of the past. Volunteers today tend to have less time, and they want to work in areas that provide them with more satisfaction, but they still want to make a difference. What does this mean? Volunteers have generally become more educated on the volunteer process, and they want to have some control over the work that they perform and the results they achieve.

The volunteer management program within the government affairs activity needs to focus not only on what needs to be done for the cause but also on what can be done to attract and retain volunteers. Developing volunteer positions that fulfill your needs as well as individual volunteers' needs will pay huge dividends. This can be done even in the traditionally difficult-to-fill volunteer roles such as fund-raising and direct contact with legislators.

The ongoing process of contacting constituents to evaluate them as potential volunteers is vital for all areas of a not-for-profit, not just the government affairs function. The more contact you have with your constituents, the more prospects that will emerge. In-person contacts are the best, but often you cannot spend the time on this for everyone. Calling constituents to thank them or to ask their advice can open the door to establishing a relationship with them. Personal letters asking for help can also open doors for future involvement.

Several years ago, I asked a volunteer to testify at a state hearing concerning an issue that we had been working on for sometime. When I asked him to testify, I didn't realize that the location of the hearing, while in-state, was several hundred miles away. The hearing was also being held early in the morning. The volunteer was the president of a midsized company and had to be in meetings late the day before and had another set of meetings to attend the day of the hearing. I was about to ask, "Should I find someone else?" when he accepted the assignment. The volunteer left his house at 3 A.M., traveled to the location of the hearing, testified on our behalf, and then traveled back in time for his afternoon meetings. This type of dedication did not suddenly happen; it was the result of a sound not-for-profit cultivation program and a volunteer's believing so deeply in a cause that he would make such a sacrifice to serve. Volunteers can be found, cultivated, and asked to do what seems impossible if they are motivated to do so.

Recommended Volunteer Structures   The volunteer structure for the government affairs function varies, depending on a number of factors, including budget, staff involvement, current volunteers, and volunteer potential. Generally, one of these four models seems to be used to create a volunteer structure:

1. A not-for-profit may use the chief professional officer as the staff director and may have a small group of volunteers who are involved with the government affairs function. These volunteers often have other volunteer roles, such as board member.

2. A consultant may be given most, or at least part, of the government affairs function. The consultant reports to the chief professional officer, and a less formal volunteer structure is in place.

3. A full-time government affairs assignment may be given to a member of the staff, who reports to the chief professional officer. A government affairs committee is in place.

4. A full-time government affairs staff may be used, with a director of government relations, who reports to the chief professional officer. A government affairs committee is in place using a multilayer approach. Volunteers are a key part of the leadership.

See Exhibit 8.7 for more detail on these models. Whatever structure you have or will select, volunteers should play an upfront role. Volunteers can

---

EXHIBIT 8.7   Organizational Models

The following government affairs models are, in a general way, the structures that a number of not-for-profit organizations use.

CEO-Driven Organization
The size of this organization can vary from small to medium. No other staff members are involved with the government affairs function. No outside consultants are involved, either. Such an organization generally does not engage in moving legislation. It operates as more of a tracking and reporting program. Some volunteer support may be used.

Consultant-Driven Organization
This kind of organization relies on an outside consultant to do most of the work. The level of work generally depends on the level of funding that is available for the consultant. The level of work falls far short of a full-blown plan. You may find more legislator visits and bill promotion here than under the CEO-driven model, however. Generally, very little volunteer support is requested.

Staff-Driven Organization
In this model, the government affairs assignment is given to a full-time staff person. It may not be a full-time effort, however. The staff person may have other duties to perform. The role of the CEO varies. It depends on the interest and job description developed. Outside consultants may be used as well. Volunteer support may be sought but generally for testimony and not for strategic thinking.

Team-Driven Organization
The organization that selects a team-driven model wishes to have the government affairs function become an intrinsic part of the organization. The government affairs function is part of the organization's strategic plan. Generally, this level of commitment takes place in organizations that have a greater sense of where they are and where they want to go. Such an organization has a government affairs department. It is staffed with a full-time director and other staff as needed. Volunteers are encouraged to be involved at all levels, including taking part in the strategic thinking process. Consultants are used, but only when needed for a special project or when time or geographic obstacles make it impossible to use staff or volunteers to do the job.

send a more powerful message to legislators and the outside world than a full-time not-for-profit professional can. Volunteers need to be on full display to make the human factor an issue. They can tell your story effectively, since most have lived it themselves. Don't undersell the volunteer factor.

Functions of Volunteers   As previously noted, the volunteer's role in the government affairs function is substantial, and volunteers can perform roles that the professional cannot. However, it is important to determine where volunteers will serve and where they will not. As previously mentioned, the volunteer should be used as the front person in a number of cases but can play other roles as well.

In looking at the front role, you need to determine how to place volunteers to best serve the not-for-profit, but don't forget that the placement you choose must serve the volunteers as well. A successful placement can be made by looking at the process in two ways:

1. What needs to be done?
2. Who can do it?

This sounds basic, but it's a matching game—matching the tasks that need to be done with the right volunteers to do them. It is always a challenge to select the right volunteer for each task.

The government affairs function is a unique area of the not-for-profit. Just as in the case of fund-raising, government affairs takes a special breed of volunteer, and, within that breed, a volunteer may have the capability to perform one or more tasks but, for the most part, cannot or will not perform all of the volunteer functions needed. That is why it is so important to carefully orchestrate each volunteer assignment. (See Exhibit 8.8.)

It is a good practice to keep a complete profile of current government affairs volunteers. This profile should be linked to the master profile that your not-for-profit is keeping on all volunteers. For government affairs purposes, you will need to know the relationship of the volunteer to the organization. This often reveals the area that the volunteer has interest in and is most passionate about. Check to see how long the volunteer has been a member and how much he or she has donated to the organization. Document past volunteer experiences, both with your organization and with others.

It is particularly interesting if you can find out how your volunteers donate their time and money outside your organization. In at least a few cases, you will be shocked to find a great deal more time being spent with other not-for-profit organizations. If that is the case, try to determine why. While you may not be able to change the ratio in your favor, you may be able to refine your approach to increase the loyalty and interest of your volunteers.

Make sure that you categorize the overall interest profile of each volunteer. This is simply your evaluation, with the data you have collected, of

EXHIBIT 8.8   Volunteer Profile Sheet

The volunteer profile sheet provides a way to gather data on existing or prospective volunteers. These records can be stored in the computer in a variety of software applications.

Name: _____

Address: _____

_____

Telephone: _____ Fax: _____

E-mail: _____

Volunteer status: _____ New prospect for organization

_____ Current volunteer but not in government affairs

Personal Background
  a. Education
  b. Family
  c. Business
  d. Civic interests and volunteer work outside organization
  e. Worth
  f. Hobbies
  g. Other

Organizational Background
  a. Member how many years? _____ Why is he/she a member? _____

_____

  b. Total contribution last year? _____ What areas of not-for-profit designated for contribution? _____

  c. Volunteer history: _____

  d. Other: _____

Individuals Whom the Prospect Admires or Respects
  a. Within the organization:

  b. Outside the organization:

Recommendations
  a. What volunteer position is the best fit for the individual?

_____

  b. Who should cultivate this individual and ask the prospect to volunteer?

_____

_____

_____

  c. When is the best time to ask? _____
     What is the best place to ask? _____

the best place each volunteer can serve your organization to bring maximum return satisfaction to both you and the volunteers.

For the average not-for-profit, keeping a volunteer profile may seem like a lot of work. It doesn't have to be. The following are some suggestions on how to get started:

1. Determine the data that you wish to seek.
2. Set up the place where you wish to deposit the information. Following are a few ideas:
   a. Use a central computer-based software package that your organization has for profiling current and prospective volunteers.
   b. If that does not exist, your organization may have a fund-raising software program that tracks givers and prospects. Chances are you can adapt that software to create a government affairs volunteer profile program.
   c. If none of the above exists, look into the basic computer software system you have in place; you can probably create a basic data system to hold your government affairs volunteer profiles.

Once you have a place to store the data, set up rules on how you are going to obtain and enter the data. Every staff member and volunteer in the organization should be in charge of obtaining the data. I receive my best information about prospective volunteers from my current volunteers. I also receive a lot of interesting information from my staff. The key is to have all channels open for receiving information.

The most important parts of data collection are who enters the information and how the information is entered—for instance, can it be retrieved easily and in a format that will benefit you the most? This is determined by both the data system's capabilities and the roles you wish the staff to play. The data system's capabilities may vary, but the system must have be able to allow staff to access the system to retrieve and enter data.

In our office, we have a central volunteer profile database. This database is located within our fund-raising software package. New files are set up by assigned support staff. The bio information is kept up-to-date by our support staff. The entire staff is able to access these records to perform a number of tasks, including entering notes about telephone converstaions, e-mails, or in-person visits with prospects. This keeps each profile timely and helps us to make educated decisions about managing our volunteer program.

Recognition Factor One of the areas that not-for-profits tend to forget is recognition of the volunteer's work. Recognition is a funny thing—

what is good for one person will turn off another. Recognition, therefore, needs to be tailored to each program you conduct and, as best as you can, to each volunteer.

The government affairs function attracts a vast array of volunteers, ranging from the most visible leaders in the nation to grassroots advocates. All volunteers are important. Each one plays a role that makes your program successful.

At my organization, we provide a wide array of recognition programs. We tend to have a core group of recognition mechanisms for everyday use, but we tailor most of our recognition programs based on the campaigns that we conduct. The following are two examples.

In Iowa, our organization conducted a campaign that required an aggressive grassroots effort, which included getting our constituents to the state capital to conduct a rally on the capital steps. We spent a lot of time motivating them to attend, and our goal was to have 500 people attend. It required us to charter five buses and to cater food. We contacted everyone by telephone and had key volunteer leaders in charge of filling each bus; however, we did one more thing: we provided each attendee with a hunter orange ball cap with our logo on it. The day of the rally, it began to snow. In Iowa, when it snows, it *really* snows. All of the buses full of volunteers started out to the state capital, but only three made it. We had our rally: a stream of orange more than 300 volunteers strong. It was one of the largest demonstrations of voter power ever held in the state. While we didn't get the bill out of committee, we were very close. It did, however, generate so much power and pride that it helped us to launch a state committee, which has continued to fight for the bill and other measures. A simple recognition like an an orange hat, or the acknowledgment that volunteers make a difference can be very powerful.

Our group ran a major campaign in Ohio, which required that $2.3 million be raised. More than 2,000 volunteers were recruited to assist, and the campaign took 2 years to complete. In the end, we raised over $2.6 million from 300,000 gifts. We gave instant recognition to all the grassroots volunteers, ranging from jackets to belt buckles. We won our issue by a 60/40 margin due to the level of funds the volunteers generated which gave us the power to develop a major media campaign. Our recognition gathering was a statewide rally, which 1,500 constituents attended. Almost 90 of the attendees were state legislative leaders. We recognized all volunteers; everyone received a special thank you. Our chairman was recognized at an event that took place outside of our organization, but the event was one of the major gatherings of key business and political leaders in the state. This provided both the chairman and our group with major visibility recognition.

You cannot sell short the impact that a recognition program can have for your volunteer management plan. Make sure that you gear the recognition to fit the various audiences that you have within your plan.

One last thing to remember is that a recognition plan cannot be effective unless others witness it. A crowded room helps you to achieve a number of goals, including the following two:

1. A recognition plan can motivate other volunteers to emulate the volunteer being recognized. This is why my group uses instant recognition programs for grassroots campaigns. We traditionally plan regular report meetings. The highlight of each of these meetings is the recognition of the volunteers who have made their goals. Volunteers enjoy being recognized in front of their peers, and it is an effective tool to motivate others to work harder to receive recognition at the next report meeting.

2. Prospective volunteers can also be motivated. In my organization, we often bring prospective volunteers to report meetings. The meeting shows them that they could be part of a team of volunteers with ample support and that everyone is having a good time and being recognized. We make sure that the prospective volunteer has a buddy or mentor to show him or her around and to help finalize the person's decision to volunteer. The professional staff members also make sure the prospective volunteers feel comfortable and that all of their questions are answered.

Evaluation Plan   Government affairs volunteer management programs need an effective evaluation plan. The following questions can help you evaluate:

1. Did the not-for-profit provide the level of support needed for the volunteers in the government affairs program?
2. Did the volunteers perform to the level needed to be successful?
3. What areas need refinement?
4. What areas should be dropped?
5. How did each volunteer do and, based on that, where should he or she be placed next?

Your not-for-profit's support of the volunteer management plan needs to be evaluated at least once a year. A lot of effort and money is put into such a program. An evaluation can help you to determine next year's approach. The staff should meet first to evaluate the government affairs volunteer management program. That meeting should generate the agenda for the key volunteer meeting. At that time, the staff members should present a report that outlines their evaluation. The volunteers should then add thoughts, make comments on the staff's evaluation, and agree on a final report.

The report should contain an evaluation of the support given to volunteers. Volunteers should be asked to comment. While you may think that this could cause more problems than it solves, I have found that this process helps to shed light on problems that no one would have stated without being asked. Most of the problems that are discovered can be solved, and improvements and exciting new ideas emerge, which can make the process more effective and less expensive.

Make sure that you place all of your programs on the table; let both staff and key volunteers evaluate the worth of existing programs. Be sure to ask their ideas on possible new programs as well. Ask them to evaluate the volunteers' overall performance, based on a scale of 1 to 9, making sure that everyone participates in the overall evaluation and that it is done so that no one gets hurt in the process.

The most important part of the evaluation process is the individual volunteer evaluation. This needs to be done as a cooperative effort between the staff and key volunteers. (See Exhibit 8.9.) This part of the evaluation plan must be conducted carefully and confidentially.

Each volunteer evaluation should review the role that the individual played. Is the job description for the position still valid or does it need refinement? Which areas did the volunteer excel in? Which areas need refinement? This is the time to be honest, particularly in the area of refinement. Provide an overall evaluation and maintain the same overall evaluation scoring method for all the volunteers whom you are evaluating.

When the process is done, the final determinations to make are:

1. Should the individual stay in the same position?
2. Should the individual be moved to another position within the government affairs role?
3. Should the individual be given an opportunity to hold a volunteer position in another area of the not-for-profit?
4. Should the individual be dropped altogether as a volunteer?

The evaluation process is a task that many not-for-profits do not perform such not-for-profits but they do a disservice to their volunteers and themselves by not completing this part of the volunteer management process.

Determining the Costs and Funding Issues

The financial burden seems to be the main reason that a number of not-for-profit organizations tend to not have a government affairs program. If the financial burden could be lifted, a lot more not-for-profits would probably take advantage of the benefits that a government affairs program can provide. To project the costs and to find a way to pay for the program, a not-for-profit needs to (1) make a cost analysis and (2) find ways to fund the program.

EXHIBIT 8.9   Volunteer Evaluation Form

Not-for-profit organizations depend on volunteers to perform a wide array of duties. The recruitment and retention of volunteers is vital to the survival of these organizations, yet a number of not-for-profits do not take the time to evaluate volunteer performance, nor do they help their volunteers to find the experience that can fulfill their goals and objectives. Volunteers are a key element in the success of a government affairs program.

Name: _____

Address: _____

_____

Telephone: _____   Fax: _____

E-mail: _____

Volunteer position: _____

Description of Duties

Areas Volunteer Excels In

Refinements/Improvements That Can Be Made

Past Recognition Given for Volunteer Achievement

Recognition   Given by Whom?   At What Function?

Overall Evaluation
  a. Volunteer rating _____ (based on a 1 to 9 scale)
  b. Explain rating: _____

Recommendations
  a. What kind of recognition should the volunteer receive?
     1. Thank-you letter
     2. Recognition published in not-for-profit's materials
     3. Personal recognition piece
        a. Standard (describe it)
        b. Special (describe it)
  b. Should the volunteer remain in the same position? _____ (yes/no)
  c. If the volunteer should not be kept in the same position, what is your recommendation?
     1. Move the volunteer to another position.
        If so, what is the position? _____
        Explain why. _____
     2. Drop the volunteer altogether.
        If so, why? _____

Other Information

_____   _____   _____
     Volunteer evaluator   Date   Staff evaluator

_____
_____

EXHIBIT 8.10   Cost Analysis Form

The cost of developing and maintaining a government affairs function often is a major block in launching and maintaining an effective program. The cost analysis form provides a starting point for you to determine the resources that will be needed.

Personnel (List)	Salary	Benefits	Other	Total Compensation

Consultants (List)	Retainer	Hourly Fee Total Time	Other	Total Fees

Overhead	Areas			Total Overhead
	a. Telephone			
	b. Travel			
	c. Promotion			
	d. Printing			
	e. Administrative			

Other				Total Other

Total expense $_____

Since government affairs programs vary in size and dimension, how can you determine the cost? (See Exhibit 8.10.) At this juncture, plan for the program that can do the job based on your analysis. It is a simple budget process that will allow you to project what it will take to proceed.

As always in a not-for-profit, staff and/or consultant time is the major expense. Be realistic when it comes to your staff's time. A successful government affairs program takes time, and you do not want to lessen the impact of other programs that you are developing.

Once you have determined the staffing expenses, most of the other budgetary items will be easier to determine. The budget needs to reflect the overall plan. If you are going to do a major issues campaign in Washington, DC, and you live in Texas, you know that your travel expenses need to reflect several trips to DC. Once you have determined your projected costs, you are ready to see if you can afford to run such a program.

Traditionally, finding ways to raise government affairs funds is harder to do than raising program funds. Obviously, you do not want to divert program funds currently being raised for other sections of your not-for-profit. Whether you're launching a government affairs program or refining one, finding the needed funds is always a challenge. Funds for these purposes can come from:

- Direct contributions
- Issue-directed contributions
- Campaign-focused contributions
- A PAC
- Other sources

Direct contributions to fund a government affairs function can be sought at any time. If you are launching a government affairs department, you may want to develop a campaign to introduce the concept to your members and ask for a onetime gift, in addition to their annual gift, to help to get the program going. A number of organizations have separate funding campaigns for the government affairs function. It's a good idea, and it keeps the program in front of the membership.

Issue-directed contributions are another way to gain funds. Funds are sought based on a major ongoing issue. AARP, for example, is deeply interested in the Social Security issue and could have an extensive campaign each year just on this issue.

Campaign-focused efforts are designed to have a start and an end. My group uses this method as well, both at the federal level and the state level. This type of effort tends to be highly charged. To fund such an effort successfully, you must be able to identify the constituents who best fit your profile and tailor your message to introduce the issue and position the message to meet their needs and passions. This can be a good way to start a government affairs program.

Political action committees are known by almost everyone. They act as a method for some not-for-profits to raise funds to make contributions to election campaigns for state and federal legislators. (Chapter 3 details the role that PACs play.) A PAC can attract new kinds of dollars for your effort and is worth looking into.

You can also explore other areas of fund-raising including a major gift effort each year to procure large donations geared to the government affairs effort and endowments to the program. A major gift program is natural for a number of organizations. Government affairs seems to attract more globally minded individuals, who tend to be wealthier than others. Do not overlook endowing the entire effort, however. You may be able to find one or more individuals who feel so strongly about your issue that they want to underwrite the entire costs.

Determining the Parameters

Determining the initial parameters of the government affairs function is an important step in launching or reinventing activity. We have discussed the volunteer requirement, the ways to fill the staff roles, the ways to determine the costs, and the possible ways of funding the operation. The next step is to begin to map out the plan. To determine the initial parameters, the following areas need to be examined:

- Ways to create a government affairs plan based on current capacity
- Ways for the organization to look bigger than it is
- Ways of building a network
- Ways of becoming a resource

Ways to Create a Government Affairs Plan Based on Current Capacity
We discussed the capacity issue earlier in this chapter, but let's look at it from a different perspective. If your organization is currently without a government affairs function and wish to add it, can it be done without increasing capacity? The answer is, maybe or maybe not. The underlining question is, what do you really want out of the government affairs function? The following are a few answers that tend to surface:

- I merely want to increase our visibility.
- I want to increase our prestige.
- I want to make more money for our organization.
- I see it as an opportunity to represent our members.
- I think our issues need to be defended and promoted.
- Our constituents will lose (or gain).
- We need to support and initiate bills to represent our members.
- We need to help elect (or help defeat) legislators to ensure that our constituents are protected.
- I want our not-for-profit to be the number one resource in our area of expertise.
- I want our organization to author bills that affect our issue.

Where do you fit into the picture? If you tend to want to focus on the first three answers of the preceding list, visibility, prestige and money, you may be able to develop a much smaller effort, almost like a public relations effort. (Chapter 4 may be able to provide you with a few ideas.) If you are more interested in representing members or defending and promoting your issues, then you probably need a government affairs function.

Formal representation can mean a lot of things. The very act of having a not-for-profit shows that your constituents want to be represented. They may not realize it, however. They may feel that the primary purpose of your organization is to provide a service. Therefore, the association needs to raise the funds and have a structure in place to dispense these services. What would your constituents say if you were not allowed to dispense your services or if your method of procuring funds were to become illegal? This is why you need to be in the government affairs arena.

As you are aware, a number of small not-for-profits are very active government affairs players at the state level. A mental health group may be making sure that funding is available for next year, while an outdoor sportsmen's group may be making sure that laws are not introduced that would curtail sound conservation principles. Representation is one of the fundamental reasons to begin to develop a government affairs program.

Defending and promoting your organization is the cornerstone of a sound government affairs program. While a CEO with government affairs background can do it, you may need additional internal or external help. At my organization, most of what we do is either defending an issue or promoting a new issue or bill. We use a number of specialized staff and outside consultants. Your organization needs to determine how extensively you wish to be involved in this part of the plan.

Multiple issues take a lot of time and skill to handle. A number of not-for-profits focus on one major issue each year. This is a good idea if your budget is limited. The trick in doing that, however, is to achieve a consensus on what the top issue will be. In government affairs, it seems that most of the time you are dealing with defensive issues—that is, fighting proposals or legislation that is trying to take away a fundamental part of your organization's mission. Because of this, it is important to have a proactive issue in the mix once in awhile. It is a great morale builder for both staff and volunteers.

If you are interested in introducing a federal or state bill on behalf of your members, you have arrived at the full-time level of a government affairs program. You should have a government affairs director, use outside consultants, and have an active group of volunteers working at both the committee and the grassroots levels. Introducing a bill can be the most exciting part of the government affairs process, but it cannot happen unless you have the right players, both staff and volunteers, in place.

The election of legislators who support your issue is vital. They can make a big difference in how future bills are passed or defeated. If your organization's IRS status permits you to do so, you should take advantage of instituting a political action committee (PAC). (Chapter 3 provides detailed information on their overall use.) A PAC can assist in raising funds from members and in giving funds to legislative campaigns. Your capacity may need to be enlarged in order to institute such a program.

As previously mentioned, becoming recognized as a state or federal resource by legislators is the highest compliment you can receive in the government affairs arena. This means that legislators and their aides come to you frequently to ask for advice, to obtain data, and to ask your organization to support legislation. This level of respect and power does not come easily, however; it comes from a lot of hard work in building relationships, providing support, and using your power as a leader in your field. Organizations that achieve this level have a highly charged and effective government affairs program.

The highest level of government affairs work is authoring legislation and helping to introduce bills that affect your issue. This can happen only when your organization is in tune with a legislator's needs. Key players who represent special interest groups often write bills, and your organization can be part of that process. The keys are your commitment and your skill in relationship building.

Ways for the Organization to Look Bigger Than It Is   In our age of technology, the Internet has taught us that you can appear to be as big as you want to be. In many cases, that has to happen in the government affairs arena as well. I am not advocating that a 50-member not-for-profit promote that it represents 10 million people, only that you need to examine whom you actually represent. You may be shocked to find that your 50-member group indirectly represents 10 million people. The key here is to determine whom you can influence through your organization. The 50-member group may, for example, be 50 other organizations, each of which has thousands of members. You may already have the power that you dream of.

Ways to Think Long-Term from the Beginning   Government affairs work is not a short term experience; you must think long term. It is a relationship-building activity. From the moment that you launch or refine your government affairs plan, think about the ways in which the plan will need to unfold six months or a year down the road. Whom will you need to influence, how will the plan be financed, and what people resources will you need?

We have discussed the financial and the people resources, but what about the ability to influence? Your entire job within the government affairs function is to influence. The two main groups you can influence are legislators and the voting public. The long-term objective needs to focus on how your organization can achieve that goal. Becoming the source and moving your agenda will take major relationship building with a number of target audiences. The only way that happens is to plan who your targets are and to begin the process.

Ways of Building a Network   The key to your success will be to build a network that will enable you to represent your constituents successfully. A good network includes the following:

- Legislators
- Legislators'aides
- Key political party officials
- The media
- Influential people
- Other organizations
- For-profit organizations
- Others

Building relationships with legislators seems obvious, but what kind of relationship do you want to build? Everyone seems to feel that a legislator's primary goal is to be re-elected. For the most part, it is. You simply have to deal with that issue. Do whatever is in your organization's power to assist. Beyond that issue, though, lies the goals and aspirations that the legislator wants to achieve. Find out how these objectives fit your agenda. If you find common ground, you are on your way to building a relationship.

Aides are the real key to your relationship with legislators. If you have dealt with a legislator's office before, you know that you work with aides more than legislators. Keep in mind that aides are confidantes of legislators. They are the insiders who feed information to legislators on a host of topics. Legislators cannot possibly keep up with all of the issues; they must rely on their aides to sort out necessary information and to give it to them. It is vital that you have a first-name working relationship with the aides of key legislators.

The political parties often play a role in what will be passed or defeated. One party may traditionally favor your issue over another. Even so, most not-for-profits should not be perceived as favoring one party over another. In most cases, your issues are the leading topics of the day. They are important to your constituents, but they are not so important that a legislator will risk party affiliations. That is why the best method of dealing with your issues is to make them as nonpartisan as possible. It is not always easy, but it is very important to have friends on both sides of the aisle.

The media play an important role in your government affairs plan. My association pays careful attention to the media. While we address the media in general, we tend to focus on the media that cover our issue, the outdoor writers. In some of our issues campaigns, we rely on the media to tell our story to the general public. The media, in many cases, are the key to winning or losing an issues campaign, particularly when we are involved in state initiative or ballot issues campaigns. The media need to be cultivated on a year-round basis. They need to know that your association is the source for information pertaining to your issue. News releases are a factor but developing a relationship with the media requires personal one-on-one contact with the press. Our organization visits key media sources regularly and attends and speaks at media organization functions, such as the Outdoor Writers Association.

Influential people play an important role in your government affairs program. They have the contacts and the means to make your plan work. Influential people can often open doors that you cannot. They can speak on your behalf to the right people at the right time, and they have the financial resources to assist you in underwriting the government affairs function. Every not-for-profit has the potential to attract influential people. In most cases, it is an essential part of not-for-profits' strategy and should be a vital part of your government affairs plan.

Other organizations play a key role in your plan as well. We have seen that grouping several organizations together to form a coalition is often the way to gather the strength needed to move your issue along. In addition, working relationships with other organizations that have a common thread can assist you in many ways. They can open doors or help you in ways that would not be possible if you were to try to run an issues campaign alone. Often, the leadership of these organizations, both staff and volunteers, can become advisors to your plan as well.

For-profit leaders and the businesses that they represent can have an impact on your government affairs program. Even though your organization is a not-for-profit, it may represent for-profit entities or at least have an effect on how they do business. For example, the issue that you are currently working on may have an indirect negative or positive effect on the bottom line of one or more businesses. If it does, you have a grand opportunity to introduce or strengthen your organization's relationship with the business community. This also provides an opportunity to meet business leaders whom you may have not had access to under other circumstances.

While it is impossible to list all of the groups and individuals with whom you need or have the opportunity to network, the important thing is that you make it a priority to do so. It is a vital part of the government affairs function. It is also a wonderful opportunity to widen your reach for the overall good of your not-for-profit.

Building relationships can be accomplished through a plan that focuses on staff and volunteers alike getting out and meeting with the key leadership of all of the target groups that you have identified. It is not a complicated process, but it is a labor-intensive exercise. The rewards, however, will outweigh the effort that is needed to create and maintain your relationship-building network.

Ways of Becoming a Resource Becoming a resource for legislators, the media, and the general public is one of the highest levels of recognition that a not-for-profit can obtain. It keeps the organization visible in the minds of your target audiences, and it provides you with greater success in your over-all endeavors. This is particularly true in the government affairs arena.

To be a resource, your organization needs to become the leading information source in your area or mission. This can be done by

- Reviewing your mission to discover the area where your organization can be the primary source of information
- Creating ways to store this information
- Developing an information system that can be easily assessed
- Marketing your organization as a resource
- Going out of your way to provide information and assistance to anyone who wishes to use your not-for-profit as a resource

Focus on what you do best. To be a resource, you need to be able to supply data and expertise better than any other source. Thousands of not-for-profits do this all the time. We can all think of examples: American Red Cross, Catholic Charities, American Society of Association Executives, and so on. These organizations have clearly defined their missions, have worked hard at keeping their target audiences informed, and have strived to be the very best in their field. Make a review of your organization to determine what will make you a resource.

Make sure that you create ways to store your information that your staff and outside interests can access. Take full advantage of current and future technology. Don't hesitate to develop a plan that constantly updates your internal technology. Your major source of power as a not-for-profit is the information that you have obtained and are currently gathering on your area of expertise.

Make sure your organization's computer, e-mail, and web page capacity is working for you, not against you. At my organization, we make it a priority to keep our information system current. We take full advantage of all the technology we can afford. Our web page is geared to inform and encourage our current and potential customers to get involved in our government affairs activities.

Marketing your organization as a resource is a must. Government affairs is a lot like your communications efforts. You have to have an ongoing plan to keep your target audiences informed of who you are and what you can bring to the table. Meeting with key players, developing ongoing news releases, and keeping in touch by telephone is needed to maintain your organization's position as a resource.

Competition in the government affairs arena is fierce. A legislator's aide, for example, will keep your organization on the radar screen only as long as you have something to offer that helps to fulfill the legislator's goal. Your job is to keep your organization in sight.

The most important part of the plan is to make sure that your organization provides information on a timely basis. The information can vary from simple to complicated. All staff must fulfill requests. The Wildlife Legislative Fund of America has gained the title as the resource for wildlife management issues by making sure that it delivers what is requested. It has become a resource for state, federal, and international information. Requests come from around the world from students, legislators, conservation professionals, business leaders, and educators.

Determining Your Prime Issue

Your prime issue is the most basic questions to determine. Focusing on the issue will help you to answer the questions of who to influence, who to ask for funding, and who may partner with you. They are not questions to take lightly. The answers to these questions will either help you to gain influence or put you in the middle of the pack, where you will be lost. To answer these questions you need to:

1. Determine your niche.
2. Build on your expertise on the issue.
3. Become the authority.
4. Stand apart from the others.

Determine Your Niche   We have discussed the advantages of having a niche; what you need to do now is discover the niche for your organization. In most fields, including not-for-profits, you have competitors who may be friendly but are certainly not interested in promoting your cause, particularly if it affects their organizations. You need to determine if your organization has a unique niche or not. Most organizations can find a niche or at least can distinguish themselves from other like organizations by a service, an activity, or a belief.

I was once involved in a professional role with a not-for-profit that performed the same service that another organization performed. Both were national organizations, but the competitor was a much bigger and more well-known organization. We were able to distinguish ourselves through the method that we used to approach the same constituents. This produced members who thought as we thought and gave us a unique way to sell legislators on our issue. We became the leading group with another approach, an approach that was not being heard in Congress or in the executive branch.

Build on Your Expertise on the Issue   Once you have discovered your niche, you need to build on it and become the expert in that area. The process of achieving that level requires development both within and outside the organization. Your organization, needs to become an information-driven entity and to attain the highest standards possible in your professional ranks. The government affairs function then builds on these results.

Become the Authority   As your organization becomes the expert, it may enter a new level on government affairs ladder—it may become the authority, a higher level than that of expert. Our nation's capital is full of experts, but few are the authority on a given issue. Being the authority makes your not-for-profit the lead group in your area. It is a great place to be and the goal to shoot for in your government affairs program.

Stand Apart from the Others   You need to design your government affairs plan to stand out. In some ways, this is the result of the marketing aspects of your plan, rather than a result of what your issue is or will become. You have to have a compelling issue, but you need to mold an exciting approach that is different from others.

If you ran a not-for-profit that stores blood, for example, would your issue center around being a blood bank, or is there a more exciting way to describe your organization and gain greater attention to blood storage issues? If you think about whom your not-for-profit represents and the impact that it has, you can make a compelling case for its existence and discover ways that can open doors to further your issues.

Ways in Which You Will Make Your Voice Heard

Once your plan and operations are in place, your primary goal needs to be getting your voice heard, a difficult task if you have not established a network. It will take time, even if you hire a consultant. Don't expect to be at the top of your game right away; it is just not realistic. Develop a plan that accomplishes this goal gradually. Use the techniques described in this chapter, and focus on the following tasks:

- Develop a clear message that everyone understands.
- Significantly increase your visibility.
- Focus on the players who can help you to succeed.
- Constantly evaluate.

Develop a Clear Message That Everyone Understands   Developing a clear message is the most important component of your organization and its government affairs program. Keep your message simple and direct, making sure that it has appeal beyond your constituents' cause or thoughts. Make the message so appealing that it has to be addressed.

Look at other examples of messages that not-for-profits have used. See if any give you an idea or two. A clear message has to describe your organization and the issue—namely, your not-for-profit is an expert and the is-sue is so compelling that it must be addressed.

Mothers Against Drunk Driving (MADD) made drunk driving its com-pelling issue. Mothers, whose sons or daughters who had died at the hands of drunk drivers, testified at hearings in all 50 states to refine laws to lower drunk driver thresholds. MADD has been very effective by developing a simple, compelling message.

Significantly Increase Your Visibility   This not the first time that increas-ing visibility has been mentioned in this book. You cannot conduct an effec-tive government affairs function without being highly visible. Since time and money are factors, you need to create an effective plan that maximizes your visibility with what you have to work with.

At my organization, we conduct a number of government affairs campaigns simultaneously. The level of visibility depends on the com-mitment of time and money to each project. For example, we are con-ducting a federal campaign to introduce legislation, as well as three state legislative issues, five initiative/ballot issues, and four legal issues. In addition, we track more than 1,000 issues each year. Each one of these is-sues takes time and money to produce the visibility needed to win. For us, visibility means getting our message to three main targets, depend-ing on the issue and the way we are approaching it. These targets include the following:

- Legislators
- The general public
- Constituents

Approaching legislators can be done directly or indirectly. Meeting with legislators or their aides is the direct way, but having the legislators' con-stituents contact them in person or by telephone, e-mail, or mail is much more effective—particularly when a quick turnaround is needed to kill a bill, for example.

The general public is becoming a more active player in getting issues approved or killed. The initiative process is one way to make law even though the legislature has already dealt with it. Ballot issues are expensive and demand high-visibility methods—namely, the media—to sell a point. If you are engaging in voter initiative campaigns, it is best to maintain a high level of visibility on an ongoing basis.

Constituents need to hear from you regularly. This can be accomplished through a plan that calls for regular mailings, telephone and e-mail con-tacts, and meetings. The key is to keep constituents informed and excited about your government affairs efforts. Ask their advice, survey them, and get them involved as much as possible.

Focus on the Players Who Can Help You to Succeed   With limited budgets and limited time to execute your plan, you need to focus on the players who will affect your issue. At the federal level, my group focuses on a very small number of members of Congress and committees. Most not-for-profits do the same. That doesn't mean that we don't cultivate the other members of Congress; we do. We will need their support from time to time to vote on bills that we support. The real work for us, however, is at the committee level. Within the committees, we focus on the key players. We also work with the leadership of both sides of the aisle. Our focus has paid off very well and has made us a major force in Washington, DC.

Constantly Evaluate   Nothing changes more quickly than a successful government affairs strategy. You need to embrace change and seize opportunities. Some of the greatest moves come well within the heat of a campaign and were not originally planned at all. That is the challenge of the process, and it's what makes it fun. Such a move can project your issue and your not-for-profit further ahead than the original plan forecasted. The evaluation process can also assist you in refining your plan and becoming better at your craft.

Your Desire Either To Lead or To Follow

Taking the lead on an issue is not always the best plan. However, if possible, taking the lead position is usually the most productive. It sounds a bit confusing, but your timing, budget, staffing, and priorities all need to be taken into account. This is particularly true in the development of a new government affairs program.

     When you plan your government affairs program, you need to consider a number of strategies:

1. In the beginning, follow.
2. Use coalitions to gain strength.
3. Set a goal to lead on at least one issue.
4. Know when to lead and when to follow.
5. Be flexible because change is constant.

In the Beginning, Follow   In the case of a new government affairs program or one that has limited resources, taking a following position may be a good strategy. This means that your organization is not the lead group working on an issue. Of course, this position will not give your organization high visibility, but it will make you a player. Often, this can be enough to fulfill your goal. Being a follower is also a good move for organizations that:

- Have several issues with which they need to be involved simultaneously
- Have a limited budget
- Are not interested in increasing their visibility
- Have other priorities, which outweigh the government affairs function
- Use the government affairs function only to show that the organization is a player for membership benefit purposes.

While some of these reasons for being a follower may not be especially noble, they are considerations in deciding to lead or to follow.

Use Coalitions to Gain Strength   Coalitions are a great way to fulfill your organization's need to be a player while acting as a follower. At our organization, we are involved in both accepting invitations to become a member of coalitions and in forming coalitions and asking other organizations to participate. We are involved in coalitions at both the state and federal levels. They are very effective tools. For the most part, my association takes the lead position in forming coalitions; it is the nature of our mission. We also will continue to be followers within coalitions as well.

Currently, my organization is involved in taking the lead position in a major federal bill. We have created a coalition that has 97 not-for-profit organizations. There will be well over 100 groups involved eventually. Most of the organizations involved in the coalition have not done a great deal to participate. To belong, these groups had to endorse our position, promote the issue to their members, and allow us to use their names. In return, they are able to say that they are players. It is a win-win situation. Each group involved can tell its members that it supports this legislation, and our association, the lead group, can use the power of the 97 not-for-profits, which represent millions of members, to push the legislation.

Be absolutely sure that the coalitions that your not-for-profit joins are in your best interest, however. Coalitions are formed for all kinds of motives, most for the right reasons, but always look for a hidden agenda. The following are some questions you can ask to evaluate a coalition your organization may wish to join:

- Who are the players? Do they generally take positions that my organization would support?
- Has the coalition presented a clearly defined plan and direction?

- Has the coalition defined what each coalition member's role will be?
- What control does each member have in the process of the coalition?
- How will the coalition use my organization's name?
- Will my organization have the opportunity to accept or reject coalition materials being made public?
- When will the coalition end?

Coalitions are designed to follow a very focused agenda , and members are attracted to that agenda. Coalition members may vary greatly by mission, yet they want to be part of the focused agenda. Coalitions need to stick to the agenda, or it can no longer be considered a coalition. Watch for any changes, particularly if hidden agendas begin to appear.

Set a Goal to Lead in at Least One Issue   Following is nice, and sometimes even necessary, but there is nothing like taking the lead on an issue. Most associations cannot take the lead on every issue, yet, to be a major force your not-for-profit needs to select at least one issue to push. One of my organization's issues, for example, took 13 years to complete. For this issue, we drafted the language and helped to secure passage in all 50 states. Generally, our issues take 1 to 3 years to complete.

Know When to Lead and When to Follow   Knowing when to lead is far more difficult than determining when to follow. Most organizations, particularly those that are new to the game, stew over this decision.

The following are some questions your organization should ask in determining if it should take the lead on an issue:

- Are we the best authority on the subject?
- Can we attract other groups to follow?
- Do we have the capacity to lead an issue?
- Can the network that we have developed help us to be successful?
- Can the issue help to fulfill our mission?

It is just as difficult for not-for-profits with seasoned government affairs programs to determine when the best time is to be a follower. At my organization, we work as much behind the scenes of campaigns as we do in leading campaigns. Our group engineered a number of key federal and state issues that produced significant results for outdoor sports enthusiasts, but those whom we represent never knew that we were involved. This is not exactly following, in the pure sense. In fact, it is more of a leadership role, but we were not the official lead group. Your organization needs to determine the role it should play in each issue. (See Exhibit 8.11.)

EXHIBIT 8.11   Role-Playing Evaluation

One of the important decisions that your organization will need to make both in its overall government affairs program and for each issue is the following: do you want to lead, do you want to follow, or do you plan to work behind the scenes? The role-playing evaluation can assist you in this decision-making process.

The issue: _____

_____

Description of Issue:

Assessment:

    a. How does the issue fit in with our organization's mission?
        1. Is it closely aligned with our mission? _____ (yes/no)
        2. Is it an opportunity to increase our visibility? _____ (yes/no)

    b. What will we gain by being involved? Explain:

    c. What role do we want to play on this issue?
        1. Do we want to lead? _____ (yes/no)
        2. Do we want to follow? _____ (yes/no)
        3. Do we want to work behind the scenes? _____ (yes/no)
        Explain your decision:

    d. Do we have the capacity to play the role we have determined? _____ (yes/no) If not, what do we need to do to get up to speed and is it worth the time and cost?

    e. Do we want to do it alone? _____ (yes/no) If not, list whom we can attract to the table:
        Organization   Contact   Reason That They Would Be Interested

    f. Do we have the financial resources to underwrite the costs? _____ (yes/no) If not, can we procure the funds needed? _____ (yes/no) What would be the source of the funds? (list)
                Source of Funds   Estimated Funds

Plan Approval

The following have approved the role that the organization will play on this issue.

_____   _____   _____
     Volunteer leader   Date   Staff person assigned

Be Flexible Because Change Is Constant   Your main objective must always be in focus to win any issue. As previously noted, your not-for-profit should determine the best role to play to that end. Once you have determined the initial role your organization will play, keep an open mind. Your organization needs to change gears and take on other roles if doing so will help to move the issue including more one-on-one visits, media buys, or fund raising.

Your Evaluation Process   One of the most important aspects of your government affairs program is the evaluation process. Exhibits 8.11, 8.12, 8.13 and 8.14 can assist you in this effort. Your evaluation process should consider:

1. First and foremost you need to evaluate the extent that your not-for-profit can be involved in government affairs work, and the extent that your leadership wishes to be involved. This requires an evaluation of your entire operation including your IRS classification.
2. Once you decide to conduct a government affairs program, you need to determine the role that you wish to play for each issue. Does the issue in question fit into your area or not?
3. After you select an issue, you need to evaluate how your not-for-profit will successfully introduce, promote and sell the issue.
4. At least annually, your not-for-profit should evaluate the total government affairs program. This evaluation will provide valuable information to help improve your government affairs activities.

Strategic Planning Models

We have discussed the areas needed to create a successful government relations function. It is now time to personalize the process. The following can help you to begin the process:

- Creating a successful model for small not-for-profits
- Creating a successful model for medium-sized or large organizations
- Breathing new life into an existing government affairs program
- Looking at examples of successful government affairs programs
- Using a template to begin the process

Creating a Successful Model for Small Not-for-Profits

We have discussed the considerations needed to conduct a successful government relations program. If you are involved with a small not-for-profit, in many ways you have a larger challenge than a medium-sized or larger organization, simply due to the level of funding that you can generate and the staff and volunteer muscle that you can allocate. (See Exhibit 8.12.)

Exhibit 8.12 will help you to begin to explore the ways you can use your current resources and to find ways to discover new resources. It will also help you to determine the priority of each issue. It will help you to decide which issues to drop because they do not fit into your parameters or because they are too large to handle.

Exhibit 8.13 provides a way to analyze each issue that comes your way. Your main areas of concern will be

- Does the issue fit into your parameters?
- How will the issue affect your constituents?
- What is your interest level?
- What needs to be done?
- Are you capable of doing what it takes to be successful?
- What is your suggested game plan?
- What are your recommendations?

The first three areas in this list are important to consider. Make sure that you carefully weigh the answers to each of these questions.

It is important that your leadership, both volunteer and professional, know the parameter of issues that organization will consider. The parameters should have been agreed on in writing and approved by your board. If an issue fits your parameters and could have a major effect on your constituents, then it may be an issue to consider. The leadership needs to be able to filter out the measures that have little to no effect so your organization can focus on the real issues of concern.

What is the level of constituent interest? There is nothing worst than developing an issues campaign and finding out that it generates little or no interest from your constituents. You should rate each issue, 1 to 9, based on your evaluation of the interest in it.

The next three areas in the preceding list of concerns—what needs to be done, are we capable of doing what needs to be done to be successful, and what is the suggested game plan—are critical to the success of the proposed issue campaign. Spend time determining what will need to be done to be a player on the issue. Consider money, staff, volunteers, and other resources issues. Determine if your not-for-profit can handle the task, or if you will need outside help. Create a game plan based on two or more contingencies—with certain elements missing or with more money and/or people added to the mix.

The final part of the evaluation process is to make a recommendation. For example, the evaluation may seem to point to your involvement with the issue but other factors either within or outside the organization make the timing bad. The recommendation part, therefore, is a very important facet

EXHIBIT 8.12   Not-for-Profit Organization Worksheet

Whatever the size of your not-for-profit, you need to develop a working government affairs plan if you wish to be successful. Use the information that you have gathered from completing the other worksheets in the chapter and the ideas you gained throughout the entire book. Now you are ready to create or refine your government affairs program.

Not-for-Profit Organization Worksheet

Name of organization: _____

Mission:

IRS considerations:

What is your IRS Status? 501(c) _____ Describe the extent of the government affairs programs permitted under IRS ruling: _____

What current government affairs budget figure is permitted, based on your overall budget and IRS status? _____

Current status (use Exhibit 8.4 to assist):

     a. Evaluate your current strengths and weaknesses.
     b. Determine your future requirements.

Budget requirements (use Exhibit 8.10 to assist):

Income:

What will be your sources of funds for the government affairs program?

     a. General funds _____
     b. Raising new funds. If new funds are needed what will be the sources?
         1. General organizational funds _____
         2. Government affairs general fund-raising campaign _____
         3. Issues-driven campaign _____
         4. Political action committee _____
         5. Other (explain) _____

Outline, briefly and with attachments, the plan to raise these funds.

Expenses:

What will be the overall costs of the government affairs program? (list details)

Staff requirements (use Exhibit 8.1 to assist):

     a. Use of current staff (list staff and role that they will play)
     b. New staff requirement (list positions needed and time line to procure)

EXHIBIT 8.12   Not-for-Profit Organization Worksheet *(continued)*

Consultant needs (use Exhibit 8.3 to assist):

    a. Do you need outside assistance? _____ (yes/no)

    b. If so, develop the profile and needs list.

Volunteer requirements (use Exhibits 8.5, 8.6, 8.8, and 8.9 to assist):

List the volunteers and the positions that need to be involved. Assign them to the tasks and issues for the year. Set plans for confirming and procuring volunteers. Develop an evaluation plan.

Task needs assessment (use Exhibits 8.2, 8.7, 8.11, and 8.13 to assist):

    a. List the task needed and develop a short overview on the role that the organization could play.

    b. Determine what role, if at all, you wish to play each issue.

Communications requirements:

    a. What is the government affairs message and overall strategy within the organization's communications message?

    b. What is the communications plan to support the government affairs program?

Timetable:

Develop a schedule that will cover all the functions of the plan, including fund procurement; issues to be sought; the people who will need to be involved, including staff, consultants, and volunteers; the outside network needs; and any other element that would make your plan a success.

Evaluate:

Take the time to go over your plan one more time before you proceed:

    a. Did you include all the items needed to be successful?

    b. Is the budget adequate, and have you kept within IRS guidelines?

    c. Are the staffing, consulting, and volunteer requirements enough?

    d. Is the communications effort adequate?

    e. Is the time line good?

Develop an ongoing evaluation plan that allows you to refine as you go.

Put into place an overall evaluation of your government affairs program.

Other Requirements:

List unique circumstances or items not covered above.

Approval:

This plan is approved by both the volunteer and professional leadership of the organization.

_____	_____	_____
Volunteer leader	Date	Staff leader

EXHIBIT 8.13   Issues Evaluation Sheet

The issue: _____

Description:

How does it fit into the organization's parameters?

How can the issue affect our constituents?
      a. What is the interest level? _____ (based on a 1 to 9 scale)
      b. Detail how it affects our constituents.

What needs to done to succeed (list the overall requirements):

Does the organization have the capacity to do what it takes to be successful?
_____ (yes/no). If not, what will it take to gain the capacity and is it worth pursuing?

Suggested game plan (you should have additional contingencies in case Plan A fails):

Recommendations (keep your answers clear and to the point):

_____	_____	_____
Submitted by	Date	Approved by

of the evaluation process. Make sure that the reason to drop the issue or to become involved is clearly stated and based on as many facts as possible.

Creating a Successful Model for Medium-Sized to Large Organizations

It is surprising to discover that not all medium-sized and large organizations have a government affairs program and that, if they do, in some cases it is not functioning as well as it could. If you are in a medium-sized or large association and your government affairs program is doing its job, you know that it takes a lot of effort to make it work.

For the most part, what I am about to suggest will be for start-up efforts. If your organization has a government affairs program but has not placed a great deal of interest in it, you may discover new ways to create more attention and even excitement into your program. If your organization is engaged in a highly developed government affairs program, maybe an idea or two will emerge. Larger associations require a lot more capacity to make the government affairs role work, but, because of this, they can take on a lot more assignments. The key is to do the same thing that smaller organizations do to evaluate capabilities. Review Exhibit 8.12, which provided areas to explore for your overall plan and which can be expanded for a more comprehensive government affairs plan. A larger organization will need more staff, volunteer support, and funding sources, and the issues list will be more extensive.

Breathing New Life into a Government Affairs Program

A number of years ago I was on the staff of an association that had a government affairs program. It was a very large national association with nearly 20,000 members. It represented a group of professionals who really needed to have representation at both the federal and state levels. At the time, I was assigned to the development department as a fund-raiser and was not involved with the government affairs program. The organization did not have a full-time government affairs director. It relied on the CEO and the part-time efforts of a communications executive. Very little was ever done. The CEO did not have the capability to perform or interest in government affairs and the communications executive was given only information-gathering duties.

Meanwhile, the field that this association represented had a large void. Competitive associations that had traditionally been in the lead position of promoting and defending issues had changed leadership, and the new directors had different interests. A major opportunity was lost to serve its members and to take the lead position on issues that directly affected its members.

This case may sound familiar to you. It could fit a number of organizations' profiles. The lack of leadership is often the problem, as it was in this case, but other issues can be factors as well including budget restraints, lack of interest, and the perception that not-for-profits cannot engage in government affairs work. (See Exhibit 8.14.)

Communications Program That Enhances Your Government Affairs Program

Your government affairs program cannot be successful without a sound communications effort behind the plan. (Chapter 4 details the communications role that needs to be played to win.) Winning is the goal, and, no matter how you stage it, losing is not winning. Your communications effort makes the process work. The following are questions that you need to ask:

1. Is our government affairs plan a key part of your overall communications effort?

EXHIBIT 8.14   Evaluation of a Not-for-Profit's Government Affairs Plan

How does an organization evaluate a government affairs program? Exhibits 8.4 and 8.12 can help you to begin the process. Exhibit 8.14 will assist you in using this information to answer the question "Where do I want to go from here?"

Issues Review (list each issue):

Issue   Won-Lost-Pending   Led-Followed-Behind the Scenes   Remarks

Financial Information:

    a. Budget $_____
    b. Funds raised $_____
    c. Total +/− $_____

(Include any information that could assist in future efforts.)

Staff Involvement:

Number of nongovernment affairs staff involved: _____
Average percent of time spent: _____

Staff   Title   Time Spent   %

Consultants Used:

Consultant   Role   Time Spent   Cost

Volunteers Involved:

Name   Role   Time Spent   Recommended Future Role

Network Involved by Issue (You should maintain a detailed listing, by issue, separately. Use this to compile your summary):

Issue   Individual   Organization   Business   Other (Explain)

Media Involvement:

Issue   Media Source   Newspaper   Magazine   Radio   TV   Other

Overall Evaluation:

Based on a 1 to 9 scale, how would you rate your government function? _____

Recommendations:

    a. List the areas that you feel:
      1. Need refinement and detail why.
      2. Need to be added and why.
    b. Develop your plan, using appropriate exhibit, for the next cycle.

2. Is a communication plan established within the government affairs program?
3. Have we developed strong ties with the media?
4. What is our working relationship with the media?
   a. Keeping the targeted public informed
   b. Changing attitudes concerning an issue
   c. Creating good will
5. Are you underestimating the power of the media?

Make the Government Affairs Plan a Key Part of Your Overall Communications Effort

A government affairs program cannot work in a vacuum; it has to be part of all the functions of the not-for-profit. The communications function is no exception. Coordinating the overall message will pay huge dividends. This means that the communications and government affairs staff and volunteers need to work together. The communications role is to make sure that everyone knows that the overall organization stands behind the government affairs effort.

Establish a Communications Plan within the Government Affairs Program

This may sound like overkill from the previous paragraph, but it isn't. While an overall communications effort needs to be made, another effort has to be made as well. The role that the communications effort plays within the government affairs program is to support the issues in play and to help those issues win. (This effort is detailed in Chapter 4.) At my association, we rely on the communications effort quite heavily. It can vary from sending postcards to creating a full-blown campaign that costs millions of dollars. Issues campaigns often need the media to help it work. Government affairs is a game of persuasion, and communications is one valuable tool to use.

Develop Strong Ties with the Media

There is no substitute for gaining exposure to your target audience through a strong relationship with the media. This is not an easy task. It is labor intensive and costly, but it pays off. At my organization, we strive to keep our contacts with the media. We send press releases, have a media e-mail program, make frequent visits to meet the media, and work and attend media-related association meetings.

Our plan pays off. For example, our organization was recently featured in four places in the same issue of a national magazine. Even though it took several months to coordinate the effort, these articles appeared in the publication in the same month that we had a key bill being introduced in Congress. That is what can happen when you have established a media relations program.

Work with the Media

The media can be a real asset to your government affairs program. The important thing is always to keep the media informed. Whatever the story is, you should be the first to break both good and bad news. If you do this, the media will come to recognize you more and more as the source for news within your area of expertise.

The media can help you change attitudes. At my association, we have worked with the media in several campaigns where we were able to change media attitudes toward a campaign and then, through their help, change the attitudes of the general public about the issue. These efforts have really made a difference.

The media have an ongoing relationship with my organization. This, in part, comes from making sure that we provide whatever the media sources need to complete the story.

Never Underestimate the Power of the Media

The media's goal is to find exciting stories that will satisfy their readers and sell their media products. If your government affairs communications effort can help the media achieve this goal, they will respond. That is why you need to know the media that you deal with, so that you can present a story or an angle that will appeal to them. On the other hand, do not try to sell a "non-story" or try to fudge anything within your story, or you will pay the price.

Conclusion

The founders of the United States placed a great deal of government control in the hands of the American people. While we sometimes think that we have lost that power, it still exists, and it is up to us to use it.

Not-for-profits that develop a government affairs program become an active part of the American process. Since the United States has a representative form of government, we, as citizens, have the power to elect or defeat legislators and to educate them on the issues that affect our constituents. We also have the right to educate voters on issues they vote on through the initiative process, as well as the right to bring legal measures against those who try to harm our constituents in any way.

Our form of government provides a blend of checks and balances, which protects each citizen. The role that not-for-profits play through government affairs programs is a noble one. Those of us who are engaged in this process should be proud to be a key element in the democratic process that is the envy of the world.

Not-for-profit leaders need to make the government affairs program a priority. If you do not have a program, start one. If your program is not working effectively, improve it. If you have developed a successful program, share your expertise with others.

The government affairs role is more important than ever. Dramatic changes are occurring in every area of interest. If your area of interest is not being adequately covered, your constituents will lose their rights and the only people who can be blamed are the ones who sat around and did nothing.

Ten Fundamental Keys to a Successful Government Affairs Program

WALTER P. PIDGEON, JR.

Government affairs does make a difference. It is a major way to add excitement and a purpose to a not-for-profit. Government affairs also opens new opportunities for the organizations that are actively engaged in the process including adding influence, increasing funding, and attracting talented people.

I hope that this book provided you with a wealth of ideas on how to create a government affairs program. If you follow the suggestions outlined in the book, you will be well on your way. As a parting summary I would like to offer the following:

1. *Plan strategically.* Creating a government affairs program is a challenging task. Establish goals that are realistic. Nothing is worse than failing to make goals, particularly when they are not based on reality. Do not be afraid to think outside the box. Those who are able to think differently often win.

2. *Be unique.* Find a niche where your organization is or could be the primary source or expert. Make this information available to legislators and the media. Become the resource on the subject.

3. *Be a leader.* Take at least one leadership role on an issue each year. Strive to author and pass a bill.

4. *Be a follower.* Know when and how to follow.

5. *Communicate.* Use all facets of communication, including traditional and grassroots efforts through letters, mailgrams, phone calls, e-mails, and personal contacts. These efforts produce results. Often, fewer than 100 letters from constituents affect a Congress member's vote.

6. *Know the legal guidelines.* Discover your legal limits and don't exceed them. Remember that the federal and states laws differ widely. Don't get so busy that you forget the boundaries.

7. *Secure appropriate financing.* You cannot afford to be in the middle of a government affairs campaign when the money runs out. Look for the money before, during, and after the campaign to make sure that you are totally funded.

8. *Secure good professional talent.* Be sure that you have the professional talent to perform the government affairs function. If your organization doesn't have sufficient talent internally, look outside for a consultant who can perform the task. In addition, make sure that all staff members know their role in the government affairs function.

9. *Never underestimate the power of volunteers.* Do not underestimate the power and the dynamics of volunteers. They can do what a professional cannot do and, sometimes, should not do. Make volunteers a key part of your plan.

10. *Form partnerships.* Most not-for-profits cannot perform a government Affairs Program alone. Look to join or form coalitions for mutual advantage.

Reference Guide to Organizational Support

American Society of Association Executives
    1575 I Street, NW
    Washington, DC 20005
    Phone: 202-626-2723
    Fax: 202-371-0870
    E-mail: asaenet.org
    www.asaenet.org

Government Affairs

Association of Fund Raising Professionals
    1101 King Street, Suite 700
    Alexandria, VA 22314
    Phone: 703-684-0410
    Fax: 703-684-0540
    E-mail: ap@nsfre.org

Fund-Raising

Points of Light Foundation
    1400 I Street, Suite 800, NW
    Washington, DC 20005
    Phone: 202-729-8000
    Fax: 202-223-9257
    E-mail: polf@aol.com

Volunteering

Wildlife Legislative Fund of America
    801 Kingsmill Parkway
    Columbus, OH 43229
    Phone: 614-888-4868
    Fax: 614-888-0326
    E-mail: info@wlfa.org
    www.wlfa.org

Government Affairs
Fund-Raising
Volunteering

The Accompanying CD-ROM and How to Use it

This book has an added feature to assist in the development of a successful government affairs program. The CD-ROM attached inside the back cover contains a number of items that can assist you.

The CD's Contents

1. The CD contains all of the exhibits in the book. A number of these exhibits can be used to develop or refine your government affairs program. Feel free to use them. If you do, please make reference to the source.

2. In addition to book-related information, the CD-ROM contains materials that have been used in successful government affairs campaigns. Also included are hyper-links to two association websites that feature government affairs programs. We encourage you to borrow an idea or two for your government affairs program.

▼ End Notes

Blum, Jared O. *Beyond Washington: An Association Guide to Shaping a State Government Affairs Program.* Washington, DC: American Society of Association Executives, 1990.

Cigler, Allan J., and Burdett A. Loomis. *Interest Group Politics,* 2d ed. Washington, DC: CQ Press, 1986.

Hunt, Frederick, D. *How Coalitions Work: Learn What You're Getting into Before You Sign Up.* Washington, DC: Association Management, American Society of Association Executives, June 1993.

Jacobs, Jerold A. *Federal Lobbying Law Handbook,* 2d ed. Washington, DC: ASAE Publications, 1993.

Mack, Charles S. *Lobbying and Government Relations: A Guide for Executives.* New York: Quorum Books, 1989.

Mayer, J.P., Alexis de Tocqueville. *Democracy in America.* Translated by George Lawence. New York: Harper & Row, 1969.

Potter, Trevor. *Political Activity, Lobbying, Laws and Gifts Rules Guide.* Vol. 2. Little Falls, NJ: Glasser Legal Works, 1999.

Ritchie, James I. *How to Work Effectively with State Legislatures.* Washington, DC: American Society of Association Executives, 1969.

Zorack, John L. *The Lobbying Handbook.* Washington, DC: Professional Lobbying and Consulting Center, 1990.

Index